Western Michigan University

First-Year Experience Seminar

Designed Specifically for Western Michigan University
First-Year Experience Seminar Students

SECOND EDITION

YOUR EXPERIENCE BEGINS HERE!

A CUSTOMIZED VERSION OF
COLLEGE & CAREER SUCCESS
BY MARSHA FRALICK
FIFTH EDITION

Kendall Hunt
publishing company

Cover images courtesy of Western Michigan University

www.kendallhunt.com
Send all inquiries to:
4050 Westmark Drive
Dubuque, IA 52004-1840

Copyright © 2014 by Kendall Hunt Publishing Company

ISBN 978-1-4652-4923-4

Printed in the United States of America

BRIEF CONTENTS

CONTENTS

Part II   College Success   97

4   Managing Time and Money   99

5   Improving Memory and Reading   143

have always believed that education provides a means for accomplishing a person's dreams. I guess I learned that idea from my parents and teachers in high school. When I started college at the University of New Mexico, it was the beginning of a great adventure which was to last my lifetime. I can still recall being a college freshman. I had attended a small school in northern New Mexico, Pojoaque High School. I was a good student in high school and was motivated to succeed in college. As a freshman, I had career goals that were pretty unrealistic and changed from week to week. I thought about becoming the first woman president or maybe a diplomat. Since Nancy Drew was my heroine, I thought about being a spy or detective like Nancy Drew. Deciding on a major and career was a monumental task.

When I started at the University of New Mexico, I was soon overwhelmed. I did not know how to take notes, remember what I read, or manage my time. I remember that I was anxious and stressed out about taking tests. I worked and went to school during the day and tried to study at night. Sometimes I studied all night and then the next day forgot what I had studied. College was not fun, and I wished that someone had written a book on how to survive in college. I decided that I would figure out how to be successful and maybe someday write a book about it so that other people would not have to struggle as much as I did.

I learned how to survive and was very successful in college, completing my bachelor's, master's, and doctorate degrees. I enjoyed the college environment so much that I ended up being a college counselor and teacher. That was pretty far from being Nancy Drew, but it has been a career that I have found very satisfying. In 1978, the vice-president of newly opened Cuyamaca College in El Cajon, California, asked if I would design a college success course for the new college. I was excited to design a course that would help students to be successful in college. I was motivated because I believed in the value of education and remembered what it was like to be a new college student. Now it is 34 years later and I am still designing and teaching college success courses. Every semester that I teach, I learn more from students and continue to develop ideas for a college success course that makes a positive difference in students' lives. My experiences as a student and faculty member have helped me design a class with proven success. I have also done research on student success and designed this textbook based on my research findings.

What do students need to be successful? First of all, they need to know how to study. This includes being able to apply memory techniques, read effectively, listen to lectures, take notes, and prepare for exams. Without these skills, students may wrongly decide that they are not capable of doing college work. If students know these techniques and apply them, they can be confident in their abilities and reach their true potential. With confidence, they can begin to relax and meet the challenges of tests and term papers. They might even learn to like education.

Being able to study is not enough. Students need to know what to study, so having a career goal is important. I have observed that students choose their career goals for a variety of reasons. Just like I wanted to be Nancy Drew, some students choose their occupations based on some person that they admire. Some choose their career based on familiarity. They choose occupations that they have observed in their families or communities. Others choose a career by accident; they obtain whatever job is available. We now have a great deal of information on how to choose a satisfying career goal. The first step is personal assessment. What are the students' personality types, interests, aptitudes, and values? Once these are determined, what careers match these personal characteristics? What careers will be a good choice for the future? These are all questions that need to be answered in order to continue to study in college.

Managing time and money and setting goals are important. Like many other students, I had always worked while attending college. While getting my master's and doctorate degrees, I worked and had a family. I have felt the pressures of these many roles and learned how to manage them. Students can learn these important life skills to make the journey easier.

Learning how to speak and write well has been a great asset to me in college and in my career. These skills did not come easily. I remember getting papers back with so many red corrections that they looked like decorated Christmas trees. I learned from the mistakes and kept practicing. These are skills that all college students need to master early in their college careers.

One of the goals of a college education is to learn to think critically and creatively. The world is full of complex issues with no easy answers. We find solutions by working with others, questioning the status quo, looking at different alternatives, respecting the opinions of others, and constructing our own personal views. Through creative thinking, we can come up with ideas to solve problems in our careers and personal lives.

I had the advantage of growing up with two cultures and speaking two languages. This has given me an appreciation for different groups of people. Appreciating others and working with diverse groups of people are skills needed by everyone today because the world is becoming more diverse. If we have hope for being able to live peacefully in the world, we will need to understand and appreciate this diversity.

Probably the most important skill for success is that of positive thinking. I truly believe that we accomplish what we think we can do. We need to become aware of our thoughts, and when they are negative, we need to change them. I often ask students to notice their negative thoughts and then, as if rewinding a tape, change their negative thoughts to positive thoughts. Positive thoughts are powerful influences on attitude and behavior.

What good does it do to attend college if students do not enjoy good health? I have resolved to emphasize achieving wellness and maintaining good health in all my college classes. In the new millennium, we are all supposed to live to be 100 years old. I collect stories about seniors who climb mountains, orbit the earth, write bestselling novels, and become famous artists. We can learn from them about how to live long, healthy, and productive lives.

Through the study of psychology, we have discovered many ways to help people to be successful. I have briefly introduced these theories and the names of the psychologists who have done research in this area. It is not enough to know the theory or idea; it is necessary to know how to apply it. This book contains many exercises designed to assist students apply the material learned.

The sections titled "Keys to Success," located near the end of each chapter, are my personal philosophies of life developed from being in education for over 40 years. Although I still remember being a college freshman, that was a long time ago, and I have learned a lot since then. If I could survive in college, you can too. I wrote that book that I thought about many years ago. I hope that it makes your journey through college, your career, and your life a little easier.

FEATURES OF THIS BOOK

- Topics regarding college, career, and lifelong success are presented in the text.

- Personality type and learning style are key themes throughout the text.

- Throughout the text, students are encouraged to build on their strengths and think positively about the future.

- Interactive activities within the text help students to practice the material learned.

- Frequent quizzes and answer keys within the chapters help students with reading comprehension and check understanding of key concepts.

- Journal entries help students think critically and apply what they have learned to their personal lives.

- Individual and group exercises are included at the end of each chapter.

Dear First-Year Student:

Congratulations and welcome to Western Michigan University. The First-Year Experience (FYE) Programs' staff looks forward to meeting and working with you as you make the transition from high school to college and become adjusted to your new home away from home. Without question, this is an amazing and exciting time in your life, while at the same time you may feel anxious, or somewhat unsure about this new beginning. This is quite normal for most, if not all new students. As director of FYE, I want to personally reassure you that as a university, we are fully committed to your academic and personal success.

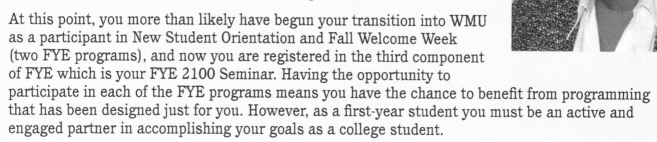

At this point, you more than likely have begun your transition into WMU as a participant in New Student Orientation and Fall Welcome Week (two FYE programs), and now you are registered in the third component of FYE which is your FYE 2100 Seminar. Having the opportunity to participate in each of the FYE programs means you have the chance to benefit from programming that has been designed just for you. However, as a first-year student you must be an active and engaged partner in accomplishing your goals as a college student.

As an active and engaged student you are:

- Assuming responsibility for consistently and appropriately attending class.
- Taking the necessary time to connect with your professors during office hours to seek assistance when required and also discuss your academic progress.
- Studying an average of 25 to 35 hours per week.
- Enjoying your first-year college experience but ensuring that you maintain a healthy balance between academics and social activity.
- Utilizing the many WMU resources available to support you academically, socially, physically, mentally and/or emotionally.
- Making connections with other students through involvement and participation in registered student organizations or maybe intramural sports.

College opens the doors to unlimited possibilities, challenges you to put forth your very best, and prepares and empowers you to achieve life's dreams. A great deal of your achievement depends on your commitment, but I want you to remember that *you are not alone* on this new journey. Everyone at WMU is cheering for your success. We positively welcome you as the newest members of the BRONCO family, and we eagerly anticipate applauding your achievements as you earn your diploma and become an alumnus of the university in a few short years.

Again welcome, welcome, welcome, we eagerly look forward to what your future holds.

Sincerely,

Toni Woolfork-Barnes, Ed.D.
Director

Welcome to WMU!

One of my greatest pleasures as president of this great university is welcoming new Broncos. We're all glad you're here. You made a great decision when you chose Western Michigan University. Your next few years will be exciting and busy ones. If you do your part, you will succeed here.

I encourage you to get it right, right from the start. Attend class, ask questions, do your homework, see your advisor, and study. A solid first semester sets the stage for achievement throughout your college career. Take advantage of everything we offer so you can realize the full WMU experience. Academics come first, of course, but being a truly successful student means knowing how to balance work and fun. It means discovering new things, meeting new people, and learning outside the classroom. Don't miss a chance to do any of that.

As you begin your life as a Bronco, I'd like you to remember three things. Take them to heart and hold them close for the next few years. You're part of WMU now.

- You're a student at one of the nation's top research universities.
- You're surrounded by people ready to help you.
- You're on your way to success.

I look forward to getting to know as many of you as possible. When you see me on campus, don't be shy about introducing yourself and talking. I try to greet as many students as I can, but I'd love it if you would approach me to say hello, tell me who you are and how your student experience is going.

As the years speed by—and believe me they will—I will watch your progress with pride. In due course, I'll be standing on the Miller Auditorium stage, ready to shake your hand and present your diploma. It will be a moment in which we both will feel a great sense of accomplishment.

Warmest regards,

John M. Dunn President

PART I

Career Success

CHAPTER 1

Understanding Motivation

Learning Objectives

Read to answer these key questions:

- What do I want from college?

- What is the value of a college education?

- How do I choose my major and career?

- How can I motivate myself to be successful?

- How can I begin habits that lead to success?

- How can I be persistent in achieving my goal of a college education?

ost students attend college with dreams of making their lives better. Some students are there to explore interests and possibilities, and others have more defined career goals. Being successful in college and attaining your dreams begin with motivation. It provides the energy or drive to find your direction and to reach your goals. Without motivation, it is difficult to accomplish anything.

Not everyone is successful in college. As a freshman in college, I attended an orientation in which I was told to look at the student to the left and the student to the right of me. The speaker said that one of us would not make it through the freshman year. I remember telling myself that the speaker must have been talking about one of the other two students and not me. That was the beginning of my motivation to be successful in college. Unfortunately, about one-third of college students drop out in the first year. Forty percent of students who start college do not finish their degrees. Having a good understanding of your gifts and talents, reasons for attending college, career goals, and how to motivate yourself will help you to reach your dreams.

What Do I Want from College?

Succeeding in college requires time and effort. You will have to give up some of your time spent on leisure activities and working. You will give up some time spent with your friends and families. Making sacrifices and working hard are easier if you know what you want to achieve through your efforts. One of the first steps in motivating yourself to be successful in college is to have a clear and specific understanding of your reasons for attending college. Are you attending college as a way to obtain a satisfying career? Is financial security one of your goals? Will you feel more satisfied if you are living up to your potential? What are your hopes and dreams, and how will college help you to achieve your goals?

When you are having difficulties or doubts about your ability to finish your college education, remember your hopes and dreams and your plans for the future. It is a good idea to write these ideas down, think about them, and revise them from time to time.

What Is the Value of a College Education?

Many college students say that getting a satisfying job that pays well and achieving financial security are important reasons for attending college. By going to college, you can get a job that pays more per hour. You can work fewer hours to earn a living and have more time for leisure activities. You can spend your time at work doing something that you like to do. A report issued by the Census Bureau in 2007 listed the following education and income statistics for all races and both genders throughout the United States.[1] Lifetime income assumes that a person works 30 years before retirement.

Average Earnings Based on Education Level

Education	Yearly Income	Lifetime Income
High school graduate	$31,286	$938,580
Some college, no degree	$33,009	$990,270
Associate degree	$39,746	$1,192,380
Bachelor's degree	$57,181	$1,715,430
Master's degree	$70,186	$2,105,580
Professional degree	$120,978	$3,629,340

Notice that income rises with educational level. A person with a bachelor's degree earns almost twice as much as a high school graduate. Of course, these are average figures across the nation. Some individuals earn higher or lower salaries. People have assumed that you would certainly be rich if you were a millionaire. College won't make you an instant millionaire, but over a lifetime, you earn over a million dollars by having an associate's degree. People fantasize about winning the lottery. The reality is that the probability of winning the lottery is very low. In the long run, you have a better chance of improving your financial status by going to college.

Let's do some further comparisons. A high school graduate earns an average of $938,580 over a lifetime. A college graduate with a bachelor's degree earns $1,715,430 over a lifetime. A college graduate earns $776,850 more than a high school graduate does over a lifetime. So, how much is a college degree worth? It is worth $776,850 over a lifetime. Would you go to college if someone offered to pay you $776,850? Here are some more interesting figures we can derive from the table on page 4:

Completing one college course is worth $19,421.
($776,850 divided by 40 courses in a bachelor's degree)

Going to class for one hour is worth $405.
($19,421 divided by 48 hours in a semester class)

Would you take a college class if someone offered to pay you $19,421? Would you go to class today for one hour if someone offered to pay you $405? Of course, if this sounds too good to be true, remember that you will receive these "payments" over a working lifetime of 30 years.

Money is only one of the values of going to college. Can you think of other reasons to attend college? Here are some less tangible reasons.

- College helps you to develop your potential.
- College opens the door to many satisfying careers.

- College prepares you to be an informed citizen and fully participate in the democratic process.
- College increases your understanding and widens your view of the world.
- College allows you to participate in a conversation with the great minds of all times and places. For example, reading the work of Plato is like having a conversation with that famous philosopher. You can continue great conversations with your faculty and fellow students.
- College helps to increase your confidence, self-esteem, and self-respect.

Journal Entry #1

What are your dreams for the future? Write a paragraph about what you hope to accomplish by going to college.

Courtesy of Western Michigan University

Choosing a Major and Career

Having a definite major and career choice is a good motivation for completing your college education. It is difficult to put in the work necessary to be successful if you do not have a clear picture of your future career; however, three out of four college students are undecided about their major. For students who have chosen a major, 30 to 75 percent of a graduating class will change that major two or more times.[2] Unclear or indefinite career goals are some of the most significant factors that identify students at risk of dropping out of college.[3] Students often drop out or extend their stay in college because they are uncertain about their major or want to change their major. Choosing an appropriate college major is one of the most difficult and important decisions that college students can make.

How do people choose a career? There are many complex factors that go into your career choice. This course will help you to become aware of these factors and to think critically about them in order to make a good choice about your career. Some of the factors involved in choosing a career include:

- **Heredity.** You inherit genes from your parents that play a role in shaping who you are.
- **Intelligence.** Every person has a unique mixture of talents and skills. You can work to develop these skills.
- **Experience.** Your experiences can either build your self-confidence or cause you to doubt your abilities.

- **Environment.** What careers have you observed in your environment? Maybe your father was a doctor and you grew up familiar with careers in medicine. Your parents may have encouraged you to choose a particular career. You may want to learn about other possibilities.
- **Social roles.** Maybe you learned that men are engineers and women are teachers because your father is an engineer and your mother is a teacher. It is important to think critically about traditional roles so that your choices are not limited.
- **Learning.** What you have learned will play a part in your career decision. You may need to learn new behaviors and establish new habits.
- **Learning style.** Knowing how you like to learn can help you be successful in college as well as on the job. Your learning style may provide options for selecting a career as well.
- **Relationships.** We sometimes choose careers to enhance relationships. For example, you may choose a career that gives you time to spend with your family or with people who are important to you.
- **Stress.** Our ability to cope with stress plays a part in career choice. Some enjoy challenges; others value peace of mind.
- **Health.** Good health increases career options and enjoyment of life.
- **Personality.** Your personality is a major factor influencing which career you might enjoy.
- **Values.** What you value determines which career you will find satisfying.
- **Culture.** Your culture has an influence on which careers you value.
- **Traditions.** Traditions often guide career choice.
- **Beliefs.** Your beliefs about yourself and the world determine your behavior and career choice.
- **Interests.** If you choose a career that matches your interests, you can find satisfaction in your career.

Figure 1.1 Factors in career choice.

How can you choose the major that is best for you? The best way is to first understand yourself: become aware of your personality traits, learning style, interests, preferred lifestyle, values, gifts, and talents. The next step is to do career research to determine the career that best matches your personal characteristics. Then, plan your education to prepare for your career. Here are some questions to answer to help you understand yourself and what career and major would be best for you.

To learn about yourself, explore these areas:

- **What is my personality type?** Assessing your personality type will help you to become more aware of your individual gifts and talents and some careers that will give you satisfaction.

- **What is my learning style?** Being aware of your learning style will help you identify learning strategies that work best for you and increase your productivity in college, on the job, and in your personal life.

- **What are my aptitudes?** Focus on your strengths by identifying your multiple intelligences.

- **What are my interests?** Knowing about your interests is important in choosing a satisfying career.

- **What kind of lifestyle do I prefer?** Think about how you want to balance work, leisure, and family.

- **What are my values?** Knowing what you value (what is most important to you) will help you make good decisions about your life.

To learn about career possibilities, research the following:

- **What careers match my personality, learning style, aptitudes, interests, lifestyle, and values?** Learn how to do career research to find the best career for you. Find a career that has a good outlook for the future.

- **How can I plan my education to get the career I want?** Once you have identified a career that matches your personal strengths and interests, consult your college catalog or advisor to make an educational plan that matches your career goals.

By following the above steps, you can find the major that is best for you and minimize the time you spend in college.

Journal Entry #2

Write a paragraph about deciding on your ideal major and career. Use any of these questions to guide your thinking: If you have chosen a major, why is it the best major for you? How does it match your interests, aptitudes, and values (what is most important to you)? Does this major help you to live your preferred lifestyle? If you have not chosen a major, what are some steps in choosing the right major and career? What qualities would you look for in an ideal career? Can you describe some of your interests, aptitudes, and values? What is your preferred lifestyle?

How to Be Motivated

There are many ways to be motivated.

- You can **think positively about the future** and take the steps necessary to accomplish your goals.
- You can begin your studies by **looking for what is interesting** to you.
- You can **improve your concentration** and motivation for studying by managing your external and internal distractions.
- You can be motivated by internal or external factors called **intrinsic or extrinsic motivation.**
- You can become aware of your **locus of control,** or where you place the responsibility for control over your life. If you are in control, you are more likely to be motivated to succeed.
- You can join a club, organization, or athletic team. **Affiliation motivation** involves taking part in school activities that increase your motivation to stay in college.
- **Achievement** and competition are motivating to some students.
- You can **use rewards** as a motivation to establish desirable behaviors.

Let's examine each type of motivation in more detail and see if some of these ideas can be useful to you.

Thinking Positively about the Future

You can motivate yourself to complete your education by thinking positively about the future. If you believe that your chances of graduating from college are good, you can be motivated to take the steps necessary to achieve your goals. Conversely, if you think that your chances of graduating are poor, it is difficult to motivate yourself to continue. The degree of optimism that you possess is greatly influenced by past experiences. For example, if you were a good student in the past, you are likely to be optimistic about the future. If you struggled with your education, you may have some negative experiences that you will need to overcome. Negative thoughts can often become a self-fulfilling prophecy: what we think becomes true.

How can you train yourself to think more optimistically? First, become aware of your thought patterns. Are they mostly negative or positive? If they are negative, rewind the tape and make them more positive. Here is an example.

Pessimism

I failed the test. I guess I am just not college material. I feel really stupid. I just can't do this. College is too hard for me. My (teacher, father, mother, friend, boss) told me I would never make it. Maybe I should just drop out of college and do something else.

Optimism

I failed the test. Let's take a look at what went wrong, so I can do better next time. Did I study enough? Did I study the right material? Maybe I should take this a little slower. How can I get help so that I can understand? I plan to do better next time.

Can a person be too optimistic? In some circumstances, this is true. There is a difference between optimism and wishful thinking, for example. Wishful thinking does not include plans for accomplishing goals and can be a distraction from achieving them. Working toward unattainable goals can be exhausting and demoralizing, especially when the resources for attaining them are lacking. Goals must be realistic and achievable. Psychologists recommend that "people should be optimistic when the future can be changed by positive thinking, but not otherwise."[4] Using optimism requires some judgment about possible outcomes in the future.

There are some good reasons to think more positively. Psychologists have done long-term studies showing that people who use positive thinking have many benefits over a lifetime, including good health, longevity, happiness, perseverance, improved problem solving, and enhanced ability to learn. Optimism is also related to goal achievement. If you are optimistic and believe a goal is achievable, you are more likely to take the steps necessary to accomplish the goal. If you do not believe that a goal is achievable, you are likely to give up trying to achieve it. Being optimistic is closely related to being hopeful about the future. If you are hopeful about the future, you are likely to be more determined to reach your goals and to make plans for reaching them. Be optimistic about graduating from college, find the resources necessary to accomplish your goal, and start taking the steps to create your success.

ACTIVITY

Are you generally an optimist or pessimist about the future? Read the following items and rate your level of agreement or disagreement:
Rate the following items using this scale:

5   I definitely agree
4   I agree
3   I neither agree or disagree (neutral)
2   I disagree
1   I strongly disagree

__5__   My chances of graduating from college are good.

__5__   I am confident that I can overcome any obstacles to my success.

__3__   Things generally turn out well for me.

__3__   I believe that positive results will eventually come from most problem situations.

__5.__ If I work hard enough, I will eventually achieve my goals.

__3__   Although I have faced some problems in the past, the future will be better.

__4__   I expect that most things will go as planned.

__5__   Good things will happen to me in the future.

__5__   I am generally persistent in reaching my goals.

__5__   I am good at finding solutions to the problems I face in life.

Add up your total points and multiply by two. My total points (× 2) are __86__.

90–100	You are an excellent positive thinker.
80–89	You are a good positive thinker.
70–79	Sometimes you think positively, and sometimes not. Can you re-evaluate your thinking?
60 and below	Work on positive thinking.

Write five positive statements about your college education and your future.

Find Something Interesting in Your Studies

If you can think positively about what you are studying, it makes the job easier and more satisfying. Begin your studies by finding something interesting in the course and your textbook. Contrast these two ideas:

I have to take economics. It is going to be difficult and boring. What do I need economics for anyway? I'll just need to get through it so I can get my degree.

I have to take economics. I wonder about the course content. I often hear about it on the news. How can I use this information in my future? What can I find that is interesting?

Make sure to attend the first class meeting. Remember that the professor is very knowledgeable about the subject and finds the content interesting and exciting. At the first class meeting, the professor will give you an overview of the course and should provide some motivation for studying the material in the course. Look at the course syllabus to find what the course is about and to begin to look for something that could be interesting or useful to you.

Skimming a textbook before you begin a course is a good way to find something interesting and to prepare for learning. Skimming will give you an organized preview of what's ahead. Here are the steps to skimming a new text:

1. **Quickly read the preface or introduction.** Read as if you were having a conversation with the author of the text. In the preface or introduction, you will find out how the author has organized the material, the key ideas, and his or her purpose in writing the text.

2. **Look at the major topics in the table of contents.** You can use the table of contents as a window into the book. It gives a quick outline of every topic in the text. As you read the table of contents, look for topics of special interest to you.

3. **Spend five to 15 minutes quickly looking over the book.** Turn the pages quickly, noticing boldfaced topics, pictures, and anything else that catches your attention. Again, look for important or interesting topics. Do not spend too much time on this step. If your textbook is online, skim through the website.

4. **What resources are included?** Is there an index, glossary of terms, answers to quiz questions, or solutions to math problems? These sections will be of use to you as you read. If your book is online, explore the website to find useful features and content.

Skimming a text or website before you begin to read has several important benefits. The first benefit is that it gets you started in the learning process. It is an easy and quick step that can help you avoid procrastination. It increases motivation by helping you notice items that have appeal to you. Previewing the content will help you to relax as you study and remember the information. Early in the course, this step will help you verify that you have chosen the correct course and that you have the prerequisites to be successful in the class.

"No pessimist ever discovered the secrets of the stars, or sailed to an uncharted land, or opened a new doorway for the human spirit."
Helen Keller

"A pessimist sees the difficulty in every opportunity; an optimist sees the opportunity in every difficulty."
Winston Churchill

Improving Your Concentration

Have you ever watched lion tamers concentrate? If their attention wanders, they are likely to become the lion's dinner. Skilled athletes, musicians, and artists don't have any trouble concentrating. They are motivated to concentrate. Think about a time when you were totally focused on what you were doing. You were motivated to continue. You can improve your concentration and motivation for studying by managing your external and internal distractions.

Manage your external environment. Your environment will either help you to study or distract you from studying. We are all creatures of habit. If you try to study in front of the TV, you will watch TV because that is what you are accustomed to doing in front of the TV. If you study in bed, you will fall asleep because your body associates the bed with sleeping. If you study in the kitchen, you will eat. Find an environment that minimizes distractions. One idea is to study in the library. In the library, there are many cues that tell you to study. There are books and learning resources and other people studying. It will be easier to concentrate in that environment. You may be able to set up a learning environment in your home. Find a place where you can place a desk or table, your computer, and your materials for learning. When you are in this place, use it for learning and studying only.

Increase your concentration and motivation as well as your retention by varying the places where you study and the content of what you are studying. Study at home, in the library, outside, in a coffee shop or any place where you can focus your attention on your studies. You can also increase learning effectiveness by varying the content and subjects that you are studying. Athletes maintain concentration and motivation by including strength, speed and skill practice in each workout. Musicians practice scales, different musical pieces and rhythm exercises in one practice session. In your studies you can do the same. For example, when studying a foreign language, spend some time on reading, some time on learning vocabulary and some practice in speaking the language. Then do some problems for your math class.

Manage your internal distractions. Many of our distractions come from within. Here are some techniques for managing these internal distractions:

1. **Be here now.** Choose where you will place your attention. As I'm sure you have experienced, your body can be attending a lecture or at the desk reading, but your mind can be in lots of different and exciting places. You can tell yourself, "Be here now." You cannot force yourself to pay attention. When your mind wanders, notice that you have drifted off and gently return your attention to your lecture or reading. This will take some practice, since attention tends to wander often.

2. **The spider technique.** If you hold a tuning fork to a spider web, the web vibrates and the spider senses that it has caught a tasty morsel and goes seeking the food. After a while, the spider discovers that there is no food and learns to ignore the vibrations caused by the tuning fork. When you are sitting in the library studying and someone walks in talking and laughing, you can choose to pay attention either to the distraction or to studying. Decide to continue to pay attention to studying.

3. **Set up a worry time.** Many times worries interfere with concentration. Some people have been successful in setting up a worry time. Here's how it works:

   a. Set a specific time each day for worrying.

   b. When worries distract you from your studies, remind yourself that you have set aside time for worrying.

Managing Internal Distractions

1. Be here now
2. Spider technique
3. Worry time
4. Checkmark technique
5. Increase activity
6. Find an incentive
7. Change topics

c. Tell yourself, "Be here now."

d. Keep your worry appointment.

e. During your worry time, try to find some solutions or take some steps to resolve the things that cause you to worry.

4. **Take steps to solve personal problems.** If you are bothered by personal problems, take steps to solve them. See your college counselor for assistance. Another strategy is to make a plan to deal with the problem later so that you can study now.

5. **Use the checkmark technique.** When you find yourself distracted from a lecture or from studying, place a checkmark on a piece of paper and refocus your attention on the task at hand. You will find that your checkmarks decrease over time.

6. **Increase your activity.** Take a break. Stretch and move. Read and listen actively by asking questions about the material and answering them as you read or listen.

7. **Find an incentive or reward.** Tell yourself that when you finish, you will do something enjoyable.

8. **Change topics.** Changing study topics may help you to concentrate and avoid fatigue.

Intrinsic or Extrinsic Motivation

Intrinsic motivation comes from within. It means that you do an activity because you enjoy it or find personal meaning in it. With intrinsic motivation, the nature of the activity itself or the consequences of the activity motivate you. For example, let's say that I am interested in learning to play the piano. I am motivated to practice playing the piano because I like the sound of the piano and feel very satisfied when I can play music that I enjoy. I practice because I like to practice, not because I have to practice. When I get tired or frustrated, I work through it or put it aside and come back to it because I want to learn to play the piano well.

You can be intrinsically motivated to continue in college because you enjoy learning and find the college experience satisfying. Look for ways to enjoy college and to find some personal satisfaction in it. If you enjoy college, it becomes easier to do the work required to be successful. Think about what you say to yourself about college. If you are saying negative things such as "I don't want to be here," it will be difficult to continue.

Extrinsic motivation comes as a result of an external reward from someone else. Examples of extrinsic rewards are certificates, bonuses, money, praise, and recognition. Taking the piano example again, let's say that I want my child to play the piano. The child does not know if he or she would like to play the piano. I give the child a reward for practicing the piano. I could pay the child for practicing or give praise for doing a good job. There are two possible outcomes of the extrinsic reward. After a while, the child may gain skills and confidence and come to enjoy playing the piano. The extrinsic reward is no longer necessary because the child is now intrinsically motivated. Or the child may decide that he or she does not like to play the piano. The extrinsic reward is no longer effective in motivating the child to play the piano.

You can use extrinsic rewards to motivate yourself to be successful in college. Remind yourself of the payoff for getting a college degree: earning more money, having a satisfying career, being able to purchase a car and a house. Extrinsic rewards can be a first step in motivating yourself to attend college. With experience and achievement, you may come to like going to college and may become intrinsically motivated to continue your college education.

If you use intrinsic motivation to achieve your goal, you will be happier and more successful. If you do something like playing the piano because you enjoy it, you are more likely to spend the time necessary to practice to achieve your goal. If you view college as something that you enjoy and as valuable to you, it is easier to spend the time to do the required studying. When you get tired or frustrated, tell yourself that you are doing a good job (praise yourself) and think of the positive reasons that you want to get a college education.

Locus of Control

Being aware of the concept of locus of control is another way of understanding motivation. The word **locus** means place. The locus of control is where you place the responsibility for control over your life. In other words, who is in charge? If you place the responsibility on yourself and believe that you have control over your life, you have an internal locus of control. If you place the responsibility on others and think that luck or fate determines your future, you have an external locus of control. Some people use the internal and external locus of control in combination or favor one type in certain situations. If you favor an internal locus of control, you believe that to a great extent your actions determine your future. Studies have shown that students who use an internal locus of control are likely to have higher achievement in college.[5] The characteristics of students with internal and external loci of control are listed below.

Students with an internal locus of control:

* Believe that they are in control of their lives.
* Understand that grades are directly related to the amount of study invested.
* Are self-motivated.
* Learn from their mistakes by figuring out what went wrong and how to fix the problem.
* Think positively and try to make the best of each situation.
* Rely on themselves to find something interesting in the class and learn the material.

Students with an external locus of control:

* Believe that their lives are largely a result of luck, fate, or chance.
* Think that teachers give grades rather than students earning grades.
* Rely on external motivation from teachers or others.
* Look for someone to blame when they make a mistake.
* Think negatively and believe they are victims of circumstance.
* Rely on the teacher to make the class interesting and to teach the material.

Internal or External Locus of Control

Decide whether the statement represents an internal or external locus of control and put a checkmark in the appropriate column.

Internal   **External**

1. Much of what happens to us is due to fate, chance, or luck.
2. Grades depend on how much work you put into it.
3. If I do badly on the test, it is usually because the teacher is unfair.
4. If I do badly on the test, it is because I didn't study or didn't understand the material.
5. I often get blamed for things that are not my fault.
6. I try to make the best of the situation.
7. It is impossible to get a good grade if you have a bad instructor.
8. I can be successful through hard work.
9. If the teacher is not there telling me what to do, I have a hard time doing my work.
10. I can motivate myself to study.
11. If the teacher is boring, I probably won't do well in class.
12. I can find something interesting about each class.
13. When bad things are going to happen, there is not much you can do about it.
14. I create my own destiny.
15. Teachers should motivate the students to study.
16. I have a lot of choice about what happens in my life.

As you probably noticed, the even-numbered statements represent internal locus of control. The odd-numbered statements represent external locus of control. Remember that students with an internal locus of control have a greater chance of success in college. It is important to see yourself as responsible for your own success and achievement and to believe that with effort you can achieve your goals.

Affiliation

Human beings are social creatures who generally feel the need to be part of a group. This tendency is called affiliation motivation. People like to be part of a community, family, organization, or culture. You can apply this motivation technique in college by participating in student activities on campus. Join an athletic team, participate in a club, or join the student government. In this way, you will feel like you are part of a group and will have a

> "I am a great believer in luck, and I find that the harder I work, the more I have of it."
>
> Thomas Jefferson

sense of belonging. College is more than going to class: it is participating in social activities, making new friends, and sharing new ideas. Twenty years after you graduate from college, you are more likely to remember the conversations held with college friends than the detailed content of classes. College provides the opportunity to become part of a new group and to start lifelong friendships.

Achievement

Some students are motivated by achievement. Individuals who are achievement-motivated have a need for success in school, sports, careers, and other competitive situations. These individuals enjoy getting recognition for their success. They are often known as the best student, the outstanding athlete, or the employee of the year. These people are attracted to careers that provide rewards for individual achievement, such as sales, law, architecture, engineering, and business. They work hard in order to enjoy the rewards of their efforts. In college, some students work very hard to achieve high grades and then take pride in their accomplishments. One disadvantage of using this type of motivation is that it can lead to excess stress. These students often need to remember to balance their time between work, school, family, and leisure so that they do not become too stressed by the need to achieve.

Using a Reward

You can use rewards to manage your own behavior. If you want to increase your studying behavior, follow it by a positive consequence or a reward. Think about what is rewarding to you (watching TV, playing sports, enjoying your favorite music). You could study (your behavior) and then watch a TV program (the reward). The timing of your reward is important. To be effective, it must immediately follow the behavior. If you watch TV and then study, you may not get around to studying. If you watch the TV program tomorrow or next week, it is not a strong reinforcement because it is not an immediate reward.

Be careful about the kinds of rewards you use so that you do not get into habits that are detrimental to your health. If you use food as a reward for studying, you may increase your studying behavior, but you may also gain a few pounds. Using alcohol or drugs as a reward can start an addiction. Buying yourself a reward can ruin your budget. Good rewards do not involve too many calories, cost too much money, or involve alcohol or drugs.

You can also use a negative consequence to decrease a behavior. If you touch a hot stove and get burned, you quickly learn not to do it again. You could decide to miss your favorite television program if you do not complete your studying. However, this is not fun and you may feel deprived. You might even rebel and watch your favorite TV show anyway. See if you can find a way to use positive reinforcement (a reward) for increasing a behavior that is beneficial to you rather than using a negative consequence.

When we are young, our attitudes toward education are largely shaped by positive or negative rewards. If you were praised for being a good reader as a child, it is likely that you enjoyed reading and developed good reading skills. Maybe a teacher embarrassed you because of your math skills and you learned to be anxious about math. Think about areas of your education in which you excel, and see if you can recall someone praising or otherwise reinforcing that behavior. If you are a good athlete, did someone praise your athletic ability when you were younger? How was it rewarded? If you are not good at math, what were some early messages about your math performance? These early messages have a powerful influence on later behavior. You may need to put in some effort to learn new and more beneficial behaviors.

As a college student, you can use a reward as a powerful motivator. Praise yourself and think positively about your achievements in college even if the achievements come in small steps.

Success Is a Habit

We establish habits by taking small actions each day. Through repetition, these individual actions become habits. I once visited the Golden Gate Bridge in San Francisco and saw a cross section of the cable used to support the bridge. It was made of small metal strands twisted with other strands; then those cables were twisted together to make a stronger cable. Habits are a lot like cables. We start with one small action, and each successive action makes the habit stronger. Have you ever stopped to think that success can be a habit? We all have learned patterns of behavior that either help us to be successful or interfere with our success. With some effort and some basic understanding of behavior modification, you can choose to establish some new behaviors that lead to success or to get rid of behaviors that interfere with it.

> "Habits are first cobwebs, then cables."
> Spanish Proverb

> "We are what we repeatedly do. Excellence, then, is not an act but a habit."
> Aristotle

Seven Steps to Change a Habit

You can establish new habits that lead to your success. Once a habit is established, it can become a pattern of behavior that you do not need to think about very much. For example, new students often need to get into the habit of studying. Following is an outline of steps that can be helpful to establish new behaviors.

1. **State the problem.** What new habit would you like to start? What are your roadblocks or obstacles? What bad habit would you like to change? Be truthful about it. This is sometimes the most difficult step. Here are two different examples:

    *   I need to study to be successful in college. I am not in the habit of studying. I easily get distracted by work, family, friends, and other things I need to do. At the end of the day, I am too tired to study.

    *   I need to improve my diet. I am overweight. I eat too much fast food and am not careful about what I eat. I have no time for exercise.

2. **Change one small behavior at a time.** If you think about climbing a mountain, the task can seem overwhelming. However, you can take the first step. If you can change one small behavior, you can gain the confidence to change another. For example:

    *   I plan to study at least one hour each day on Mondays through Fridays.

    *   I plan to eat more fruits and vegetables each day.

Seven Steps to
Change a Habit

1. State the problem
2. Change one small
   behavior at a time
3. Be positive
4. Count the behavior
5. Picture the change
6. Practice the behavior
7. Reward yourself

State the behavior you would like to change. Make it small.

3. **State in a positive way the behavior you wish to establish.** For example, instead of the negative statements "I will not waste my time" or "I will not eat junk food," say, "I plan to study each day" or "I plan to eat fruits and vegetables each day."

4. **Count the behavior.** How often do you do this behavior? If you are trying to establish a pattern of studying, write down how much time you spend studying each day. If you are trying to improve your diet, write down everything that you eat each day. Sometimes just getting an awareness of your habit is enough to begin to make some changes.

Ten Habits of Successful College Students

Starting your college education will require you to establish some new habits to be successful.

1. Attend class.

College lectures supplement the material in the text, so it is important to attend class. Many college instructors will drop you if you miss three hours of class. After three absences, most students do not return to class. If your class is online, log in frequently.

2. Read the textbook.

Start early and read a little at a time. If you have a text with 400 pages, read 25 pages a week rather than trying to read it all at once.

3. Have an educational plan.

Counselors or advisors can assist you in making an educational plan so that you take the right classes and accomplish your educational goal as soon as possible.

4. Use college services.

Colleges offer valuable free services that help you to be successful. Take advantage of tutoring, counseling, health services, financial aid, the learning resources center (library) and many other services.

5. Get to know the faculty.

You can get to know the faculty by asking questions in class or meeting with your instructors during office hours. Your instructors can provide extra assistance and write letters of recommendation for scholarships, future employment, or graduate school.

6. Don't work too much.

Research has shown that full-time students should have no more than 20 hours of outside employment a week to be successful in college. If you have to work more than 20 hours a week, reduce your college load. If you are working 40 hours a week or more, take only one or two classes.

7. Take one step at a time.

If you are anxious about going to college, remember that each class you attend takes you another step toward your goal. If you take too many classes, especially in the beginning, you may become overwhelmed.

8. Have a goal for the future.

Know why you are in college and what you hope to accomplish. What career will you have in the future? Imagine your future lifestyle.

9. Visualize your success.

See yourself walking across the stage and receiving your college diploma. See yourself working at a job you enjoy.

10. Ask questions if you don't understand.

Asking questions not only helps you to find the answers, but it shows you are motivated to be successful. Starting your college education will require you to establish some new habits to be successful.

5. **Picture in your mind the actions you might take.** For example:

- I picture myself finding time to study in the library. I see myself walking to the library. I can see myself in the library studying.

- I see myself in the grocery store buying fruits and vegetables. I see myself packing these fruits and vegetables in my lunch. I see myself putting these foods in a place where I will notice them.

6. **Practice the behavior for 10 days.** In 10 days, you can get started on a new pattern of behavior. Once you have started, keep practicing the behavior for about a month to firmly establish your new pattern of behavior. The first three days are the most difficult. If you fail, don't give up. Just realize that you are human and keep trying for 10 days. Think positively that you can be successful. Write a journal entry or note on your calendar about what you have accomplished each day.

7. **Find a reward for your behavior.** Remember that we tend to repeat behaviors that are rewarded. Find rewards that do not involve too many calories, don't cost too much money, and don't involve alcohol or drugs. Also, rewards are most effective if they directly follow the behavior you wish to reinforce.

"The difference in winning and losing is most often . . . not quitting."

Walt Disney

"It's not that I'm so smart; it's just that I stay with problems longer."

Albert Einstein

QUIZ

Motivation

Test what you have learned by selecting the correct answers to the following questions:

1. If the behavior is followed by a reward

    a. it is likely to be increased.
    b. it is likely to be decreased.
    c. there will probably be no effect.

2. For rewards to be effective, they must occur

    a. before the behavior.
    b. immediately after the behavior.
    c. either before or after the behavior.

3. Manage your internal distractions by

    a. forcing yourself to concentrate.
    b. telling yourself not to worry about your problems.
    c. noticing when your attention has wandered and choosing where you want to focus your attention.

4. To be successful in college, it is best to use

    a. intrinsic motivation.
    b. extrinsic motivation.
    c. an external locus of control.

5. To change a habit,

    a. set high goals.
    b. focus on negative behavior.
    c. begin with a concrete behavior that can be counted.

How did you do on the quiz? Check your answers: 1. a, 2. b, 3. c, 4. a, 5. c

Persistence

There is an old saying that persistence will get you almost anything eventually. This saying applies to your success in life as well as in college. The first two to six weeks of college are a critical time in which many students drop out. Realize that college is a new experience and that you will face new challenges and growth experiences. Make plans to persist, especially in the first few weeks. Get to know a college counselor or advisor. These professionals can help you to get started in the right classes and answer any questions you might have. It is important to make a connection with a counselor or faculty member so that you feel comfortable in college and have the resources to obtain needed help. Plan to enroll on time so that you do not have to register late. It is crucial to attend the first class. In the first class, the professor explains the class requirements and expectations and sets the tone for the class. You may even get dropped from the class if you are not there on the first day. Get into the habit of studying right away. Make studying a habit that you start immediately at the beginning of the semester or quarter. If you can make it through the first six weeks, it is likely that you can finish the semester and complete your college education.

It has been said that 90 percent of success is just showing up. Any faculty member will tell you that the number one reason for students dropping out of college is lack of attendance. They know that when students miss three classes in a row, they are not likely to return. Even very capable students who miss class may find that they are lost when they come back. Many students are simply afraid to return. Classes such as math and foreign languages are sequential, and it is very difficult to make up work after an absence. One of the most important ways you can be successful is to make a habit of consistently showing up for class.

You will also need commitment to be successful. Commitment is a promise to yourself to follow through with something. In athletics, it is not necessarily the one with the best physical skills who makes the best athlete. Commitment and practice make a great athlete. Commitment means doing whatever is necessary to succeed. Like the good athlete, make a commitment to accomplishing your goals. Spend the time necessary to be successful in your studies.

When you face difficulties, persistence and commitment are especially important. History is full of famous people who contributed to society through persistence and commitment. Consider the following facts about Abraham Lincoln, for example.

- Failed in business at age 21.
- Was defeated in a legislative race at age 22.
- Failed again in business at age 24.
- Overcame the death of his sweetheart at age 26.
- Had a nervous breakdown at age 27.
- Lost a congressional race at age 34.
- Lost a congressional race at age 36.
- Lost a senatorial race at age 45.
- Failed in an effort to become vice president at age 47.
- Lost a senatorial race at age 49.
- Was elected president of the United States at age 52.[6]

You will face difficulties along the way in any worthwhile venture. The successful person keeps on trying. There are some precautions about persistence, however. Make sure that the goal you are trying to reach is attainable and valuable to you. As you learn more about yourself, you may want to change your goals. Also, persistence can be misguided if it involves other people. For example, if you decide that you want to marry someone and this someone does not want to marry you, it is better to focus your energy and attention on a different goal.

One of the best ways to be persistent is to accomplish your goals one step at a time. If you look at a mountain, it may seem too high to climb, but you can do it one step at a time. Araceli Segarra became the first Spanish woman to climb Mount Everest. At 29,028 feet, Mount Everest is the highest mountain in the world. It is so high that you need an oxygen tank to breathe at the top. So how did Araceli climb the mountain? She says that it took strength and concentration. She put one foot in front of the other. When she was near the top of the mountain, she was more tired

continued

than she had ever been in her life. She told herself that she would take 10 more steps. When she had taken 10 steps, she said, "I'm OK. I made it." Then she took 10 more steps until she reached the top of the mountain.

The goal of getting a college education may seem like a mountain that is difficult to climb. Break it into smaller steps that you can accomplish. See your college counselor or advisor, register for classes, attend the first class, read the first chapter, do the first assignment, and you will be on the road to your success. Then continue to break tasks into small, achievable steps and continue from one step to the next. And remember, persistence will get you almost anything eventually.

Courtesy of Western Michigan University

Journal Entry #5

What will you do if you are tempted to drop out of college? What steps can you take to be persistent in achieving your college goals? Are there times when it is best to change goals rather than to be persistent if your efforts are not working? Write a paragraph about how you will be persistent in reaching your college goals.

JOURNAL ENTRIES

Understanding Motivation

Go to http://www.collegesuccess1.com/JournalEntries.htm for Word files of the Journal Entries

Success over the Internet

Visit the *College Success Website* at http://www.collegesuccess1.com/

The *College Success Website* is continually updated with new topics and links to the material presented in this chapter. Topics include:

- How to improve concentration
- Motivation
- Positive attitude
- Balancing work, school, and social life
- Success factors for new college students
- How to change a habit
- Dealing with cravings and urges

Contact your instructor if you have any problems accessing the *College Success Website*.

Notes

1. W. Lewallen, "The Impact of Being Undecided on College Persistence," *Journal of College Student Development* 34 (1993): 103–12.

2. Marsha Fralick, "College Success: A Study of Positive and Negative Attrition," *Community College Review* 20 (1993): 29–36.

3. Ideas from Lina Rocha, Personal Development Instructor, Cuyamaca College, El Cajon, CA.

4. Christopher Peterson, *A Primer in Positive Psychology* (New York: Oxford University Press, 2006), 127.

5. M. J. Findlay and H. M. Cooper, "Locus of Control and Academic Achievement: A Literature Review," *Journal of Personality and Social Psychology* 44 (1983): 419–27.

6. Anthony Robbins, *Unlimited Power* (New York: Ballantine Books, 1986), 73.

Name _____ Date _____

A good way to begin your success in college is to assess your present skills to determine your strengths and areas that need improvement. Complete the following assessment to get an overview of the topics presented in the textbook and to measure your present skills.

Measure Your Success

The following statements represent major topics included in the textbook. Read the following statements and rate how true they are for you at the present time. At the end of the course, you will have the opportunity to complete this assessment again to measure your progress.

5 Definitely true
4 Mostly true
3 Somewhat true
2 Seldom true
1 Never true

_____ I am motivated to be successful in college.

_____ I know the value of a college education.

_____ I know how to establish successful patterns of behavior.

_____ I can concentrate on an important task until it is completed.

_____ I am attending college to accomplish my own personal goals.

_____ I believe to a great extent that my actions determine my future.

_____ I am persistent in achieving my goals.

_____ **Total points for Motivation**

_____ I can describe my personality type.

_____ I can list careers that match my personality type.

_____ I can describe my personal strengths and talents based on my personality type.

_____ I understand how my personality type affects how I manage my time and money.

_____ I know what college majors are most in demand.

_____ I am confident that I have chosen the best major for myself.

_____ Courses related to my major are interesting and exciting to me.

_____ **Total points for Personality and Major**

_____ I can describe my learning style.

_____ I can list study techniques that match my learning style.

_____ I understand how my personality affects my learning style.

_____ I understand the connection between learning and teaching style.

_____ I understand the concept of multiple intelligences.

_____ I can list my multiple intelligences.

_____ I create my own success.

_____ **Total points for Learning Style and Intelligence**

_____ I can describe my vocational interests.

_____ I can list careers that match my vocational interests.

_____ I can list my top five values.

_____ I generally consider my most important values when making decisions.

_____ My actions are generally guided by my personal values.

_____ My personal values motivate me to be successful.

_____ I can balance work, study, and leisure activities.

_____ **Total points for Interests and Values**

_____ I understand how current employment trends will affect my future.

_____ I know what work skills will be most important for the 21st century.

_____ I have an educational plan that matches my academic and career goals.

_____ I know the steps in making a good career decision.

_____ I have a good resume.

_____ I know how to interview for a job.

_____ I know how to choose a satisfying career.

_____ **Total points for Career and Education**

_____ I have a list or mental picture of my lifetime goals.

_____ I know what I would like to accomplish in the next four years.

_____ I spend my time on activities that help me accomplish my lifetime goals.

_____ I effectively use priorities in managing my time.

_____ I can balance study, work, and recreation time.

_____ I generally avoid procrastination on important tasks.

_____ I am good at managing my money.

_____ **Total points for Managing Time and Money**

_____ I know memory techniques and can apply them to my college studies.

_____ I can read a college textbook and remember the important points.

_____ I know how to effectively mark a college textbook.

_____ I can quickly survey a college text and select the main ideas.

_____ I generally have good reading comprehension.

_____ I can concentrate on the material I am reading.

_____ I am confident in my ability to read and remember college-level material.

_____ **Total points for Memory and Reading**

_____ I know how to listen for the main points in a college lecture.

_____ I am familiar with note-taking systems for college lectures.

_____ I know how to review my lecture notes.

_____ I feel comfortable with writing.

_____ I know the steps in writing a college term paper.

_____ I know how to prepare a speech.

_____ I am comfortable with public speaking.

_____ **Total points for Taking Notes, Writing, and Speaking**

_____ I know how to adequately prepare for a test.

_____ I can predict the questions that are likely to be on the test.

_____ I know how to deal with test anxiety.

_____ I am successful on math exams.

_____ I know how to make a reasonable guess if I am uncertain about the answer.

_____ I am confident of my ability to take objective tests.

_____ I can write a good essay answer.

_____ **Total points for Test Taking**

_____ I understand how my personality affects my communication style.

_____ I know how to be a good listener.

_____ I can use some basic techniques for good communication.

_____ I can identify some barriers to effective communication.

_____ I know how to deal with conflict.

_____ I feel confident about making new friends in college and on the job.

_____ I am generally a good communicator.

_____ **Total points for Communication and Relationships**

_____ I have the skills to analyze data, generate alternatives, and solve problems.

_____ I can identify fallacies in reasoning.

_____ I can apply the steps of critical thinking to analyze a complex issue.

_____ I am willing to consider different points of view.

_____ I can use brainstorming to generate a variety of ideas.

_____ I am good at visualization and creative imagination.

_____ I am generally curious about the world and can spot problems and opportunities.

_____ **Total points for Critical and Creative Thinking**

_____ I understand the basics of good nutrition.

_____ I understand how to maintain my ideal body weight.

_____ I exercise regularly.

_____ I avoid addictions to smoking, alcohol, and drugs.

_____ I protect myself from sexually transmitted diseases.

_____ I generally get enough sleep.

_____ I am good at managing stress.

_____ **Total points for Health**

_____ I understand the concept of diversity and know why it is important.

_____ I understand the basics of communicating with a person from a different culture.

_____ I understand how the global economy will affect my future career.

_____ I understand how the concept of the electronic village will affect my future.

_____ I am familiar with the basic vocabulary of diversity.

_____ I try to avoid stereotypes when dealing with others who are different than me.

_____ I try to understand and appreciate those who are different from me.

_____ **Total points for Diversity**

_____ I understand the theories of life stages.

_____ I can describe my present developmental stage in life.

_____ I have self-confidence.

_____ I use positive self-talk and affirmations.

_____ I have a visual picture of my future success.

_____ I have a clear idea of what happiness means to me.

_____ I usually practice positive thinking.

_____ **Total points for Future**

_____ I am confident of my ability to succeed in college.

_____ I am confident that my choice of a major is the best one for me.

_____ **Total additional points**

Total your points:

_____ Motivation

_____ Personality and Major

_____ Learning Style and Intelligence

_____ Interests and Values

_____ Career and Education

_____ Managing Time and Money

_____ Memory and Reading

_____ Taking Notes, Writing, and Speaking

_____ Test Taking

_____ Communication and Relationships

_____ Critical and Creative Thinking

_____ Health

_____ Diversity

_____ Future

_____ Additional Points

_____ **Grand total points**

If you scored

450–500   You are very confident of your skills for success in college. Maybe you do not need this class?

400–449   You have good skills for success in college. You can always improve.

350–399   You have average skills for success in college. You will definitely benefit from taking this course.

Below 350   You need some help to survive in college. You are in the right place to begin.

Use these scores to complete the Success Wheel that follows this assessment. Note that the additional points are not used in the chart.

Success Wheel

Name _____ Date _____

Use your scores from the Measure Your Success assessment to complete the following Success Wheel. Use different colored markers to shade in each section of the wheel.

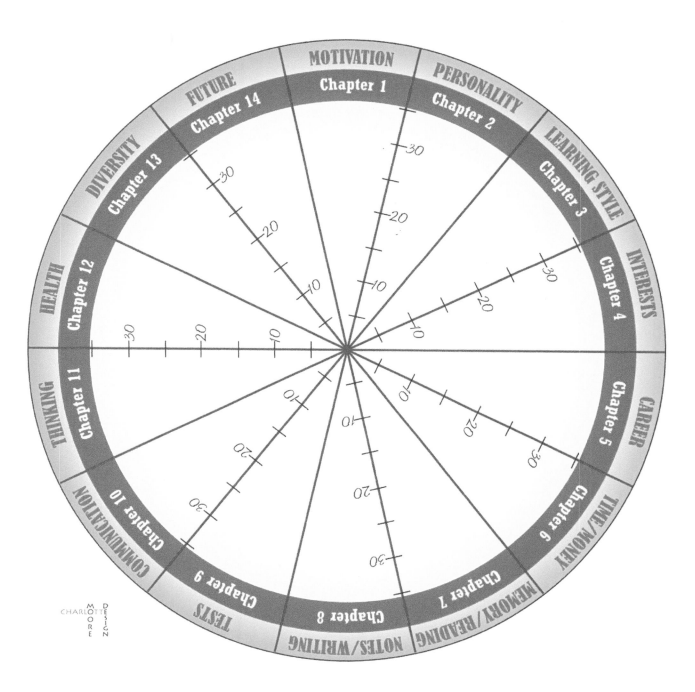

1. What are your best areas?

2. What are areas that need improvement?

Name _____   Date _____

Justin

It is the first day of class in the college success course. Justin is feeling excited and a little apprehensive as he walks into the class on the first day. He wonders if this is the right course for him. He managed to be successful in high school without much effort and thinks that college should be the same. His college advisor has recommended the course for all new students. He thinks that this course should be at least an easy A grade and it is not too important to attend every class. Justin has just graduated from high school and is looking forward to more freedom and independence. Justin has just been employed at a local sporting goods store. He is enjoying the job and the extra spending money. He started out working on Saturday only, but has now agreed to work 30 hours a week so that he can buy a new truck. School is not one of his top priorities, but his parents are insisting that he attend college so that he can get a better job in the future. How can Justin motivate himself to be successful in this course?

Anna

Anna walks into the classroom on the first day with a great deal of anxiety. She is returning to school 15 years after her high school graduation. Her children are getting a little older and she has decided to return to school to finish that degree that she has always wanted. Although having a college degree has been a lifelong dream of hers, she is uncertain about which major would be best. She is hoping to choose a major that leads to a well-paying job so that she can help her children with college expenses in the near future. She has a busy family life and is not sure how to add all the college activities to her schedule. The college success course seems like a good place to start. She looks around the classroom, notices that she is one of the older students in class, and hopes she can keep up with the younger students who have just graduated from high school. What steps can Anna take to be successful in this course?

What Do I Want from College?

Name _____ Date _____

Read the following list and place checkmarks next to your reasons for attending college. Think about why you are attending college and add your own personal reasons to the list.

_____ 1. To have financial security

_____ 2. To find a satisfying career

_____ 3. To explore possibilities provided by college

_____ 4. To expand my options

_____ 5. To become an educated person

_____ 6. To figure out what I want to do with my life

_____ 7. To develop my potential

_____ 8. To become a role model for my children

_____ 9. To make my parents happy

_____ 10. To respect myself

_____ 11. To feel good about myself

_____ 12. To see if I can do it

_____ 13. To meet interesting people

_____ 14. To have something to do and prevent boredom

_____ 15. To become the best I can be

_____ 16. To have better job opportunities

_____ 17. To have no regrets later on

_____ 18. To prepare for a good job or profession

_____ 19. To have job security

_____ 20. To gain confidence in myself

_____ 21. To get a degree

_____ 22. To gain a greater understanding of the world

_____ 23. To have fun

_____ 24. To understand myself

_____ 25. To learn how to think

_____ 26. To enjoy what I do for a living

_____ 27. To reach my potential

_____ 28. Because my parents want me to get a degree

_____ 29. For my own personal satisfaction

_____ 30. To make a difference in other people's lives

_____ 31. To have a position of power

_____ 32. To have respect

_____ 33. To have prestige

_____ 34. To have time and money for travel

_____ 35. To acquire knowledge

_____ 36. _____

_____ 37. _____

What are your top six reasons for attending college? You may include reasons not listed above. If you are tempted to give up on your college education, read this list and think about the reasons you have listed below.

1. _____   4. _____

2. _____   5. _____

3. _____   6. _____

How to Change a Habit

Name _____ Date _____

The following exercise will help you to practice the process of beginning successful new habits. Choose *one* of these simple 10-day projects:

- Monitor how many minutes you study each day.
- Monitor how many minutes you exercise each day.
- Monitor how you spend your money each day. Write down all your expenditures.
- Make a goal of eating breakfast. Write down what you eat for breakfast each day.
- Keep a list of the fruits and vegetables you eat each day.
- Count how many sodas you drink each day.
- Keep a log of time you sleep each night and make a note of how rested you feel the next day.
- Make a goal of making your bed or picking up your clothes. Record your progress each day.
- You can choose another behavior as long as it is realistic and achievable. You must be able to count it or describe the outcome. Consult with your instructor if you choose this option.

1. First, state the problem. Describe the behavior you want to change. What are your roadblocks or obstacles?

   For example: I get stressed when I run out of money before my next paycheck. I would like to manage my money better. One obstacle is my attitude that if I have money, I can spend it.

2. Choose one small behavior at a time. If you can change one small behavior, you can gain the confidence to change another.

   For example: A goal like improving money management is broad and vague. A good way to begin is to choose a small first step. A good first step is to keep track of expenditures so that you can begin to understand how you spend your money. The projects listed earlier are examples of small behaviors. If you are working on a different project, is it a small behavior that can be counted and one that can realistically be accomplished? List the small behavior that you will use for this project.

3. State in a positive way the behavior you wish to establish.

   For example: Instead of saying, "I will not spend all of my money before payday," say, "I will keep a money monitor for 10 days." Of course, the next step would be to work on a budget. If necessary, rewrite your goal in a positive way.

4. Count the behavior. Sometimes just becoming aware of your habit is enough to begin making some changes.

   For example: For the next 10 days, I will write down all my expenditures.

5. Picture in your mind the actions you might take to accomplish your goal and write them down in the following space.

   For example: I see myself writing down all my expenses on a sheet of paper. I will do this each day so that I can find out where I spend my money and begin to manage my money better. I see myself less stressed because I will have money for the things I need.

6. What reward will you use to reinforce the behavior? Rewards are most effective if they directly follow the behavior you wish to reinforce. Remember that good rewards do not have too many calories, cost too much money, or involve alcohol or drugs. List your rewards.

7. Practice the behavior for *10 days*. The first three days are the most difficult. If you fail, don't give up. Just realize that you are human and keep trying for 10 days. Think positively that you can be successful. Use the space below or a separate sheet of paper to count how many times you did the behavior each day and what happened. Remember, you can get started on a new habit in 10 days, but you will need to continue for about a month to firmly establish your new pattern of behavior.

Day 1: _____
_____
_____

Day 2: _____
_____
_____

Day 3: _____
_____
_____

Day 4: _____
_____
_____

Day 5: _____
_____
_____

Day 6: _____
_____
_____

Day 7: _____
_____
_____

Day 8: _____
_____
_____

Day 9: _____
_____
_____

Day 10: _____
_____
_____

How did this project work for you?

Name _____ Date _____

Use this text or any new text to answer the following questions. Challenge yourself to do this exercise quickly. Remember that a textbook survey should take no longer than five to 15 minutes. Try to complete this exercise in 15 minutes to allow time for writing. Notice the time when you start and finish.

1. Write two key ideas found in the introduction or preface to the book.

2. Looking at the table of contents, list the first five main ideas covered in the text.

3. Write down five interesting topics that you found in the book.

4. What did you find at the back of the book (e.g., index, glossary, appendixes)?

5. How long did it take you to do this exercise? _____

6. Briefly, what did you think of this textbook skimming exercise?

Learning Style and Intelligence

Learning Objectives

Read to answer these key questions:

- What is my learning style?

- What is the best learning environment for me?

- What are some specific learning strategies that match my learning style?

- How is learning style connected to personality type?

- What are some specific learning strategies that are based on personality type?

- How can I understand and adapt to my professor's personality type (or "psych out" the professor)?

- What kinds of intelligence do I have?

- How can I create my success?

Alec Kraus

Majoring in Economics and Criminal Justice

Hometown: Orland Park, IL

FYS Intern, Student Ambassador, CJSA member, Alpha Lambda Delta member

I hope you are so excited to be starting your college career here at WMU! College is a time that **you will be continually challenged in many ways**. No matter what you are here to study, you can **always benefit from what Western has to offer**!

When I took many of my general requirement classes, I was not as motivated as I would have been in a class for my major, simply because the material wasn't always as interesting to me. What always helped me was realizing that **there was a reason for me to be there**, even if it wasn't obvious. Sometimes a class might show you how to see things from a different perspective, **help you think critically** in different ways, or teach you how to **manage your time** and efforts when you might not be as driven. Even when it is not completely noticeable, **there is always a way you can benefit from a class!**

When you realize how to **make WMU your home**, you will be driven more to succeed. There is always a club, an activity, or an event going on for every interest. Being **surrounded by good friends** and a community that is **focused on your success** will help drive you to **be the best you can**! I encourage you to **find your home here** and let yourself succeed. Don't ever convince yourself that you can't do something, because then you won't. **Trust yourself** and don't be afraid to make mistakes. **If you slip, you only fail when you don't pick yourself back up!**

Bronco Pride!

> "Learning is a treasure that will follow its owner anywhere."
> Chinese Proverb

Knowing about your learning style can help you to choose effective strategies for learning in school and on the job. Knowing about your preferred learning environment can help you increase productivity. Discovering your multiple intelligences will help you to gain an appreciation of your gifts and talents that can be used to develop your self-confidence and choose the career that is right for you.

What Is Learning Style?

Just as each individual has a unique personality, each individual has a unique learning style. It is important to remember that there are no good or bad learning styles. Learning style is simply your preferred way of learning. It is how you like to learn and how you learn best. By understanding your learning style, you can maximize your potential by choosing the learning techniques that work best for you. This chapter explores the many factors that determine how you learn best. Each individual also has a preferred learning environment. Knowing about your preferred learning environment and learning style helps you be more productive, increase achievement, be more creative, improve problem solving, make good decisions, and learn effectively. Personality type also influences how we learn. Another way to think about learning style is through an awareness of the many kinds of intelligences that we possess. Knowing about how you learn best helps to reduce frustration and increase your confidence in learning.

Gary Price has developed the Productivity Environmental Preference Survey (PEPS), which is included with your textbook. It identifies 20 different elements of learning style and environment, including the immediate environment, emotional factors, sociological needs, and physical needs. As you read the description of each of these elements, think about your preferences.[1]

1. **Sound.** Some students need a quiet environment for study, whereas others find it distracting if it is too quiet.

- If you prefer quiet, use the library or find another quiet place. If you cannot find a quiet place, sound-blocking earphones or earplugs may be helpful. Remember that not all people need a quiet environment for study.
- If you study better with sound, play soft music or study in open areas. Use headphones for your music if you are studying with those who prefer quiet.

2. **Light.** Some students prefer bright light to see what they are studying, whereas others find bright light uncomfortable or irritating.
   - If you prefer bright light, study near a window with light shining over your shoulder or invest in a good study lamp.
   - If you prefer dim lights, sit away from direct sunlight or use a shaded light.

3. **Temperature.** Some students perform better in cool temperatures and others prefer warmer temperatures.
   - If you prefer a warm environment, remember to bring your sweater or jacket. Sit near a window or other source of heat.
   - If you prefer a cooler environment, study in a well-ventilated environment or even outside in the shade.

4. **Design.** Some students study best in a more formal environment or less formal environment.
   - If you prefer a formal environment, sit in a straight chair and use a desk.
   - If you prefer an informal environment, sit on the sofa or a soft chair or on some pillows on the floor.

5. **Motivation.** Some students are self-motivated to learn, and others lack motivation.
   - If you are self-motivated, you usually like school and enjoy learning on your own.
   - If you lack motivation, think about your reasons for attending college and review the material in the motivation chapter of this book.

6. **Persistence.** Some students finish what they start, whereas others have many things going on at once and may not finish what they have started.
   - If you are persistent, you generally finish what you start.
   - If you lack persistence, you may get bored or distracted easily. You may find it easier to break tasks into small steps and work steadily toward completing assignments on time. Think about your college and career goals to increase motivation and persistence.

7. **Responsibility (conforming).** This element has a unique meaning in the area of learning style.
   - Some students like to please others by doing what is asked of them. They complete assignments to please the professor.
   - Other students are less likely to conform. They prefer to complete assignments because they want to rather than because someone else wants the assignment done. These students may need to look for something interesting and personally meaningful in school assignments.

8. **Structure.** Students prefer more or less structure.
   - Students who prefer structure want the teacher to give details about how to complete the assignment. They need clear directions before completing an assignment.
   - Students who prefer less structure want the teacher to give assignments in which the students can choose the topic and organize the material on their own.

9. **Alone/peer.** Some students prefer to study alone, and others prefer to study with others.
   - You may find other people distracting and prefer to study alone. You need to study in a private area.
   - You may enjoy working in a group because talking with others helps you to learn.

10. **Authority figures present.** Some students are more or less independent learners.
    - Some students prefer to have the professor available to guide learning. In the college environment, students may prefer traditional face-to-face classes.
    - Others prefer to work on their own. In the college environment, students may prefer online classes or independent study.

11. **Several ways.** Some students learn in several ways, and others have definite preferences.
    - Some students like variety and can learn either on their own or with others.
    - Some students definitely prefer learning on their own or prefer learning with others.

12. **Auditory.** Some students prefer to learn through listening and talking.
    - Those who prefer auditory learning find it easier to learn through lectures, audio materials, discussion, and oral directions.
    - Those who do not prefer auditory learning may find their minds wandering during lectures and become confused by oral directions. They do not learn through others talking about the topic. These students should read the material before the lecture and take notes during the lecture. Review the notes periodically to remember the material.

13. **Visual.** Some students learn through reading or seeing things.
    - Those who prefer visual learning benefit from pictures and reading.
    - Those who are not visual learners may dislike reading. If auditory learning is preferred, attend the lecture first to hear the lecturer talk about the subject and then do the reading. It is important to do the reading because not all the material is covered in the lecture.

14. **Tactile.** Some students prefer to touch the material as they learn.
    - Students who prefer tactile learning prefer manipulative and three-dimensional materials. They learn from working with models and writing. Taking notes is one of the best tactile learning strategies.
    - Students who are not tactile learners can focus on visual or auditory strategies for learning.

15. **Kinesthetic.** Kinesthetic learning is related to tactile learning. Students learn best by acting out material to be learned or moving around while learning.
    - Students who prefer kinesthetic learning enjoy field trips, drama, and becoming physically involved with learning. For example, they can learn fractions by slicing an apple into parts or manipulating blocks. It is important to be actively involved in learning.
    - Students who are not kinesthetic learners will use another preferred method of learning such as auditory or visual.

16. **Intake.** Some students need to chew or drink something while learning.
    - If you prefer intake while learning, drink water and have nutritious snacks such as fruits and vegetables.
    - Some students do not need intake to study and find food items distracting.

17. **Evening/morning.** Some students are more awake in the morning and prefer to go to bed early at night. If this is your preference, schedule your most challenging studying in the morning and do your routine tasks later.

18. **Late morning.** Some students are more awake from 10:00 A.M. until noon. If this is your preference, use this time for studying. Use other times for more routine tasks.

19. **Afternoon.** Some students are most productive in the afternoon. If this is your preference, schedule your study time in the afternoon. Do your routine tasks at other times.

20. **Mobility.** Some students like to move around while studying.

- If you prefer mobility, you may find it difficult to sit still for a long time. Take a break every 15 or 20 minutes to move around. When choosing an occupation, consider one that requires you to move around.

- If you don't need to move around while studying, a stationary desk and chair are sufficient to help you concentrate on learning.

Learning Techniques

It is important to connect specific learning strategies to your preferred learning style. Even if you have definite preferences, you can experiment with other styles to improve your learning. If you become frustrated with a learning task, first try a familiar technique that you have used successfully in the past. If that does not work, experiment with different ways of learning. If one technique does not work, try another. It is powerful to combine techniques. For example, it is a good idea to make pictures of what you want to remember (visual), recite the ideas you want to remember (auditory), and take notes (tactile).

The following are specific techniques for each type of learner. Underline or highlight techniques that are useful to you.

> "What I hear, I forget.
> What I see, I remember.
> What I do, I know."
> Chinese Proverb

Visual Learning Techniques

- Make a mental photograph or mental video of what you want to remember. Put action and color in the picture.
- Use flash cards and look at them frequently.
- Use different colors to highlight or underline your reading and lecture notes.
- Draw pictures to remember what you are learning.
- Use symbols or pictures in the margin to emphasize important points.
- Draw a map or outline of important points.

Auditory Learning Techniques

- Discuss what you have learned with others.
- Participate in study groups.
- Teach others what you want to learn.
- Use music to study if it does not distract you or break your concentration.
- Use music as a study break.
- Add rhythm or music to the items you are trying to remember.
- Recite aloud or silently in your mind while you are reading.
- Use flash cards and say the items on the cards.
- Use a tape recorder to recite and review important points from the reading or lecture.

Kinesthetic and Tactile Learning Techniques

- Read while walking or pacing.
- Study outside when practical.
- Take notes on lectures.
- Highlight or underline your reading material and lecture notes.
- Write summaries of the material to be learned.
- Outline chapters.
- Think of practical applications for abstract material.
- Act out the material as in a play.
- Use puzzles, games, and computers.
- Make a game out of flash cards. Count the number of answers you get correct. Set a time limit and see if you can get through the cards in the time allowed.
- Take something apart and put it together again.

Journal Entry #2

List five useful learning strategies based on your visual, auditory, or kinesthetic and tactile learning preferences. For example, the physical act of writing or taking notes helps kinesthetic and tactile learners remember what they are trying to learn.

Developing Your E-Learning Style

"The illiterate of the 21st century will not be those who cannot read and write, but those who cannot learn, unlearn, and relearn."

Alvin Toffler

There are many opportunities for learning online, including online courses, professional development, or learning for your personal life. Students who are independent learners or introverts who enjoy individual learning in a quiet place may prefer online learning. Students who prefer having a professor to guide learning with immediate feedback and extraverts who are energized by social interaction may prefer traditional classroom education. Because of work, family, and time constraints, online learning might be a convenient way to access education. No matter what your learning style, you are likely to be in situations where you may want to take advantage of online learning.

If you have never taken an online course, be aware of some of the myths of online learning. One of the most popular myths is than online courses are easier than traditional courses. Online courses cover the same content and are just as rigorous as traditional face-to-face courses. It is likely that your online course will require more writing; instead of responding verbally in discussions, you will have to write your answer. Online courses generally require the same amount of time as traditional courses. However, you will save time in commuting to class and have the added convenience of working on your class at any time or place where you can access the Internet.

Here are some suggestions for a successful e-learning experience.

- The most important factor in online learning is to **log in regularly** and complete the work in a systematic way. Set goals for what you need to accomplish each week and do the work a step at a time. Get in the habit of regularly doing your online study, just as you would attend a traditional course each week.

- It is important to **carefully read the instructions** for the assignments and **ask for help** if you need it. Your online professor will not know when you need help.

- Begin your online work by getting familiar with the requirements and components of the course. Generally online courses have reading material, quizzes, discussion boards, chat rooms, assignments, and multimedia presentations. Make sure that you **understand all the resources, components, and requirements** of the course.

- **Have a backup plan** if your computer crashes or your Internet connection is interrupted. Colleges generally have computer labs where you can do your work if you have technical problems at home.

- Remember to **participate** in the online discussions or chats. It is usually part of your grade and a good way to learn from other students and apply what you have learned. The advantage of online communication is that you have time to think about your responses.

- **Check your grades** online to make sure you are completing all the requirements. Celebrate your success as you complete your online studies. Online learning becomes easier with experience.

Personality and Learning Preferences

Learning preferences are also connected to personality type. As a review, according to the work of Carl Jung, Katherine Briggs, and Isabel Myers, personality has four dimensions:

1. Extraversion or Introversion

2. Sensing or Intuition

3. Thinking or Feeling

4. Judging or Perceiving

What is your personality type? To review, read the following brief descriptions and think about your preferences:

Extraverts focus their energy on the world outside themselves. They enjoy interaction with others and get to know a lot of different people. They enjoy and are usually good at communication. They are energized by social interaction and prefer being active. These types are often described as talkative and social.

Introverts focus their energy on the world inside of themselves. They enjoy spending time alone and think about the world in order to understand it. Introverts like more limited social contacts, preferring smaller groups or one-on-one relationships. These types are often described as quiet or reserved.

Sensing persons prefer to use the senses to take in information (what they see, hear, taste, touch, smell). They focus on "what is" and trust information that is concrete and observable. They learn through experience.

INtuitive persons rely on instincts and focus on "what could be." While we all use our five senses to perceive the world, the intuitive person is interested in relationships, possibilities, meanings, and implications. They value inspiration and trust their "sixth sense" or hunches. We all use our senses and intuition in our daily lives, but we usually have a preference for one mode or another.

Thinking individuals make decisions based on logic. They are objective and analytical. They look at all the evidence and reach an impersonal conclusion. They are concerned with what they think is right.

ACTIVITY

Your Personality Style

Circle your personality type.

Extravert	or	Introvert
Sensing	or	Intuitive
Thinking	or	Feeling
Judging	or	Perceptive

Each personality type has a natural preference for how to learn. When learning something new, it may be easiest and most efficient to use the style that matches your personality type. It is also a good idea to experiment with using new techniques commonly used by other types. There is no learning style that works best in all situations. You may need to adapt your learning style based on the learning activity. As you look at the chart below, think about your personality type and learning preferences:

Learning Preferences Associated with Personality Types[2]

Extraversion	Introversion
Learn best when in action	Learn best by pausing to think
Value physical activity	Value reading
Like to study with others	Prefer to study individually
Say they're above average in verbal and interpersonal skills	Say they're below average in verbal expression
Say they need training in reading and writing papers	Say they need training in public speaking
Background sounds help them study	Need quiet for concentration
Want faculty who encourage discussion	Want faculty who give clear lectures

Sensing	INtuition
Seek specific information	Seek quick insights
Memorize facts	Use imagination to go beyond facts
Value what is practical	Value what is original
Follow instructions	Create their own directions
Like hands-on experience	Like theories to give perspective
Trust material as presented	Read between the lines
Want faculty who give clear assignments	Want faculty who encourage independent thinking

Thinking		Feeling	
Want objective material to study		Want to be able to relate to the material personally	
Logic guides learning		Personal values are important	
Like to critique new ideas		Like to please instructors	
Can easily find flaws in an argument		Can easily find something to appreciate	
Learn by challenge and debate		Learn by being supported and appreciated	
Want faculty who make logical presentations		Want faculty who establish personal rapport with students	

Judging		Perceiving	
Like formal instructions for solving problems		Like to solve problems informally	
Value dependability		Value change	
Plan work well in advance		Work spontaneously	
Work steadily toward goals		Work impulsively with bursts of energy	
Like to be in charge of events		Like to adapt to events	
Drive toward closure (finish)		Stay open to new information	
Want faculty to be organized		Want faculty to be entertaining and inspiring	

Feeling individuals make decisions based on what is important to them and matches their personal values. They are concerned about what they feel is right.

Judging types like to live in a structured, orderly, and planned way. They are happy when their lives are structured and matters are settled. They like to have control over their lives. Judging does not mean to judge others. Think of this type as orderly and organized.

Perceptive types like to live in a spontaneous and flexible way. They are happy when their lives are open to possibilities. They try to understand life rather than control it. Think of this type as spontaneous and flexible.

Learning Strategies for Different Personality Types

Based on the above descriptions of learning preferences, the following learning strategies are suggested along with some cautions for each type. As you read these descriptions, think about those suggestions and cautions that apply to you.

Extravert

1. Since extraverts learn best when talking, discuss what you have learned with others. Form a study group.

2. Extraverts like variety and action. Take frequent breaks and do something active during your break such as walking around.

3. *Caution!* You may become so distracted by activity and socialization that your studying does not get done.

Introvert

1. Since introverts like quiet for concentration, find a quiet place to study by yourself.

2. Plan to study for longer periods of time and in a way that minimizes interruptions. Unplug the phone or study in the library.

3. *Caution!* You may miss out on sharing ideas and the fun social life of college.

Sensing

1. Sensing types are good at mastering facts and details.

2. Think about practical applications in order to motivate yourself to learn. Ask, "How can I use this information?"

3. *Caution!* You may miss the big picture or general outline by focusing too much on the facts and details. Make a general outline to see the relationship and meaning of the facts.

Intuitive

1. Intuitive types are good at learning concepts and theories.

2. As you are reading, ask yourself, "What is the main point?"

3. *Caution!* Because this type focuses on general concepts and theories, they are likely to miss details and facts. To learn details, organize them into broad categories that have meaning for you.

Thinking

1. Thinking types are good at logic.

2. As you are reading, ask yourself, "What do I think of these ideas?" Discuss or debate your ideas with others.

3. Allow time to think and reflect on your studies.

4. If possible, pick instructors whom you respect and who are intellectually challenging.

5. *Caution!* Others may be offended by your logic and love of debate. Learn to respect the ideas of others.

Feeling

1. Feeling types need a comfortable environment in order to concentrate.

2. For motivation, search for personal meaning in your studies. Ask how the material affects you or others. Look for a supportive environment or study group.

3. Help others to learn.

4. When possible, choose classes that relate to your personal interests.

5. If possible, select instructors who get to know the students and establish a positive learning environment.

6. *Caution!* You may neglect studying because of time spent helping others or may find it difficult to pay attention to material that is not personally meaningful.

Judging

1. Judging types are orderly and organized. Find ways to organize the material to learn it easier.

2. If possible, select instructors who present material in an organized way.

3. Set goals and use a schedule to motivate yourself. This type is naturally good at time management.

4. Use a daily planner, calendar, or to-do list.

5. *Caution!* Being too structured and controlled may limit your creativity and cause conflict with others who are different. Judging types are sometimes overachievers who get stressed easily.

Perceptive

1. Perceptive students are good at looking at all the possibilities and keeping options open.

2. Allow enough time to be thorough and complete your work.

3. Keep learning fun and interesting.

4. Study in groups that have some perceptive types and some judging types. In this way, you can explore possibilities, have fun, and be organized.

5. *Caution!* Work on managing your time to meet deadlines. Be careful not to overextend yourself by working on too many projects at once.

Journal Entry #3

Write a paragraph about your personality type and how it affects your learning style. Begin your paragraph by listing the four letters of your personality type. Tell how these personal characteristics affect your learning style. Include at least four learning strategies that match your personality type. For example:

My personality type is ISFJ. Being an introvert, I like quiet for concentration and prefer to study quietly in the library. I am also a sensing type . . .

Understanding Your Professor's Personality

Different personality types have different expectations of teachers.

- Extraverts want faculty who encourage class discussion.
- Introverts want faculty who give clear lectures.
- Sensing types want faculty who give clear assignments.
- Intuitive types want faculty who encourage independent thinking.
- Thinking types want faculty who make logical presentations.
- Feeling types want faculty who establish personal rapport with students.
- Judging types want faculty to be organized.
- Perceptive types want faculty to be entertaining and inspiring.

"The wisest mind has something yet to learn."
George Santayana

"Tell me and I forget.
Teach me and I remember.
Involve me and I learn."
Benjamin Franklin

What can you do if your personality and the professor's personality are different? This is often the case. In a study reported by *Consulting Psychologist Press,* college faculty were twice as likely as students to be introverted intuitive types interested in abstractions and learning for its own sake.[3] College students are twice as likely as faculty to be extraverted sensing types who are interested in practical learning. There are three times more sensing and perceptive students than faculty. Faculty tend to be intuitive and judging types. Students expect faculty to be practical, fun, and flexible. Faculty tend to be theoretical and organized. In summary:

College faculty tend to be	College students tend to be
Introverted	Extraverted
Intuitive	Sensing
Judging	Perceptive

Of course, the above is not always true, but there is a good probability that you will have college professors who are very different from you. First, try to understand the professor's personality. This has been called "psyching out the professor." You can usually tell the professor's personality type on the first day of class by examining class materials and observing his or her manner of presentation. If you understand the professor's personality type, you will know what to expect. Next, try to appreciate what the professor has to offer. You may need to adapt your style to fit. If you are a perceptive type, be careful to meet the due dates of your assignments. Experiment with different study techniques so that you can learn the material presented.

Courtesy of Western Michigan University

Journal Entry #4

How can you use your knowledge of personality type to understand your professor's teaching style and expectations? What should you do if your personality does not match the professor's personality? For example, if your professor is a judging type and you are a perceptive type, how can you adapt to be successful in this course?

Learning Style

Test what you have learned by selecting the correct answers to the following questions.

1. The best environment for learning

   a. matches your learning style.
   b. is a straight chair and a desk.
   c. includes music in the background.

2. Kinesthetic types learn best by

   a. listening to lectures.
   b. reading the textbook.
   c. taking notes and reviewing them.

3. If you become frustrated in learning, it is best to

   a. keep trying.
   b. take a long break.
   c. take a short break and then apply your preferred learning style.

4. Introverts would probably prefer

   a. studying quietly in the library.
   b. participating in a study group.
   c. learning through classroom discussions.

5. When working on a term paper, perceptive types would probably prefer

   a. organizing the project and completing it quickly.
   b. making a plan and finishing early.
   c. looking at all the possibilities and keeping their options open.

How did you do on the quiz? Check your answers: 1. a, 2. c, 3. c, 4. a, 5. c

Multiple Intelligences

In 1904, the French psychologist Alfred Binet developed the IQ test, which provided a single score to measure intelligence. This once widely used and accepted test came into question because it measured the intelligence of individuals in schools in a particular culture. In different cultures and different situations, the test was less valid. As an alternative to traditional IQ tests, Harvard professor Howard Gardner developed the theory of multiple intelligences. He looked at intelligence in a broader and more inclusive way than people had done in the past.

Howard Gardner observed famous musicians, artists, athletes, scientists, inventors, naturalists, and others who were recognized contributors to society to formulate a more meaningful definition of intelligence. He defined intelligence as **the human ability to solve problems or design or compose something valued in at least one culture**. His definition broadens the scope of human potential. He identified eight different intelligences: musical, interpersonal, logical-mathematical, spatial, bodily-kinesthetic, linguistic, intrapersonal, and naturalist. He selected these intelligences because they are all represented by an area in the brain and are valued in different cultures. Howard Gardner has proposed adding existential intelligence to the list. He defines existential intelligence as the capacity to ask profound questions about the meaning of life and death. This intelligence is the cornerstone of art, religion, and philosophy.[4] His theory can help us to understand and use many different kinds of talents.

Within the theory of multiple intelligences, learning style is defined as intelligences put to work. These intelligences are measured by looking at performance in activities associated with each intelligence. A key idea in this theory is that most people can develop all of their intelligences and become relatively competent in each area. Another key idea is that these intelligences work together in complex ways to make us unique. For example, an athlete uses bodily-kinesthetic intelligence to run, kick, or jump. They use spatial intelligence to keep their eye on the ball and hit it. They also need linguistic and interpersonal skills to be good members of a team.

Developing intelligences is a product of three factors:

1. Biological endowment based on heredity and genetics

2. Personal life history

3. Cultural and historical background[5]

For example, Wolfgang Amadeus Mozart was born with musical talent (biological endowment). Members of his family were musicians who encouraged Mozart in music (personal life history). Mozart lived in Europe during a time when music flourished and wealthy patrons were willing to pay composers (cultural and historical background).

Each individual's life history contains **crystallizers** that promote the development of the intelligences and **paralyzers** that inhibit the development of the intelligences. These crystallizers and paralyzers often take place in early childhood. For example, Einstein was given a magnetic compass when he was four years old. He became so interested in the compass that he started on his journey of exploring the universe. An example of a paralyzer is being embarrassed or feeling humiliated about your math skills in elementary school so that you begin to lose confidence in your ability to do math. Paralyzers involve shame, guilt, fear, and anger and prevent intelligence from being developed.

Describing Your Multiple Intelligences

Below are some definitions and examples of the different intelligences. As you read each section, think positively about your intelligence in this area. Place a checkmark in front of each item that is true for you.

Musical

Musical intelligence involves hearing and remembering musical patterns and manipulating patterns in music. Some occupations connected with this intelligence include musician, performer, composer, and music critic. Place a checkmark next to each skill that you possess in this area.

_____ I enjoy singing, humming, or whistling.

_____ One of my interests is playing recorded music.

_____ I have collections of recorded music.

_____ I play or used to play a musical instrument.

_____ I can play the drums or tap out rhythms.

_____ I appreciate music.

_____ Music affects how I feel.

_____ I enjoy having music on while working or studying.

_____ I can clap my hands and keep time to music.

_____ I can tell when a musical note is off key.

_____ I remember melodies and the words to songs.

_____ I have participated in a band, chorus, or other musical group.

Look at the items you have checked above and summarize your musical intelligence.

_____

_____

_____

Interpersonal

Interpersonal intelligence is defined as understanding people. Occupations connected with this intelligence involve working with people and helping them, as in education or health care. Place a checkmark next to each skill that you possess in this area.

_____ I enjoy being around people.

_____ I am sensitive to other people's feelings.

_____ I am a good listener.

_____ I understand how others feel.

_____ I have many friends.

_____ I enjoy parties and social gatherings.

_____ I enjoy participating in groups.

_____ I can get people to cooperate and work together.

_____ I am involved in clubs or community activities.

_____ People come to me for advice.

_____ I am a peacemaker.

_____ I enjoy helping others.

Look at the items you have checked above and summarize your interpersonal intelligence.

_____

_____

_____

Logical-Mathematical

Logical-mathematical intelligence involves understanding abstract principles and manipulating numbers, quantities, and operations. Some examples of occupations associated with logical-mathematical intelligence are mathematician, tax accountant, scientist, and computer programmer. Place a checkmark next to each skill that you possess. Keep an open mind. People usually either love or hate this area.

_____ I can do arithmetic problems quickly.

_____ I enjoy math.

_____ I enjoy doing puzzles.

_____ I enjoy working with computers.

_____ I am interested in computer programming.

_____ I enjoy science classes.

_____ I enjoy doing the experiments in lab science courses.

_____ I can look at information and outline it easily.

_____ I understand charts and diagrams.

_____ I enjoy playing chess or checkers.

_____ I use logic to solve problems.

_____ I can organize things and keep them in order.

Look at the items you have checked above and summarize your logical-mathematical intelligence.

_____

_____

_____

Spatial

Spatial intelligence involves the ability to manipulate objects in space. For example, a baseball player uses spatial intelligence to hit a ball. Occupations associated with spatial intelligence include pilot, painter, sculptor, architect, inventor, and surgeon. This intelligence is often used in athletics, the arts, or the sciences. Place a checkmark next to each skill that you possess in this area.

_____ I can appreciate a good photograph or piece of art.

_____ I think in pictures and images.

_____ I can use visualization to remember.

_____ I can easily read maps, charts, and diagrams.

_____ I participate in artistic activities (art, drawing, painting, photography).

_____ I know which way is north, south, east, and west.

_____ I can put things together.

_____ I enjoy jigsaw puzzles or mazes.

_____ I enjoy seeing movies, slides, or photographs.

_____ I can appreciate good design.

_____ I enjoy using telescopes, microscopes, or binoculars.

_____ I understand color, line, shape, and form.

Look at the items you have checked above and summarize your spatial intelligence.

_____

_____

_____

Bodily-Kinesthetic

Bodily-kinesthetic intelligence is defined as being able to use your body to solve problems. People with bodily-kinesthetic intelligence make or invent objects or perform. They learn by doing, touching, and handling. Occupations connected to this type of intelligence include athlete, performer (dancer, actor), craftsperson, sculptor, mechanic, and surgeon. Place a checkmark next to each skill that you possess in this area.

_____ I am good at using my hands.

_____ I have good coordination and balance.

_____ I learn best by moving around and touching things.

_____ I participate in physical activities or sports.

_____ I learn new sports easily.

_____ I enjoy watching sports events.

_____ I am skilled in a craft such as woodworking, sewing, art, or fixing machines.

_____ I have good manual dexterity.

_____ I find it difficult to sit still for a long time.

_____ I prefer to be up and moving.

_____ I am good at dancing and remember dance steps easily.

_____ It was easy for me to learn to ride a bike or skateboard.

Look at the items you checked above and describe your bodily-kinesthetic intelligence.

_____

_____

_____

Linguistic

People with linguistic intelligence are good with language and words. They have good reading, writing, and speaking skills. Linguistic intelligence is an asset in any occupation. Specific related careers include writing, education, and politics. Place a checkmark next to each skill that you possess in this area.

_____ I am a good writer.

_____ I am a good reader.

_____ I enjoy word games and crossword puzzles.

_____ I can tell jokes and stories.

_____ I am good at explaining.

_____ I can remember names, places, facts, and trivia.

_____ I'm generally good at spelling.

_____ I have a good vocabulary.

_____ I read for fun and relaxation.

_____ I am good at memorizing.

_____ I enjoy group discussions.

_____ I have a journal or diary.

Look at the items you have checked above and summarize your linguistic intelligence.

_____

_____

_____

Intrapersonal

Intrapersonal intelligence is the ability to understand yourself and how to best use your natural talents and abilities. Examples of careers associated with this intelligence include novelist, psychologist, or being self-employed. Place a checkmark next to each skill that you possess in this area.

_____ I understand and accept my strengths and weaknesses.

_____ I am very independent.

_____ I am self-motivated.

_____ I have definite opinions on controversial issues.

_____ I enjoy quiet time alone to pursue a hobby or work on a project.

_____ I am self-confident.

_____ I can work independently.

_____ I can help others with self-understanding.

_____ I appreciate quiet time for concentration.

_____ I am aware of my own feelings and sensitive to others.

_____ I am self-directed.

_____ I enjoy reflecting on ideas and concepts.

Look at the items you have checked above and summarize your intrapersonal intelligence.

_____

_____

_____

Naturalist

The naturalist is able to recognize, classify, and analyze plants, animals, and cultural artifacts. Occupations associated with this intelligence include botanist, horticulturist, biologist, archeologist, and environmental occupations. Place a checkmark next to each skill you possess in this area.

_____ I know the names of minerals, plants, trees, and animals.

_____ I think it is important to preserve our natural environment.

_____ I enjoy taking classes in the natural sciences such as biology.

_____ I enjoy the outdoors.

_____ I take care of flowers, plants, trees, or animals.

_____ I am interested in archeology or geology.

_____ I would enjoy a career involved in protecting the environment.

_____ I have or used to have a collection of rocks, shells, or insects.

_____ I belong to organizations interested in protecting the environment.

_____ I think it is important to protect endangered species.

_____ I enjoy camping or hiking.

_____ I appreciate natural beauty.

Look at the items you have checked above and describe your naturalist intelligence.

_____

_____

_____

Journal Entry #5

According to Gardner's theory, what are your most developed intelligences? Are there any you need to improve?

Multiple Intelligences

Test what you have learned by selecting the correct answers to the following questions.

1. Multiple intelligences are defined as

   a. the many parts of intelligence as measured by an IQ test.
   b. the ability to design something valued in at least one culture.
   c. the ability to read, write, and do mathematical computations.

2. The concept of multiple intelligences is significant because

   a. it measures the intelligence of students in schools.
   b. it does not use culture in measuring intelligence.
   c. it broadens the scope of human potential and includes all cultures.

3. Intelligences are measured by

   a. IQ tests.
   b. performance in activities related to the intelligence.
   c. performance in the classroom.

4. Each individual's life history contains crystallizers that

   a. promote the development of the intelligences.
   b. inhibit the development of the intelligences.
   c. cause the individual to be set in their ways.

5. Multiple intelligences include

   a. getting good grades in college.
   b. bodily kinesthetic skills.
   c. good test-taking skills.

How did you do on the quiz? Check your answers: 1. b, 2. c, 3. b, 4. a, 5. b

"The best years of your life are the ones in which you decide your problems are your own. You do not blame them on your mother, the ecology, or the president. You realize that you control your own destiny."

Albert Ellis

Create Your Success

We are responsible for what happens in our lives. We make decisions and choices that create the future. Our behavior leads to success or failure. Too often we believe that we are victims of circumstance. When looking at our lives, we often look for others to blame for how our lives are going:

- My grandparents did it to me. I inherited these genes.
- My parents did it to me. My childhood experiences shaped who I am.
- My teacher did it to me. He gave me a poor grade.
- My boss did it to me. She gave me a poor evaluation.
- The government did it to me. All my money goes to taxes.
- Society did it to me. I have no opportunity.

These factors are powerful influences in our lives, but we are still left with choices. Concentration camp survivor Viktor Frankl wrote a book, *Man's Search for Meaning,* in which he describes his experiences and how he survived his ordeal. His parents, brother, and wife died in the camps. He suffered starvation and torture. Through all of his sufferings and imprisonment, he still maintained that he was a free man because he could make choices.

We who lived in concentration camps can remember the men who walked through the huts comforting others, giving away their last piece of bread. They may have been few in number, but they offer sufficient proof that everything can be taken from a man but one thing: the last of the human freedoms—to choose one's attitude in any given set of circumstances, to choose one's own way. . . . Fundamentally, therefore, any man can, even under such circumstances, decide what shall become of him—mentally and spiritually. He may retain his human dignity even in a concentration camp.[6]

Viktor Frankl could not choose his circumstances at that time, but he did choose his attitude. He decided how he would respond to the situation. He realized that he still had the freedom to make choices. He used his memory and imagination to exercise his freedom. When times were the most difficult, he would imagine that he was in the classroom lecturing to his students about psychology. He eventually did get out of the concentration camp and became a famous psychiatrist.

Christopher Reeve is another example of a person who maintained his freedom to make choices in difficult circumstances. Reeve, who once played the character Superman, was paralyzed from the neck down as the result of an accident he suffered when he was thrown from his horse. When he first awoke after the accident, he saw little reason for living. With the help of his family, he made the decision to keep fighting and do as much as he could to promote research on spinal cord injuries. He succeeded in raising awareness and money for this cause. As a result, there have been many advancements in the study and treatment of spinal cord injuries. Reeve believed that he and others in similar circumstances would walk again some day. Sadly, Reeve passed away in 2004. However, his advocacy for the cause of finding a cure for spinal injuries has led to research that will help others in the future.

Hopefully none of you will ever have to experience the circumstances faced by Viktor Frankl or Christopher Reeve, but we all face challenging situations. It is empowering to think that our behavior is more a function of our decisions than of our circumstances. It is not productive to look around and find someone to blame for your problems. Psychologist Abraham Maslow says that instead of blaming, we should see how we can make the best of the situation.

One can spend a lifetime assigning blame, finding a cause, "out there" for all the troubles that exist. Contrast this with the responsible attitude of confronting the situation, bad or good, and instead of asking, "What caused the trouble? Who was to blame?" asking, "How can I handle the present situation to make the best of it?"[7]

Author Stephen Covey suggests that we look at the word responsibility as "response-ability."[8] It is the ability to choose responses and make decisions about the future. When you are dealing with

continued

a problem, it is useful to ask yourself what decisions you made that led to the problem. How did you create the situation? If you created the problem, you can create a solution.

At times, you may ask, "How did I create this?" and find that the answer is that you did not create the situation. We certainly do not create earthquakes or hurricanes, for example. But we do create or at least contribute to many of the things that happen to us. Even if you did not create your circumstances, you can create your reaction to the situation. In the case of an earthquake, you can decide to panic or find the best course of action at the moment.

Stephen Covey believes that we can use our resourcefulness and initiative in dealing with most problems. When his children were growing up and they asked him how to solve a certain problem, he would say, "Use your R and I!" He meant resourcefulness and initiative. He notes that adults can use this R and I to get good jobs.

> *But the people who end up with the good jobs are the proactive ones who are solutions to problems, not problems themselves, who seize the initiative to do whatever is necessary, consistent with correct principles, to get the job done.*[9]

Use your resourcefulness and initiative to create the future that you want.

Courtesy of Western Michigan University

Go to http://www.collegesuccess1.com/JournalEntries.htm for Word files of the Journal Entries

Success over the Internet

Visit the *College Success Website* at http://www.collegesuccess1.com/

The *College Success Website* is continually updated with new topics and links to the material presented in this chapter. Topics include:

- Learning style assessments
- Learning style and memory
- Learning style and personality type

Contact your instructor if you have any problems in accessing the *College Success Website*.

Notes

1. Gary E. Price, "Productivity Environmental Preference Survey," Price Systems, Inc., Box 1818, Lawrence, KS 66044-8818.

2. Modified and reproduced by special permission of the Publisher, Consulting Psychologist Press, Inc., Palo Alto, CA 94303, from *Introduction to Type in College* by John K. Ditiberio and Allen L. Hammer. Copyright 1993 by Consulting Psychologist Press, Inc. All rights reserved. Further reproduction is prohibited without the Publisher's written consent.

3. John K. Ditiberio and Allen L. Hammer, *Introduction to Type in College* (Palo Alto, CA: Consulting Psychologist Press, 1993), 7.

4. Howard Gardner, *Intelligence Reframed: Multiple Intelligences for the Twenty-First Century* (Boulder, CO: Basic Books, 1999).

5. Thomas Armstrong, *Multiple Intelligences in the Classroom* (Alexandria, VA: Association for Curriculum Development, 1994).

6. Viktor Frankl, *Man's Search for Meaning* (New York: Pocket Books, 1963), 104–5.

7. Quoted in Rob Gilbert, ed., *Bits and Pieces*, November 4, 1999.

8. Stephen Covey, *The Seven Habits of Highly Effective People* (New York: Simon and Schuster, 1989), 71.

9. Ibid., 75.

Name _____ Date _____

Read the following questions and circle the letter of the best answer for each in your opinion. There are no right or wrong answers in this quiz. Just circle what you usually prefer.

1. When learning how to use my computer, I prefer to
   a. read the manual first.
   b. have someone explain how to do it first.
   c. just start using the computer and get help if I need it.

2. When getting directions to a new location, it is easier to
   a. look at a map.
   b. have someone tell me how to get there.
   c. follow someone or have him or her take me there.

3. To remember a phone number, I
   a. look at the number and dial it several times.
   b. repeat it silently or out loud to myself several times.
   c. remember the number by the pattern pressed on the keypad, the tones of each number, or writing it down.

4. For relaxation, I prefer to
   a. read a book or magazine.
   b. listen to or play music.
   c. go for a walk or do something physical.

5. I am better at
   a. reading.
   b. talking.
   c. physical activities.

6. In school, I learn best by
   a. reading.
   b. listening.
   c. hands-on activities.

7. I tend to be a
   a. thinker.
   b. talker.
   c. doer.

8. When I study for a test, it works best when I
   a. read and picture the information in my head.
   b. read and say the ideas out loud or silently.
   c. highlight, write notes, and outline.

9. It is easier for me to remember
   a. faces.
   b. names.
   c. events.

10. On a Saturday, I would prefer to
    a. see a movie.
    b. go to a concert.
    c. participate in athletics or be outside.

11. In a college class, it is most important to have
    a. a good textbook with pictures, graphs, and diagrams.
    b. a good teacher who gives interesting lectures.
    c. hands-on activities.

12. It is easier for me to study by
    a. reading and reviewing the material.
    b. discussing the subject with others.
    c. writing notes or outlines.

13. When I get lost, I prefer to
    a. look at the map.
    b. call or ask for directions.
    c. drive around the area until I recognize familiar landmarks.

14. When cooking, I often
    a. look for new recipes.
    b. talk to others to get new ideas.
    c. just put things together and it generally comes out okay.

15. When assembling a new toy or piece of furniture, I usually
    a. read the instructions first.
    b. talk myself through each step.
    c. start putting it together and read the directions if I get stuck.

16. When solving a problem, it is more useful to
    a. read a bestselling book on the topic.
    b. talk over the options with a trusted friend.
    c. do something about it.

17. Which statement do you like the best?
    a. A picture is worth a thousand words.
    b. Talk to me and I can understand.
    c. Just do it.

18. When I was a child, my mother said I
    a. spent a lot of time reading, taking photos, or drawing.
    b. had lots of friends and was always talking to someone on the phone.
    c. was always taking things apart to see how they worked.

Score your quiz:
Number of A answers   _____   Visual Learner
Number of B answers   _____   Auditory Learner
Number of C answers   _____   Kinesthetic/Tactile Learner

What did you discover as a result of taking this quiz?

Name _____ Date _____

How would you use the knowledge of your learning style to deal with the following college situations? Your instructor may use this exercise for a group activity and class discussion.

1. You have just been assigned a 10-page term paper.

2. You have to study for a challenging math test.

3. You have to write up a lab report for a biology class. It includes drawings of a frog you have dissected.

4. You are taking a required course for your major and it is taught by only one professor. You dislike this professor.

5. You are taking a business class and have been assigned a group project to design a small business. It is worth 50 percent of your grade.

6. You have signed up for an economics course and find it difficult to stay awake during the lecture.

7. You signed up for a philosophy course to meet a humanities requirement. The vocabulary in this course is unfamiliar.

8. As part of the final exam, you have to prepare a five-minute presentation for your art history class.

Name _____ Date _____

Complete the "Describing Your Multiple Intelligences" activity in this chapter before doing this exercise.

Each individual's life history contains **crystallizers** that promote the development of intelligences. Look at your highest scores on the multiple intelligences activity. List your highest scores below. Write down at least two crystallizers you experienced that may have helped you to develop these intelligences. For example, you may have been praised for your athletic skills and developed your bodily-kinesthetic intelligence.

My highest scores:

Crystallizers:

Each individual's life history also contains **paralyzers** that inhibit the development of intelligences. Look at your lowest scores on the multiple intelligences activity. Write down two paralyzers that may have discouraged you from developing this intelligence. For example, you may have been corrected many times during your piano lessons and given up learning the piano. Paralyzers often involve shame, guilt, fear, or anger.

My lowest scores:

Paralyzers:

How can you overcome some of your paralyzers if they are interfering with your success?

Are there some scores that you need to improve to accomplish your career and educational goals?

Based on the above analysis, write a discovery statement about what you have learned. I discovered that I . . . .

CHAPTER 3

Thinking Critically and Creatively

Learning Objectives

Read to answer these key questions:

- What is critical thinking?

- What are fallacies in reasoning?

- What is moral reasoning?

- What are some techniques for critical thinking?

- What is creativity?

- How can I improve my creativity?

- How is laughter a key to success?

Name: Courtney Conrad

Major: Organizational Communication

Year: Junior

Hometown: Darien, IL

Involvement: 2011 Medallion Scholar, Sigma Kappa Sorority, 2014 Rho Gamma, Order of Omega, 2012 Orientation Student Leader, 2013 Student Orientation Coordinator, 2014 New Student Orientation Intern, Fall Welcome Ambassador, First-Year Seminar Student Instructor, Omicron Sigma Lambda, Drive Safe Kalamazoo, Alpha Lambda Delta

Deciding to come to Western Michigan University was one of the **best decisions I have made** in my entire life. I have been able to push myself outside of my comfort zone and **challenge myself** both academically and in leadership opportunities.

I started off my first-year not sure where my place was at Western. I initially **focused on my academics** and **building relationships** with other first-year students. During the first semester, **I got involved** in Greek Life and **found a home** away from home in my organization. I continued to **get involved on campus** and also **found a place for me within the First-Year Experience Programs**. I believe that there is a place for every student at Western. WMU is made up of a many diverse programs, departments and organizations. I would encourage everyone to find somewhere to get involved that would **enhance their own personal college experience**.

Being **highly involved at WMU** has kept me very busy. It is important to **keep a positive mindset** and **believe in yourself** while you balance everything in college. This will be your motivation and what drives you. With that being said, **know your limits**, and **only take on what you can handle**. You will get what you put in. Put your all into **your experience at WMU** and **you will be amazed** at what you will get out of it.

Your college experience will help you to develop critical thinking, moral reasoning, and creative thinking skills. Critical thinking involves analyzing data, generating alternatives, and solving problems. Moral reasoning guides thought and action to help you live an ethical life. Creative thinking helps you to find new ideas to solve problems in your personal and professional life.

Critical Thinking

Critical thinking involves questioning established ideas, creating new ideas, and using information to solve problems. In critical thinking, reasoning is used in the pursuit of truth. Part of obtaining a college education is learning to think critically. Understanding the concepts of critical thinking will help you succeed in college courses in which critical thinking is used.

Beyond college, critical thinking is helpful in being a good citizen and a productive member of society. Throughout history, critical thinkers have helped to advance civilization. Thoughts that were once widely accepted were questioned, and newer and more useful ideas were introduced. For example, it was once assumed that bloodsucking leeches were helpful in curing diseases. Some critical thinkers questioned this practice, and the science of medicine was advanced. It was not so long ago that women were not allowed to vote. Critical thinkers questioned this practice so that women could participate in a democratic society.

A lack of critical thinking can lead to great tragedy. In his memoirs, Adolf Eichmann, who played a central role in the Nazis' killing of six million Jews during World War II, wrote:

> "A person's mind stretched to a new idea never goes back to its original dimensions."
> Oliver Wendell Holmes

> "I think, therefore I am (Cogito, ergo sum)."
> Descartes

"From my childhood, obedience was something I could not get out of my system. When I entered the armed services at the age of 27, I found being obedient not a bit more difficult than it had been during my life at that point. It was unthinkable that I would not follow orders. Now that I look back, I realize that a life predicated on being obedient and taking orders is a very comfortable life indeed. Living in such a way reduces to a minimum one's own need to think."[1]

Critical and creative thinking are closely related. If you can think critically, you have the freedom to be creative and generate new ideas. The great American jurist and philosopher Oliver Wendell Holmes noted:

"There are one-story intellects, two-story intellects, and three-story intellects with skylights. All fact-collectors who have no aim beyond their facts are one-story men. Two-story men compare, reason, generalize, using the labor of the fact-collectors as their own. Three-story men idealize, imagine, predict—their best illumination comes from above through skylights."

Use the information in this chapter to become a three-story intellect with skylights. And by the way, even though Oliver Wendell Holmes talked about men, women can be three-story intellects too.

Fallacies in Reasoning

To think critically, you need to be able to recognize fallacies in reasoning.[2] Fallacies are patterns of incorrect reasoning. Recognizing these fallacies can help you to avoid them in your thinking and writing. You can also become aware of when others are using these fallacies to persuade you. They may use these fallacies for their own purpose, such as power or financial gain. As you read through these fallacies in reasoning, think about examples you have experienced in your personal life.

- **Appeal to authority.** It is best to make decisions by reviewing the information and arguments and reaching our own conclusions. Sometimes we are encouraged to rely on experts for a recommendation because they have specialized information. Obviously, we need to have trust in the experts to accept their conclusions. However, when we cite some person as an authority in a certain area when they are not, we make an appeal to a questionable authority. For example, when a company uses famous sports figures to endorse a product, a particular brand of athletic shoes or breakfast cereal, they are appealing to a questionable authority. Just because the athletes are famous does not mean they are experts on the product they are endorsing. They are endorsing the product to earn money. Many commercials you see on TV use appeals to a questionable authority.

- **Jumping to conclusions.** When we jump to conclusions, we make hasty generalizations. For example, if a college student borrows money from a bank and does not pay it back, the manager of the bank might conclude that all college students are poor risks and refuse to give loans to other college students.

- **Making generalizations.** We make generalizations when we say that all members of a group are the same, as in:

    All lawyers are greedy.
    All blondes are airheads.

Of course, your occupation does not determine whether or not you are greedy, and the color of your hair does not determine your intelligence. Such thinking leads to harmful stereotypes and fallacies in reasoning. Instead of generalizing, think of people as unique individuals.

- **Attacking the person rather than discussing the issues.** To distract attention from the issues, we often attack the person. Political candidates today are routinely asked about personal issues such as extramarital affairs and drug use. Of course

> "The function of education is to teach one to think intensively and to think critically. Intelligence plus character—that is the goal of true education."
> Martin Luther King, Jr.

Fallacies in Reasoning

- Appeal to authority
- Jumping to conclusions
- Making generalizations
- Attacking the person
- Appeal to common belief
- Appeal to common practice
- Appeal to tradition
- Two wrongs
- Domino theory
- Wishful thinking
- Scare tactics
- Appeal to pity
- Appeal to loyalty
- Appeal to prejudice
- Appeal to vanity
- False causes
- Straw man/woman
- Cult behavior

personal integrity in politicians is important, but attacking the person can serve as a smokescreen to direct attention away from important political issues. Critical thinkers avoid reacting emotionally to personalities and use logical thinking to analyze the issues.

- **Appeal to common belief.** Just because something is a common belief does not mean that it is true. At one time people believed that the world was flat and that when you got to the edge of the earth, you would fall off. If you were to survey the people who lived in that period in history, the majority would have agreed that the earth was flat. A survey just tells us what people believe. The survey does not tell us what is true and accurate.

- **Appeal to common practice.** Appealing to common practice is the "everyone else is doing it" argument. Just because everyone else does it doesn't mean that it is right. Here are some common examples of this fallacy:

    It is okay to cheat in school. Everyone else does it.
    It is okay to speed on the freeway. Everyone else does it.
    It is okay to cheat on your taxes. Everyone else does it.

- **Appeal to tradition.** Appeal to tradition is a variation of the "everyone else is doing it" argument. The appeal to tradition is "we've always done it that way." Just because that is the way it has always been done doesn't mean it is the best way to do it. With this attitude, it is very difficult to make changes and improve our ways of doing things. While tradition is very important, it is open to question. For example, construction and automotive technology have traditionally been career choices for men, but not for women. When women tried to enter or work in these careers, there was resistance from those who did not want to change traditions. This resistance limited options for women.

- **Two wrongs.** In this fallacy, it is assumed that it is acceptable to do something because other people are doing something just as bad. For example, if someone cuts you off on the freeway, you may assume that it is acceptable to zoom ahead and cut in front of his or her car. The "two wrongs" fallacy has an element of retribution, or getting back at the other person. The old saying, "Two wrongs do not make a right," applies in this situation.

- **The slippery slope or domino theory.** The slippery slope or domino theory is best explained with an example. A student might think: If I fail the test, I will fail this class. If I fail this class, I will drop out of college. My parents will disown me and I will lose the respect of my friends. I will not be able to get a good job. I will start drinking and end up homeless. In this fallacy, the negative consequences of our actions are only remotely possible, but are assumed to be certain. These dire consequences influence people's decisions and change behavior. In this situation, it is important to evaluate these consequences. One does not necessarily lead to the other. If you fail the test,

Courtesy of Western Michigan University

Practice Matching Fallacies in Reasoning, Part I

The column on the left contains examples of fallacies in reasoning. Match each example with the name of the fallacy on the right.

Example:

_____ 1. Women should not be automotive mechanics.

_____ 2. The best sports shoes are those endorsed by famous athletes.

_____ 3. It is OK for athletes to take drugs to enhance their performance. They all do it.

_____ 4. All women with red hair get angry easily.

_____ 5. If you fail the test, you are a failure for life.

_____ 6. To defeat a politician, research his personal background and let the public know of any past mistakes.

_____ 7. Since some children steal, children should not be allowed into the store without their parents.

_____ 8. All sharks are dangerous and should be killed.

_____ 9. If someone insults you, you should insult them back.

Fallacy:

A. Appeal to authority

B. Appeal to tradition

C. Common practice

D. Two wrongs

E. Attack the person

F. Making generalizations

G. Appeal to a common belief

H. Slippery slope

I. Jumping to conclusions

Answers: 1. B, 2. A, 3. C, 4. F, 5. H, 6. E, 7. I, 8. G, 9. D

you could study and pass the next test. As a child you were probably cautioned about many slippery slopes in life:

Brush your teeth or your teeth will fall out.
Do your homework or you will never get into college and get a good job.

- **Wishful thinking.** In wishful thinking, an extremely positive outcome, however remote, is proposed as a distraction from logical thinking. For example, a new sports stadium may be proposed. Extremely positive outcomes may be presented, such as downtown redevelopment, the attraction of professional sports teams, increased revenue, and the creation of jobs. Opponents, on the other hand, might foresee increased taxes, lack of parking, and neglect of other important social priorities such as education and shelter for the homeless. Neither position is correct if we assume that the outcomes are certain and automatic. Outcomes need to be evaluated realistically.

Wishful thinking is often used in commercials to sell products. Here are a few examples:

Eat what you want and lose weight.
Use this cream and look younger.

Use this cologne and women will be attracted to you.

Invest your money and get rich quick.

- **Appeal to fear or scare tactics.** Sometimes people appeal to fear as a way of blocking rational thinking. I once saw a political commercial that showed wolves chasing a person through the forest. It was clearly designed to evoke fear. The message was to vote against a proposition to limit lawyers' fees. The idea was that if lawyers' fees were limited, the poor client would be a victim of limited legal services.

This commercial used scare tactics to interfere with rational thinking about the issue.

- **Appeal to pity.** In an appeal to pity, emotion is used to replace logic. It is what is known as a "sob story." Appeals to pity may be legitimate when used to foster charity and empathy. However, the sob story uses emotion in place of reason to persuade and is often exaggerated. College faculties often hear sob stories from students having academic difficulties:

Please don't disqualify me from college. I failed all my classes because I was emotionally upset when my grandmother died.

Please don't fail me in this class. If you fail me, my parents will kick me out of the house and I will not be able to get health insurance.

If you fail me in this class, I won't be eligible to play football and my future as a professional will be ruined.

- **Appeal to loyalty.** Human beings are social creatures who enjoy being attached to a group. We feel loyalty to our friends, families, schools, communities, teams, and favorite musicians. Appeals to loyalty ask you to act according to a group's best interests without considering whether the actions are right or wrong. Critical thinkers, however, do not support an idea just to show support for a group with which they identify.

Peer pressure is related to the loyalty fallacy. With peer pressure, members of a group may feel obliged to act in a certain way because they think members of the group act that way. Another variation of the loyalty fallacy is called the bandwagon argument. It involves supporting a certain idea just to be part of the group. This tendency is powerful when the group is perceived to be powerful or "cool." In elections, people often vote for the candidate that is perceived to be the most popular. If everyone else is voting for the candidate, they assume the candidate must be the best. This is not necessarily true.

- **Appeal to prejudice.** A prejudice is judging a group of people or things positively or negatively, even if the facts do not agree with the judgment. A prejudice is based on a stereotype in which all members of a group are judged to be the same. Speakers sometimes appeal to prejudice to gain support for their causes. Listen for the appeal to prejudice in hate speeches or literature directed against different ethnicities, genders, or sexual orientations.

- **Appeal to vanity.** The appeal to vanity is also known as "apple polishing." The goal of this strategy is to get agreement by paying compliments. Students who pay compliments to teachers and then ask for special treatment are engaging in apple polishing.

- **Post hoc reasoning, or false causes.** Post hoc reasoning has to do with cause and effect. It explains many superstitions. If I play a good game of golf whenever I wear a certain hat, I might conclude that the hat causes me to play a good golf game. The hat, however, is a false cause of playing a good game of golf. I may feel more comfortable wearing my lucky hat, but it is a secondary reason for playing well. I play well because I practice my golf skills and develop my self-confidence. In scientific research, care is taken to test for false causes. Just because an event regularly follows another event does not mean that the first event caused the second event. For example, when the barometer falls, it rains. The falling barometer does not cause the rain; a drop in atmospheric pressure causes the rain. If falling barometers caused the rain, we could all be rainmakers by adjusting our barometers.

- **Straw man or woman.** Watch for this fallacy during election time. Using this strategy, a politician creates a misleading image of someone else's statements, ideas, or beliefs to make them easy to attack. For example, politicians might accuse their opponents of raising taxes. That may only be part of the story, however. Maybe their opponents also voted for many tax-saving measures. When politicians or anyone else use the straw man fallacy, they are falsifying or oversimplifying. Use your critical thinking to identify the straw man or woman (political opponent) in the next election. Of course you don't have to be a politician to use this strategy. People use this strategy when they spread gossip or rumors about someone they want to discredit.

- **Cult behavior.** Cults and doomsday forecasters spread unorthodox and sometimes harmful beliefs with great fervor. These thoughts are perpetuated through mind-control techniques. With mind control, members of a group are taught to suppress natural emotions and accept the ideas of the group in exchange for a sense of belonging. These groups do not allow members to think critically or question the belief system. Mind control is the opposite of critical thinking. It is important to use critical thinking when you encounter beliefs for which there is no hard evidence. An example is the Heaven's Gate cult:

    > It all seems perfectly ludicrous: 39 people don their new sneakers, pack their flight bags and poison themselves in the solemn belief that a passing UFO will whisk them off to Wonderland.

ACTIVITY

Practice Matching Fallacies in Reasoning, Part II

The column on the left contains examples of fallacies in reasoning. Match each example with the name of the fallacy on the right.

Example:

_____1. You look really nice today. Can I ask you a favor?

_____2. I'll vote for a woman because I am a woman.

_____3. Earn $10,000 a month by working part time at home.

_____4. If you fail me on this test, the coach will not let me play next week.

_____5. I'm more likely to win if I wear my lucky socks.

_____6. If you vote for this politician, she will raise taxes.

_____7. If you don't buy this car, you are putting your family at risk.

_____8. All large dogs are dangerous.

_____9. The leader knows what is best for me.

Fallacy:

A. Wishful thinking

B. Scare tactics

C. Appeal to pity

D. Appeal to loyalty

E. Appeal to prejudice

F. Appeal to vanity

G. Post hoc reasoning

H. Straw man or woman

I. Cult behavior

Answers: 1. F, 2. D, 3. A, 4. C, 5. G, 6. H, 7. B, 8. E, 9. I

Journal Entry #1

Fallacies in reasoning are frequently used in advertisements and politics. From your personal experience, describe an example of a fallacy in reasoning.

How to Become a Critical Thinker

The Critical Thinking Process

When thinking about a complex problem, use these steps in the critical thinking process:

1. **State the problem in a clear and simple way.** Sometimes the message is unclear or obscured by appeals to emotion. Stating the problem clearly brings it into focus so that you can identify the issue and begin to work on it.

2. **Identify the alternative views.** In looking at different views, you open your mind to a wider range of options. The diagram entitled "Alternative Views" below gives a perspective on point of view. For every issue, there are many points of view. The larger circle represents these many points of view. The individual point of view is represented by a dot on the larger circle. Experience, values, beliefs, culture, and knowledge influence an individual's point of view.

3. **Watch for fallacies** in reasoning when looking at alternative views.

4. **Find at least three different answers.** In searching for these different answers, you force yourself to look at all the possibilities before you decide on the best answer.

5. **Construct your own reasonable view.** After looking at the alternatives and considering different answers to the problem, construct your own reasonable view. Practice this process using the critical thinking exercises at the end of this chapter.

ISSUE PERSON TOPIC

Individual Point of View Based on:
· Experience
· Values
· Beliefs
· Culture
· Knowledge

Figure 3.1 Alternative Views

Tips for Critical Thinking

1. **Be aware of your mindset.** A mindset is a pattern of thought that you use out of habit. You develop patterns of thinking based on your personal experiences, culture, and environment. When the situation changes, your old mindset may need to change as well.

2. **Be willing to say, "I don't know."** With this attitude you are open to exploring new ideas. In today's rapidly changing world, it is not possible to know everything. Rather than trying to know everything, it is more important to be able to find the information you need.

3. **Practice tolerance for other people's ideas.** We all have different views of the world based on our own experiences and can benefit from an open exchange of information.

4. **Try to look for several answers and understand many points of view.** The world is not either-or or black-and-white. Looking at all the possibilities is the first step in finding a creative solution.

5. **Understand before criticizing.** Life is not about justifying your point of view. It is important to understand and then offer your suggestions.

6. **Realize that your emotions can get in the way of clear thinking.** We all have beliefs that are important to us. It is difficult to listen to a different point of view when someone questions your personal beliefs. Open your mind to see all the alternatives. Then construct your reasonable view.

7. **Notice the source of the information you are analyzing.** Political announcements are required to include information about the person or organization paying for the ad. Knowing who paid for an advertisement can help you understand and evaluate the point of view that is being promoted.

8. **Ask the question, "What makes the author think so?"** In this way, you can discover what premises the author is using to justify his or her position.

9. **Ask the question, "So what?"** Ask this question to determine what is important and how the author reached the conclusion.

> "If there is any secret of success, it lies in the ability to get the other person's point of view and see things from his angle as well as from your own."
> Henry Ford

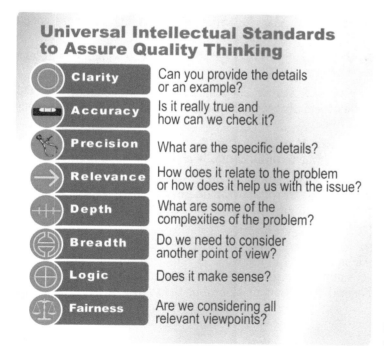

Figure 3.2
Adapted from the Foundation for Critical Thinking[3]

Critical Thinking over the Internet

The Internet is revolutionizing the way we access and retrieve information today. Through the use of search engines, websites, electronic periodicals, and online reference materials, it is possible to find just about any information you need. The Internet is also full of scams, rumors, gossip, hoaxes, exaggerations, and illegal activity. Anyone can put anything on the Internet. You will need to apply critical thinking to the information that you find on the Internet. Author Reid Goldsborough offers these suggestions for thinking critically about material on the Internet:

- **Don't be fooled by appearances.** It is easy to create a flashy and professional-looking website. Some products and services are legitimate, but some are scams.
- **Find out about the person or organization providing the information.** There should be links to a home page that lists the author's background and credentials. You need to be skeptical if the author is not identified. If you cannot identify the person who authored the website, find out what organization sponsored the site. Most of the Internet resources cited in this text are provided by educational or government sources. It is the goal of these organizations to provide the public with information.
- **Look for the reason the information was posted.** What is the agenda? Keep this in mind when evaluating the information. Many websites exist to sell a product or influence public opinion.
- **Look for the date that the information was created or revised.** A good website posts the date of creation or revision.
- **Try to verify the information elsewhere,** especially if the information is at odds with common sense or what you believe to be true. Verify the information through other websites or your local library.[4]

How to Recognize a Scam

Use your critical thinking skills to recognize a scam or hoax. How can you recognize a scam? Here are some signs to watch for:

- **Be aware of big promises.** If something sounds too good to be true, it probably is a hoax. If you are promised $5,000 a month for working part time out of your home, be careful. If you are offered a new TV in a box for $50, the box may contain stolen goods or even rocks!
- **The word "free" is often used to catch your attention to make a sale.** Few things in life are free.
- **A similar tactic is to offer money or a prize.** The scam goes like this: "Congratulations! You have just won a . . ." Be especially careful if you have to pay money to claim your prize.
- **Beware of high-pressure tactics.** A common scam is to ask you to pay money now or the price will go up. Take your time to think carefully about your expenditures. If the deal is legitimate, it will be there tomorrow.
- **To avoid identity theft, be careful about disclosing personal information** such as Social Security numbers and credit card numbers. Disclose this information only to people and organizations you know and trust.
- **If you suspect a scam, research the offer on the Internet.** Use a search engine such as yahoo.com or google.com and type in the word "scam." You can find descriptions of many different types of scams. You can also find information on the latest scams or file a complaint at the Federal Trade Commission website at www.ftc.gov.

Critical Thinking

Test what you have learned by selecting the correct answers to the following questions.

1. Critical thinking involves

   a. being critical of others' opinions.
   b. identifying alternative views.
   c. finding only one correct answer.

2. To be a critical thinker it is important to

   a. understand before criticizing.
   b. justify your point of view.
   c. tell yourself that you know the answer.

3. Construct your reasonable view by

   a. advocating for your point of view.
   b. always defending your mindset.
   c. first considering different answers.

4. An Internet site is legitimate if it

   a. looks professional.
   b. has useful information.
   c. has an identifiable and reputable source.

5. If you are offered something that is too good to be true,

   a. be thankful for your good fortune.
   b. suspect that it could be a scam.
   c. it could be a good investment.

How did you do on the quiz? Check your answers: 1. b, 2. a, 3. c, 4. c, 5. b

Journal Entry #2

How can you apply critical thinking in your college courses?

Critical Thinking and Moral Reasoning

Beyond recognizing fallacies in reasoning, critical thinking involves rationally deciding what to believe, how to act, and what is right or wrong. It involves assessing personal views and the views of others in order to make good decisions about living your life in an ethical manner. Psychologist Lawrence Kohlberg studied stages of moral reasoning by investigating the reactions of individuals to moral dilemmas. Here is an example of Kohlberg's most famous dilemma:

Heinz Steals the Drug

In Europe, a woman was near death from a special kind of cancer. There was one drug that the doctors thought might save her. It was a form of radium that a druggist in the same town had recently discovered. The drug was expensive to make, but the druggist was charging 10 times what the drug cost him to make. He paid $200 for the radium and charged $2,000 for a small dose of the drug.

"It is the mark of an educated mind to be able to entertain a thought without accepting it."
Aristotle

"Education's purpose is to replace an empty mind with an open one."
Malcolm Forbes

The sick woman's husband, Heinz, went to everyone he knew to borrow the money, but he could only get together about $1,000 which was half of what it cost. He told the druggist that his wife was dying and asked him to sell it cheaper or let him pay later. But the druggist said, "No, I discovered the drug and I'm going to make money from it." So Heinz got desperate and broke into the man's store to steal the drug for his wife. Should the husband have done that?[5]

Journal Entry #3

> What would you do in the Heinz dilemma? Would you steal the drug? Why?

Kohlberg was not interested in the question of whether what Heinz did what was right or wrong, but the reasoning used in reaching a decision. He found that children moved through different levels and stages of moral reasoning, from an egocentric view of the world in which they made decisions based on what was good for the individual, to a more socially responsible view of the world in which decisions were made based on what was good for society, and finally to decisions based on the universal principles of fairness and justice. Individuals progress through these stages as they gain experience thinking about moral problems.

Level 1. Pre-Conventional Morality

This stage of reasoning is common in children, but is sometimes used by adults. At this level, morality is determined by consequences to the individual involved.

Stage 1: Obedience and Punishment

At this stage, children obey the rules to avoid punishment. In the case of the Heinz dilemma, here are possible actions:

- Heinz should not steal the drug because it is against the law.
- Heinz should steal the drug because the pharmacist is asking too much money for it.

Stage 2: Individualism and Exchange

At this stage, children make decisions based on how it will best serve their needs as an individual: "How will it affect me?"

- Heinz should not steal the drug because he will be unhappy if he goes to prison.
- Heinz should steal the drug because he will be happier if he can save his wife.

Level 2. Conventional Morality

Conventional morality is more typical of adolescents and adults. People take into consideration society's views and expectations in making decisions about moral behavior. The individual follows society's conventions about what is right or wrong without questioning the fairness or appropriateness of the rule.

Stage 3: Interpersonal Relationships

At this stage, individuals attempt to live up to societal expectations and are concerned about others. The child attempts to be a "good boy" or a "good girl." Adults attempt to "be nice" or conform to the rules of society.

- Heinz should not steal the drug because stealing is bad and he is not a criminal.
- Heinz should steal the drug because he is a good husband and wants to take care of his wife.

Stage 4: Maintaining Social Order

At this stage it is important to do one's duty, respect authority, and follow the rules to maintain law and order. If one person violates a law, others will do it also and society will cease to function in an orderly way.

- Heinz should not steal the drug because the law prohibits stealing. If everyone broke the law, there would be no order in society.
- Heinz should steal the drug, but be prepared to accept the punishment for his actions and to repay the druggist.

Level 3. Post-Conventional Morality

In this level of morality, individuals are seen as separate entities from society and live by the highest principles based on basic human rights such as life, liberty, and justice. Rules are viewed as useful, but changeable in order to protect human rights and maintain social order. Rules and laws are not absolute dictates that must be obeyed without question. A totalitarian society where everyone followed the rules would be well organized, but unjust.

Stage 5: Social Contract and Individual Rights

Rules are important for maintaining a society, but there are differing values, opinions, and beliefs about what is right and wrong. Laws are regarded as social contracts, and individuals should agree on them. If laws do not promote the general welfare, they should be changed to promote what is best for most people. It is important to protect human rights and resolve differences through democratic processes.

- Heinz should not steal the drug because a scientist has a right to fair compensation for the discovery. Fair compensation encourages further drug development.
- Heinz should steal the drug because everyone has the right to life, regardless of the law.

Stage 6: Universal Principles

Democratic processes do not always work as when the majority votes for laws that harm the minority. Laws are only valid if they result in justice and respect for all people; people should disobey unjust laws. The individual acts because it is right, not because is expected, legal, or agreed upon by the majority. Examples of individuals who operated at this level include Gandhi, Martin Luther King, and Cesar Chavez, who all used civil disobedience to achieve just laws. Kohlberg found it difficult to find people who consistently operated at this level.

- Heinz should not steal the drug because others may need the drug just as badly and all lives are equally important.
- Heinz should steal the drug because saving a human life is more important than property rights.

At this stage, Kohlberg suggests that we reach decisions by taking an impartial look at the situation through one another's eyes. When the druggist looks at the situation from Heinz's perspective, he might realize that human life is more important than property rights and agree to give the drug to the wife. When Heinz looks at the situation from the druggist's perspective, he might agree to make payments for the drug. This would be a fair and just solution in which everyone is given full and equal respect.

What Is Creativity?

To see creativity in action, all we need to do is to look at young children. Movie producer Steven Spielberg describes their creativity:

> "The greatest quality that we can possess is curiosity, a genuine interest in the world around us. The most used word—and I have five kids, so I know what I'm talking about—the most used word in a child's vocabulary is 'why.' A child doesn't blindly accept things as they are, doesn't blindly believe in limits, doesn't blindly believe in the words spoken by some authority figure like me."[6]

Creativity involves both divergent and convergent thinking. **Divergent thinking** is the ability to discover many alternatives. The creative individual looks for problems, asks why, and comes up with many different answers. J. P. Guilford, a researcher on creativity, said that "the person who is capable of producing a large number of ideas per unit of time, other things being equal, has a greater chance of having significant ideas."[7] After many ideas are created, **convergent thinking** is used to combine the ideas to find new and creative solutions. These creative ideas are used to make a new plan of action.

Creative thinking is useful in fields such as the arts, science, and business. Creativity helps in the enjoyment of outside activities, such as hobbies, that help us to lead satisfying lives. Creativity is important in generating alternatives necessary for effective problem solving and coming up with creative solutions to the challenges we all face in life. Creative individuals are motivated, engaged, and open to new ideas. Guilford defines creative behavior as follows:

> "The individual who behaves creatively is oriented toward selecting and solving meaningful problems, using an inner drive to recombine his or her storehouse of experiences in new ways. In attacking problems, he or she does not act as a conformist; instead, he or she pioneers often, is not afraid to fail frequently, but is productive in the long run."[8]

The Three S's of Creativity: Sensitivity, Synergy, and Serendipity

The creative process involves sensitivity, synergy, and serendipity. Creative persons use their **sensitivity** to discover the world and spot problems, deficiencies, and incongruities. A person who is sensitive asks, "Why does this happen?" Sensitive persons are also inventive and ask the question, "How can I do this?" They are problem finders as well as problem solvers.

Synergy occurs when two or more elements are associated in a new way and the result is greater than the sum of the parts. For example, imagine a machine that combines the telephone, the computer, the television, and a music player. The combining of these familiar devices into one machine is changing the way we live. Another example of synergy is the old saying, "Two heads are better than one." When two or more people work together and share ideas, the result is often greater than what one person could produce alone. This is the essence of creativity.

The word **serendipity** is attributed to Horace Walpole, who wrote a story about the Persian princes of Serendip. The princes made unexpected discoveries while they were looking for something else. Serendipity is finding something by a lucky accident. You can only take advantage of a lucky accident if you look around and find new meaning and opportunity in the event. An example of serendipity comes from a story about the famous musician Duke Ellington. He was playing at an outdoor concert when a noisy plane flew over the stage. He changed the tempo of the music to go with the sounds of the airplane and directed the plane along with the orchestra. Another example of serendipity is Alexander Fleming's discovery of penicillin. He was growing bacteria in his lab when a spore of *penicillium notatum* blew in the window, landed on the bacteria, and killed it. Instead of throwing away a ruined experiment, he discovered the antibiotic penicillin, one of the most important medical discoveries ever made. Serendipitous people are flexible and open

"Questions are the creative acts of intelligence."
Frank Kingdon

"Happiness lies in the joy of achievement and the thrill of creative effort."
Franklin Roosevelt

"The real voyage of discovery consists not in making new landscapes but in having new eyes."
Marcel Proust

to possibilities as well as fearless in trying something new. They learn to seize the opportunities that just happen in life.

Figure 3.3 Sensitivity, synergy, and serendipity are the three S's of creativity.

Creative Thinking Techniques

- **Brainstorming.** One of the most important components of creativity is the ability to use divergent thinking to generate many ideas or alternatives. Brainstorming is one of the most frequently used techniques to develop divergent thinking. The key to brainstorming is to delay critical judgment to allow for the spontaneous flow of ideas. Critical judgment about the merit of ideas can hinder the creative process if it is applied too early. Here are the rules of brainstorming:
  - Generate a large quantity of ideas without regard to quality. This increases the likelihood that some of the ideas will be good or useful.
  - Set a time limit to encourage quick thinking. The time limit is generally short, from three to five minutes.
  - Set a goal or quota for the number of ideas you want to generate. The goal serves as a motivator.
  - The wilder and more unusual the ideas, the better. It is easier to tame down crazy ideas than to think up new ideas.
  - Use synergy by brainstorming with a group of people. Build on other people's ideas. Sometimes two ideas combined can make one better idea.
  - Select the best ideas from the list.

Courtesy of Western Michigan University

- **Relaxed attention.** Can you imagine being relaxed and paying attention at the same time? Robert McKim describes this as the paradox of the Ho-hum and the Aha![8] To be creative, it is first necessary to relax. The brain works better when it is relaxed. By relaxing, the individual releases full energy and attention to the task at hand. Athletes and entertainers must master the art of relaxation before they can excel in athletics or entertainment. If the muscles are too tense, blood flow is restricted and energy is wasted. However, totally relaxed individuals cannot think at all. They might even be asleep!

  Some tension, but not too much, is needed to think and be creative; hence the term "relaxed attention." In the creative process, the person first thinks about a task, problem, or creation and then relaxes to let the ideas incubate. During this incubation period, the person often gets a flash of insight or feeling of "Aha!" Famous artist Pablo Picasso described this process:

  "For me creation first starts with contemplation, and I need long, idle hours of meditation. It is then that I work most. I look at flies, at flowers, at leaves and trees around me. I let my mind drift at ease, just like a boat in the current. Sooner or later, it is caught by something. It gets precise. It takes shape . . . my next painting motif is decided."[9]

  As a student you can apply the principle of relaxed attention to improve your creativity. If you are thinking about a problem and get stuck, relax and come back to it later. Take a break, do something else, or even sleep on it. You are likely to come up with creative inspiration while you are relaxing. Then get back to solving the problem and pay attention to it.

- **Use idea files.** Keep files of ideas that you find interesting. People in advertising call these "swipe files." No one creates in a vacuum. Some of the best creative ideas involve recombining or building on the ideas of others or looking at them from a different perspective. This is different from copying other people's ideas; it is using them as the fertilizer for creative thinking.

  As a college student, you might keep files of the following:
  - Interesting ideas and their sources for use in writing term papers
  - Information about careers
  - Information for your resume
  - Information that you can use to apply for scholarships
  - Ideas related to your hobbies
  - Ideas for having fun
  - Ideas for saving money

- **Practice using visualization and imagination.** Visualizing and imagining are important in the creative process. Young children are naturally good at these two skills. What happens as we grow older? As we grow older, we learn to follow the rules and color between the lines. We need rules to have an orderly society, yet we need visualization and imagination to move forward and create new ideas. Don't forget to use and practice visualization and imagination.

> "The best way to have a good idea is to have lots of ideas."
>
> Linus Pauling

Creative Thinking Techniques

- Brainstorming
- Relaxed attention
- Idea files
- Visualization and imagination
- Read
- Keep a journal
- Think critically

Visualization and imagination can be fun and interesting activities to help you relax. We have often been told not to daydream, but daydreams can be a tool for relaxation as well as creativity. It is important to come back to reality once we are finished daydreaming. The last step in the creative process is doing something with the best of our creative ideas.

- **Read.** One of the best ways to trigger your creativity is to read a wide variety of materials, including newspapers, magazines, novels, nonfiction books, and articles on the Internet. The ideas that you discover will provide background information, helping you gain perspective on the world, and give you ideas for making your own contributions. When you read, you expose your mind to the greatest people who have ever lived. Make reading a habit.

- **Keep a journal.** Keep a journal of your creative ideas, thoughts, and problems. Writing often will help you think clearly. When you write about your problems, it is almost like having your own private therapist. In college, your journal can be a source of creative ideas for writing term papers and completing assignments.

- **Think critically.** Approach learning with a sense of awe, excitement, and skepticism. Here is another paradox! Creative and critical thinkers have much in common. Both ask questions, look at the world from different perspectives, and generate new alternatives.

> "To dream anything that you want to dream, that is the beauty of the human mind. To do anything that you want to do, that is the strength of the human will. To trust yourself to test the limits, that is the courage to succeed."
> Bernard Edmonds

> "Creativity is allowing yourself to make mistakes. Art is knowing which ones to keep."
> Scott Adams

> "Imagination is everything. It is the preview of life's coming attractions."
> Albert Einstein

QUIZ

Creative Thinking

Test what you have learned by selecting the correct answers to the following questions.

1. Divergent thinking is a creative thinking technique that involves:

   a. defending the correct answer.
   b. selecting the one best alternative.
   c. the ability to discover many different alternatives.

2. The following saying is a good definition for synergy:

   a. Seeing is believing.
   b. Two heads are better than one.
   c. Practice makes perfect.

3. Serendipity is:

   a. finding something by a lucky accident.
   b. finding something humorous in the situation.
   c. improvising while playing music.

4. When using relaxed attention as a creative process,

   a. the creative person is totally relaxed.
   b. the creative person is focusing attention.
   c. the creative person first thinks about the problem and then relaxes.

5. For brainstorming, it is important to:

   a. select the best ideas as a last step.
   b. consider only the good ideas.
   c. consider only the workable ideas.

How did you do on the quiz? Check your answers: 1. c, 2. b, 3. a, 4. c, 5. a

Journal Entry #4

Describe at least two creativity techniques that you use or are willing to try. Creativity techniques include brainstorming, using relaxed attention, idea files, visualization, imagination, reading, keeping a journal, and thinking critically.

KEYS TO SUCCESS   Learn to Laugh at Life

"Have a laugh at life and look around you for happiness instead of sadness. Laughter has always brought me out of unhappy situations. Even in your darkest moment, you usually can find something to laugh about if you try hard enough." Red Skelton

All of us face difficult times in life; but if we can learn the gift of laughter and have a good sense of humor, it is easier to deal with the difficulties. Laughter has important physical as well as emotional benefits. Laughter relaxes the body, boosts the immune system, and even improves the function of blood vessels and increases blood flow, which can protect the heart. It adds joy and zest to life, reduces anxiety, relieves stress, improves mood, and enhances resilience. Being more relaxed can help you to shift perspective, solve problems, and be more creative.

Just putting a smile on your face can help. German psychologist Fritz Strack had his subjects watch a cartoon with a pencil in their mouths. Half of his subjects held the pencil between their teeth, which made them smile. The other half of his subjects held the pencil between their lips, which made them frown. The smiling group thought that the cartoon was funnier. It seems that there is a connection between our physical responses and our internal feelings. The physical act of smiling actually makes you feel happier.[10]

If you do not feel happy, smile and pretend to feel happy. Neurophysicist Richard Hamilton says that if you pretend to be happy, you actually feel better because positive thoughts and behavior impact the biochemistry of the brain. Positive thinking helps the brain produce serotonin, a neurotransmitter linked with feelings of happiness.[11]

Humor has several components. Humor involves looking at the incongruities of life and laughing at them. It is looking at adversity and finding the humor in the situation. It is a playful attitude and the ability to make other people smile. Most children are playful, but socialization reduces their playfulness. You can develop your sense of humor by taking yourself less seriously and being grateful for the good things in your life. Learn to laugh at yourself by sharing your embarrassing moments and laughing at them. Be careful not to use humor that puts down other people or groups. Surround yourself with people who enjoy humor and laughter. Look for the humor in difficult situations. Life is full of irony and absurdity, and laughing about it unites people during difficult times. By laughing at the situation, you will be in a better position to deal with it. Keep a positive perspective by focusing on the good things that are happening in your life rather than dwelling on the negatives.

The author Mark Twain was a good example of using humor in life. Mark Twain said that he had never worked a day in his life. He said, "What I have done I have done because it has been play. If it had been work, I shouldn't have done it." He used humor throughout his life despite facing many adversities. His father died when he was 11 years old and he started work at age 12 as a printer's apprentice. He was constantly in trouble and spent some time in jail. He served in the Civil War. His wife died at an early age, and three out of four of his children died before he did.

As a child, Twain enjoyed playing pranks on his mother, and she responded with a sense of humor. After he played a prank on his mother,

continued

she told him that he gave her more trouble than all the other children. He replied, "I suppose you were afraid I wouldn't live," and she responded, "No, afraid you would." When Mark Train almost drowned in the river, she pulled him out and said, "I guess there wasn't much danger. People born to be hanged are safe in water." Mark Twain's children described him as "a very good man, and a very funny one . . .He does tell perfectly delightful stories." He started every day by making jokes at the breakfast table, and his humor is reflected in his famous books, including *Huckleberry Finn* and *Tom Sawyer.* He wrote that "humor is a great thing . . . the saving thing after all. The minute it crops up, all our hardnesses yield, all our irritations, and resentments flit away, and a sunny spirit takes their place."[12]

The path to achieving your goals is much smoother if you choose to be happy. So relax, smile, and be happy. Then work on making positive changes in your life.

Courtesy of Western Michigan University

Journal Entry #5

How can you learn to relax and laugh at life a little more?

JOURNAL ENTRIES

Thinking Critically and Creatively

Go to http://www.collegesuccess1.com/JournalEntries.htm for Word files of the Journal Entries

Success over the Internet

Visit the *College Success Website* at http://www.collegesuccess1.com/

The *College Success Website* is continually updated with new topics and links to the material presented in this chapter. Topics include:

- Critical thinking in college-level courses
- Techniques for thinking excellently
- The core concepts of critical thinking
- Avoiding scams

Contact your instructor if you have any problems accessing the *College Success Website*.

Notes

1. Roger Cohen, "Nazi Leader's Notes Cite 'Obedience' as Reason for His Genocidal Actions," *San Diego Union Tribune,* 13 August 1999.

2. Information in this section is adapted from the Institute for Teaching and Learning website Mission Critical, http://www.sjsu.edu/depts/itl/index.html.

3. Richard Paul and Linda Elder, "The Miniature Guide to Critical Thinking," The Foundation for Critical Thinking, http://www.criticalthinking.org.

4. Reid Goldsborough, "Teaching Healthy Skepticism about Information on the Internet," *Technology and Learning,* January 1998.

5. W.C. Crain, *Theories of Development* (New York: Prentice-Hall, 1985), 118–136, http://faculty.plts.edu/gpence/html/kohlberg.htm.

6. Steven Spielberg, commencement address at the University of Southern California, 1994.

7. Sidney Parnes, Ruth Noller, and Angelo Biondi, *Guide to Creative Action* (New York: Charles Scribner's Sons, 1977), 52.

8. Ibid., 9.

9. Robert McKim, *Experiences in Visual Thinking* (Monterey, CA: Brooks/Cole, 1972).

10. Joan Smith, "Nineteen Habits of Happy Women," *Redbook Magazine,* August 1999, 68.

11. Ibid.

12. Christopher Peterson and Martin Seligman, *Character Strengths and Virtues: A Handbook and Classification* (Oxford: University Press, 2004), 583–584.

Name _____ Date _____

In 1974, at the age of 19, Doris Drugdealer was arrested for selling $200 worth of heroin to an undercover police officer in Michigan. She received a 10- to 20-year prison sentence for this crime. After serving about eight months of her sentence, she decided that she could not tolerate prison, and with the help of her grandfather, plotted an escape. She used a work pass to walk away from prison. In May 2008, after 34 years, Doris was captured again by detectives who matched fingerprints from her driver's license to her prison records.

Doris said that in 1974, she was a "stupid little . . . hippie-ish girl . . . a pothead." During the 34 years that Doris evaded prison, she worried every day that she would be caught. While looking at a sunset, she would marvel at her freedom and wonder if the past would catch up with her. She was very careful to lead the life of a model citizen and even volunteered for Common Cause, an organization that promotes government ethics and accountability. She married an executive and had three children and lived a comfortable life in an upper-middle-class neighborhood in California. She never told her family about her past. Her husband of 23 years stated that he loved his wife as much as he had the day they were married and that she was a "person of the highest integrity and compassion" and had dedicated her life to raising her children. She taught her children to be responsible citizens and to avoid drugs. Her husband said that the arrest "was the next worst thing to having a death in the family." Doris worried about the effect of her arrest on her son, who had just graduated from high school and her older daughters. A neighbor commented that it would not be useful to society to send Doris back to prison.

Undercover drug officers believed that Doris had connections to "higher-ups" in the drug world and was a teenage leader in a 1970s drug ring. They had found $600, paraphernalia for cutting heroin, and pictures of her with other drug dealers in her apartment. Doris described herself as a recent high school graduate who was strapped for cash, working at a minimum-wage job, and driving a $400 car. She said that every day of her life she regretted getting herself into this situation. She was extradited back to Michigan to serve her original prison term. Her family and friends submitted a plea for clemency to the governor of Michigan. Should the governor grant her clemency?

Use your critical thinking to analyze this situation. Your professor may use this exercise as a group discussion. Use the Critical Thinking Worksheet that follows for your analysis.

This exercise is based on excerpts from "Former Fugitive Drawing Sympathy" and "Captured Fugitive Now Waiting for Extradition, and to Learn Fate" from the *San Diego Union Tribune*, May 1 and 2, 2008. From *CollegeScope/College and Career Success* by Dr. Marsha Fralick.

Critical Thinking Worksheet: Crime and Punishment

Name _____ Date _____

Use the summary of the news article on crime and punishment to answer the questions below. Discuss the issues with a group of students in your class and then write your reasonable point of view.

1. State the problem as simply and clearly as you can.

2. Describe the values and point of view of Doris Drugdealer.

3. Describe the values and point of view of her husband.

4. Describe the values and point of view of her children.

5. Describe the values and point of view of her neighbors.

6. Describe the legal and societal issues.

7. After discussing the issues and looking at different points of view, what is your reasonable point of view? Why? Include a brief description of your values. Use the back of this sheet of paper to explain your point of view.

From *CollegeScope/College and Career Success* by Dr. Marsha Fralick.

Name _____   Date _____

Brainstorming Rules

- Quantity is more important than quality.
- Do not censure your ideas or the ideas of others.
- See if you can generate 10 ideas in five minutes.
- Feel free to be wild and crazy.
- When brainstorming in a group, you may build on other people's ideas and combine them in new ways.
- Select your best ideas when you are finished.

How is this peanut like you (the college student)?

1.

2.

3.

4.

5.

6.

7.

8.

9.

10.

Put an asterisk (*) next to your best ideas. If all of your ideas are best, give yourself the freedom to put down some of your not-so-good ideas on the next try. Share them with the class.

How is this peanut like going to college?

1.

2.

3.

4.

5.

6.

7.

8.

9.

10.

Put an asterisk (*) next to your best ideas. Share your best ideas with the class.

A Moral Dilemma

Name _____ Date _____

Mr. Allen's son was seriously injured, but he had no car to take him to the hospital. He approached a stranger and asked to borrow his car, but the stranger refused, saying that he had to go to an important appointment. Mr. Allen stole the car by force to take his son to the hospital. Was it right for Mr. Allen to steal the car?

Assume you are Mr. Allen. Explain why it was right for him to steal the car.

Assume you are the stranger. Explain why it was right to refuse to lend your car.

Can you provide an answer for each of Kohlberg's stages of moral development? You may want to do this exercise as a group activity in your classroom.

Stage 1: What is the reward or punishment for both Mr. Allen and the stranger?

Stage 2: What is in the best interest of Mr. Allen? Of the stranger?

Stage 3: What would a nice person do?

Stage 4: What would a good citizen do?

Stage 5: What is the greatest good?

Stage 6: What universal ethical principles are involved?

What is Kohlberg's suggestion for resolving the issue?

PART II

College Success

CHAPTER 4

Managing Time and Money

Learning Objectives

Read to answer these key questions:

- What are my lifetime goals?

- How can I manage my time to accomplish my goals?

- How much time do I need for study and work?

- How can I make an effective schedule?

- What are some time management tricks?

- How can I deal with procrastination?

- How can I manage my money to accomplish my financial goals?

- What are some ways to save money?

- How can I pay for my education?

- How can I use priorities to manage my time?

S uccess in college requires that you manage both time and money. You will need time to study and money to pay for your education. The first step in managing time and money is to think about the goals that you wish to accomplish in your life. Having goals that are important to you provides a reason and motivation for managing time and money. This chapter provides some useful techniques for managing time and money so that you can accomplish the goals you have set for yourself.

What Are My Lifetime Goals?

Setting goals helps you to establish what is important and provides direction for your life. Goals help you to focus your energy on what you want to accomplish. Goals are a promise to yourself to improve your life. Setting goals can help you turn your dreams into reality. Steven Scott, in his book *A Millionaire's Notebook,* lays out five steps in this process:

1. Dream or visualize.

2. Convert the dream into goals.

3. Convert your goals into tasks.

4. Convert your task into steps.

5. Take your first step, and then the next.[1]

As you begin to think about your personal goals in life, make your goals specific and concrete. Rather than saying, "I want to be rich," make your goal something that you can break into specific steps. You might want to start learning about money management or begin a savings plan. Rather than setting a goal for happiness, think about what brings you happiness. If you want to live a long and healthy life, think about the health habits that will help you to accomplish your goal. You will need to break your goals down into specific tasks to be able to accomplish them.

Here are some criteria for successful goal setting:

1. **Is it achievable?** Do you have the skills, abilities, and resources to accomplish this goal? If not, are you willing to spend the time to develop the skills, abilities, and resources needed to achieve this goal?

2. **Is it realistic?** Do you believe you can achieve it? Are you positive and optimistic about this goal?

3. **Is it specific and measurable?** Can it be counted or observed? The most common goal mentioned by students is happiness in life. What is happiness, and how will you know when you have achieved it? Is happiness a career you enjoy, owning your own home, or a travel destination?

4. **Do you want to do it?** Is this a goal you are choosing because it gives you personal satisfaction, rather than meeting a requirement or an expectation of someone else?

5. **Are you motivated to achieve it?** What are your rewards for achieving it?

6. **Does the goal match your values?** Is it important to you?

7. **What steps do you need to take to begin?** Are you willing to take action to start working on it?

8. **When will you finish this goal?** Set a date to accomplish your goal.

"A goal is a dream with a deadline."

Napoleon Hill

A Goal or a Fantasy?

One of the best questions ever asked in my class was, "What is the difference between a goal and a fantasy?" As you look at your list of lifetime goals, are some of these items goals or fantasies? Think about this question as you read the following scenario:

When Linda was a college student, she was walking through the parking lot, noticed a beautiful red sports car, and decided that it would become a lifetime goal for her to own a similar car one day. However, with college expenses and her part-time job, it was not possible to buy the car. She would have to be content with the used car that her dad had given her so that she could drive to college. Years passed by, and Linda now has a good job, a home, and a family. She is reading a magazine and sees a picture of a similar red sports car. She cuts out this picture and tapes it to the refrigerator. After it has been on the refrigerator for several months, her children ask her why the picture is on the refrigerator. Linda replies, "I just like to dream about owning this car." One day, as Linda is driving past a car dealership, she sees the red sports car on display and stops in for a test drive. To her surprise, she decides that she does not like driving the car. It doesn't fit her lifestyle, either. She enjoys outdoor activities that would require a larger car. Buying a second car would be costly and reduce the amount of money that the family could spend on vacations. She decides that vacations are more important than owning the sports car. Linda goes home and removes the picture of the red sports car from the refrigerator.

There are many differences between a goal and a fantasy. A fantasy is a dream that may or may not become a reality. A goal is something that we actually plan to achieve. Sometimes we begin with a fantasy and later it becomes a goal. A fantasy can become a goal if steps are taken to achieve it. In the preceding example, the sports car is a fantasy until Linda actually takes the car for a test drive. After driving the car, she decides that she really does not want it. The fantasy is sometimes better than the reality. Goals and fantasies change over a lifetime. We set goals, try them out, and change them as we grow and mature and find out what is most important in life. Knowing what we think is important, and what we value most, helps us make good decisions about lifetime goals.

What is the difference between a goal and a fantasy? A goal is something that requires action. Ask yourself if you are willing to take action on the goals you have set for yourself. Begin to take action by thinking about the steps needed to accomplish the goal. Then take the first step and continue. Change your goals if they are no longer important to you.

"Vision without action is a daydream. Action without vision is a nightmare."
Japanese Proverb

"In life, as in football, you won't go far unless you know where the goalposts are."

Arnold Glasgow

Journal Entry #2

Write a paragraph about how you will accomplish one of your important lifetime goals. Start your paragraph by stating an important goal from the previous journal entry. What is the first step in accomplishing this goal? Next, list some additional steps needed to accomplish it. How can you motivate yourself to begin taking these steps?

For example:

One of my important lifetime goals is _____. The first step in accomplishing this goal is . . . Some additional steps are . . . I can motivate myself to accomplish this goal by . . .

The ABCs of Time Management

Using the ABCs of time management is a way of thinking about priorities. Priorities are what you think is important. An A priority is a task that relates to your lifetime goal. For example, if my goal is to earn a college degree, studying becomes an A priority. This activity would become one of the most important tasks that I could accomplish today. If my goal is to be healthy, an A priority would be to exercise and plan a healthy diet. If my goal is to have a good family life, an A priority would be to spend time with family members. Knowing about your lifetime goals and spending time on those items that are most important to you will help you to accomplish the goals that you have set for yourself. If you do not spend time on your goals, you may want to look at them again and decide which ones are fantasies that you do not really value or want to accomplish.

A B priority is an activity that you have to do, but that is not directly related to your lifetime goal. Examples of B priorities might be getting out of bed, taking a shower, buying groceries, paying bills, or getting gas for the car. These activities are less important, but still are necessary for survival. If I do not put gas in the car, I cannot even get to school or work. If I do not pay the bills, I will soon have financial difficulties. While we often cannot postpone these activities in order to accomplish lifetime goals, we can learn efficient time management techniques to accomplish these tasks quickly.

A C priority is something that I can postpone until tomorrow with no harmful effect. For example, I could wait until tomorrow or another day to wash my car, do the laundry, buy groceries, or organize my desk. As these items are postponed, however, they can move up the list to a B priority. If I cannot see out of my car window or have no clean clothes to wear, it is time to move these tasks up on my list of priorities.

Have you ever been a victim of "C fever"? This is an illness in which we do the C activities first and do not get around to doing the A activities that are connected to lifetime goals. Tasks required to accomplish lifetime goals are often ones that are more difficult, challenge our abilities, and take some time to accomplish. These tasks are often more difficult than the B or C activities. The C activities can fill our time and exhaust the energy we need to accomplish the A activities. An example of C fever is the student who cleans the desk or organizes the CD collection instead of studying. C fever is doing the endless tasks that keep us from accomplishing goals that are really important to us. Why do we fall victim to C fever? C activities are often easy to do and give us a sense of accomplishment. We can see immediate progress without too much effort. I can wash my car and get a sense of accomplishment and satisfaction in my shiny clean car. The task is easy and does not challenge my intellectual capabilities.

Setting Priorities

To see how the ABCs of time management work, read the profile of Justin, a typical college student, below.

Justin is a 19-year-old college student who plans to major in physical therapy. He is athletic and values his good health. He cares about people and likes helping others. He has a part-time job working as an assistant in the gym, where he monitors proper use of the weightlifting machines. Justin is also a member of the soccer team and practices with the team every afternoon.

Here is a list of activities that Justin would like to do today. Label each task as follows:

A if it relates to Justin's lifetime goals
B if it is something necessary to do
C if it is something that could be done tomorrow or later

_____ Get up, shower, get dressed

_____ Eat breakfast

_____ Go to work

_____ Go to class

_____ Visit with friends between classes

_____ Buy a new battery for his watch

_____ Go shopping for new gym shoes

_____ Attend soccer practice

_____ Do weightlifting exercises

_____ Study for biology test that is tomorrow

_____ Meet friends for pizza at lunch

_____ Call girlfriend

_____ Eat dinner

_____ Unpack gear from weekend camping trip

_____ Watch football game on TV

_____ Play video games

_____ Do math homework

While Justin is the only one who can decide how to spend his time, he can take some steps toward accomplishing his lifetime goal of being healthy by eating properly, exercising, and going to soccer practice. He can become a physical therapist by studying for the biology test and doing his math homework. He can gain valuable experience related to physical therapy by working in the gym. He cares about people and likes to maintain good relationships with others. Any tasks related to these goals are high-priority A activities.

What other activities are necessary B activities? He certainly needs to get up, shower, and get dressed. What are the C activities that could be postponed until tomorrow or later? Again, Justin needs to decide. Maybe he could postpone shopping for a new watch battery and gym shoes until the weekend. He would have to decide how much time to spend visiting with friends, watching TV, or playing video games. Since he likes these activities, he could use them as rewards for studying for the biology test and doing his math homework.

How to Estimate Study and Work Time

Students are often surprised at the amount of time necessary for study to be successful in college. A general rule is that you need to study two hours for every hour spent in a college class. A typical weekly schedule of a full-time student would look like this:

Typical College Schedule

15 hours of attending class
+30 hours of reading, studying, and preparation
45 hours total

A full-time job involves working 40 hours a week. A full-time college student spends 45 hours or more attending classes and studying. Some students will need more than 45 hours a week if they are taking lab classes, need help with study and learning skills, or are taking a heavy course load.

Some students try to work full-time and go to school full-time. While some are successful, this schedule is extremely difficult.

The Nearly Impossible Schedule

15 hours attending class
30 hours studying
+40 hours working
85 hours total

This schedule is the equivalent of having two full-time jobs! Working full-time makes it very difficult to find the time necessary to study for classes. Lack of study causes students to do poorly on exams and to doubt their abilities. Such a schedule causes stress and fatigue that make studying difficult. Increased stress can also lead to problems with personal relationships and emotional problems. These are all things that lead to dropping out of college.

Many students today work and go to college. Working during college can provide some valuable experience that will help you to find a job when you finish college. Working can teach you to manage your time efficiently and give you a feeling of independence and control over your own future. Many people need to work to pay for their education. A general guideline is to work no more than 20 hours a week if you plan to attend college full-time. Here is a workable schedule.

Part-Time Work Schedule

12 hours attending class
24 hours studying
+20 hours working
56 hours total

A commitment of 56 hours a week is like having a full-time job and a part-time job. While this schedule takes extra energy and commitment, many students are successful with it. Notice that the course load is reduced to 12 hours. This schedule involves taking one less class per semester. The class missed can be made up in summer school, or the time needed to graduate can be extended. Many students take five years to earn the bachelor's degree because they work part-time. It is better to take longer to graduate than to drop out of college or to give up because of frustration. If you must work full-time, consider reducing your course load to one or two courses. You will gradually reach your goal of a college degree.

> "The key is not to prioritize what's on the schedule, but to schedule your priorities."
>
> Stephen Covey

> "When you do the things you have to do when you have to do them, the day will come when you can do the things you want to do when you want to do them."
>
> Zig Ziglar

Part-Time Student Schedule

6 hours attending class
12 hours studying
+40 hours working
58 hours total

Add up the number of hours you are attending classes, double this figure for study time, and add to it your work time, as in the above examples. How many hours of commitment do you have? Can you be successful with your current level of commitment to school, work, and study?

To begin managing your schedule, use the weekly calendar located at the end of this chapter to write in your scheduled activities such as work, class times, and athletics.

> "The bad news is time flies. The good news is you're the pilot."
> Michael Althsuler

Schedule Your Success

If you have not used a schedule in the past, consider trying a schedule for a couple of weeks to see if it is helpful in completing tasks and working toward your lifetime goals. There are several advantages to using a schedule:

- It gets you started on your work.
- It helps you avoid procrastination.
- It relieves pressure because you have things under control.
- It frees the mind of details.
- It helps you find time to study.
- It eliminates the panic caused by doing things at the last minute.
- It helps you find time for recreation and exercise.

Once you have made a master schedule that includes classes, work, and other activities, you will see that you have some blanks that provide opportunities for using your time productively. Here are some ideas for making the most of your schedule:

1. Fill in your study times. Use the time immediately before class for previewing and the time immediately after class for reviewing. Remember that you need to study two hours or more for each hour spent in a college class.

2. Break large projects such as a term paper or test into small tasks and begin early. Double your time estimates for completion of the project. Larger projects often take longer than you think. If you finish early, use the extra time for something fun.

3. Use the daylight hours when you are most alert for studying. It may take you longer to study if you wait until late in the day when you're tired.

4. Think about your day and see if you can determine when you are most alert and awake. Prime time differs with individuals, but it is generally earlier in the day. Use the prime time when you are most alert to accomplish your most challenging tasks. For example, do your math homework during prime time. Wash your clothes during nonprime time, when you are likely to be less alert.

5. Set priorities. Make sure you include activities related to your lifetime goals.

6. Allow time for sleep and meals. It is easier to study if you are well rested and have good eating habits.

7. Schedule your time in manageable blocks of an hour or two. Having every moment scheduled leads to frustration when plans change.

8. Leave some time unscheduled to use as a shock absorber. You will need unscheduled time to relax and to deal with unexpected events.

9. Leave time for recreation, exercise, and fun.

Return to the schedule at the end of this chapter. After you have written in classes, work times, and other scheduled activities, use the scheduling ideas listed earlier to write in your study times and other activities related to your lifetime goals. Leave some unscheduled time to provide flexibility in the schedule.

> "The only thing even in this world is the number of hours in a day. The difference in winning or losing is what you do with these hours."
>
> Woody Hayes

If You Dislike Schedules

Some personality types like more freedom and do not like the structure that a schedule provides. There are alternatives for those who do not like to use a schedule. Here are some additional ideas.

1. A simple and fast way to organize your time is to use a to-do list. Take an index card or small piece of paper and simply write a list of what you need to do during the day. You can prioritize the list by putting an A or star by the most important items. Cross items off the list as you accomplish them. A list helps you focus on what is important and serves as a reminder not to forget certain tasks.

2. Another idea is to use monthly or yearly calendars to write down important events, tasks, and deadlines. Use these calendars to note the first day of school, when important assignments are due, vacations, and final exams. Place the calendars in a place where they are easily seen.

3. Alan Lakein, who wrote a book titled *How to Get Control of Your Time and Your Life*, suggests a simple question to keep you on track.[2] Lakein's question is, "What is the best use of my time right now?" This question works well if you keep in mind your goals and priorities.

4. Use reminders and sticky notes to keep on track and to remind yourself of what needs to be done each day. Place the notes in a place where you will see them, such as your computer, the bathroom mirror, or the dashboard of your car.

5. Some families use their refrigerators as time management devices. Use the refrigerator to post your calendars, reminders, goals, tasks, and to-do lists. You will see these reminders every time you open the refrigerator.

6. Invent your own unique ideas for managing time. Anything will work if it helps to accomplish your goals.

Manage Your Time with a Web Application

There are thousands of new web applications available to organize your life. You can use a web application on your phone, laptop, computer, or other mobile device to:

- Create a to-do list or schedule.
- Send reminders when assignments are due.
- Organize your calendar and plan your tasks.
- Organize your study time and plan assignments.
- Avoid procrastination.
- Create a virtual assistant to keep you organized.

Time Management, Part I

Test what you have learned by selecting the correct answers to the following questions.

1. The most important difference between a goal and a fantasy is

    a. imagination.
    b. procrastination.
    c. action.

2. An A priority is

    a. related to your lifetime goals.
    b. something important.
    c. something you have to do.

3. A general rule for college success is that you must spend ____ hours studying for every hour spent in a college class.

    a. one
    b. four
    c. two

4. For a workable study schedule,

    a. fill in all the blank time slots.
    b. leave some unscheduled time to deal with the unexpected.
    c. plan to study late at night.

5. To complete a large project such as a term paper,

    a. break the project into small tasks and begin early.
    b. schedule large blocks of time the day before the paper is due.
    c. leave time for exercise, recreation, and fun before beginning on the project.

How did you do on the quiz? Check your answers: 1. c, 2. a, 3. c, 4. b, 5. a

Time Management Tricks

- Divide and conquer
- Do the first small step
- 80/20 rule
- Aim for excellence, not perfection
- Make learning fun
- Take a break
- Study in the library
- Learn to say no

Time Management Tricks

Life is full of demands for work, study, family, friends, and recreation. Time management tricks can help you get started on the important tasks and make the most of your time. Try the following techniques when you are feeling frustrated and overwhelmed.

Divide and Conquer

When large tasks seem overwhelming, think of the small tasks needed to complete the project and start on the first step. For example, suppose you have to write a term paper. You have to take out a paper and pencil, log onto your computer, brainstorm some ideas, go to the library to find information, think about your main ideas, and write the first sentence. Each of these steps is manageable. It's looking at the entire project that can be intimidating.

I once set out hiking on a mountain trail. When I got to the top of the mountain and looked down, I enjoyed a spectacular view and was amazed at how high I had climbed. If I had thought about how high the mountain was, I might not have attempted the hike. I climbed the mountain by taking it one step at a time. That's the secret to completing any large project: break it into small, manageable parts, then take the first step and keep going.

Learning a small part at a time is also easy and helps with motivation for learning. While in college, carry around some material that you need to study. Take advantage of five or ten minutes of time to study a small part of your material. In this way you make good use of your time and enhance memory by using distributed practice. Don't wait until you have large blocks of uninterrupted study time to begin your studies. You may not have the luxury of large blocks of time, or you may want to spend that time in other ways.

Do the First Small Step

The most difficult step in completing any project is the first step. If you have a challenging project to do, think of a small first step and complete that small step. Make the first step something that you can accomplish easily and in a short amount of time. Give yourself permission to stop after the first step. However, you may find that you are motivated to continue with the project. If you have a term paper to write, think about some small step you can take to get started. Log onto your computer and look at the blank screen. Start writing some ideas. Type the topic into a computer search engine and see what information is available. Go to the library and see what is available on your topic. If you can find some interesting ideas, you can motivate yourself to begin the project. Once you have started the project, it is easier to continue.

The 80/20 Rule

Alan Lakein is noted for many useful time management techniques. One that I have used over the years is the 80/20 rule. Lakein says, "If all items are arranged in order of value, 80 percent of the value would come from only 20 percent of the items, while the remaining 20 percent of the value would come from 80 percent of the items."[3] For example, if you have a list of ten items to do, two of the items on the list are more important than the others. If you were to do only the two most important items, you would have accomplished 80 percent of the value. If you are short on time, see if you can choose the 20 percent of the tasks that are the most valuable. Lakein noted that the 80/20 rule applies to many situations in life:

- 80 percent of file usage is in 20 percent of the files.
- 80 percent of dinners repeat 20 percent of the recipes.
- 80 percent of the washing is done on the 20 percent of the clothes worn most frequently.
- 80 percent of the dirt is on the 20 percent of the floor used most often.

Think about how the 80/20 rule applies in your life. It is another way of thinking about priorities and figuring out which of the tasks are C priorities. This prioritizing is especially important if you are short on time. The 80/20 rule helps you to focus on what is most important.

Aim for Excellence, Not Perfection

Are you satisfied with your work only if it is done perfectly? Do you put off a project because you cannot do it perfectly? Aiming for perfection in all tasks causes anxiety and procrastination. There are times when perfection is not necessary. Dave Ellis calls this time management technique "It Ain't No Piano."[4] If a construction worker bends a nail in the framing of a house, it does not matter. The construction worker simply puts in another nail. After all, "it ain't no piano." It is another matter if you are building a fine cabinet or finishing a piano. Perfection is more important in these circumstances. We need to ask: Is the task important enough to invest the time needed for perfection? A final term paper needs to be as perfect as we can make it. A rough draft is like the frame of a house that does not need to be perfect.

In aiming for excellence rather than perfection, challenge yourself to use perspective to see the big picture. How important is the project and how perfect does it need to be? Could your time be better invested accomplishing other tasks? This technique requires flexibility and the ability to change with different situations. Do not give up if you cannot complete a project perfectly. Do the best that you can in the time available. In some situations, if life is too hectic, you may need to settle for completing the project and getting it in on time rather than doing it perfectly. With this idea in mind, you may be able to relax and still achieve excellence.

Make Learning Fun by Finding a Reward

Time management is not about restriction, self-control, and deprivation. If it is done correctly, time can be managed to get more out of life and to have fun while doing it. Remember that behavior is likely to increase if followed by a reward. Think about activities that you find rewarding. In our time management example with Justin who wants to be a physical therapist, he could use many tasks as rewards for completing his studies. He could meet friends for pizza, call his girlfriend, play video games, or watch TV. The key idea is to do the studying first and then reward the behavior. Maybe Justin will not be able to do all of the activities we have mentioned as possible rewards, but he could choose what he enjoys most.

Studying first and then rewarding yourself leads to peace of mind and the ability to focus on tasks at hand. While Justin is out having pizza with his friends, he does not have to worry about work that he has not done. While Justin is studying, he does not have to feel that he is being deprived of having pizza with friends. In this way, he can focus on studying while he is studying and focus on having a good time while relaxing with his friends. It is not a good idea to think about having pizza with friends while studying or to think about studying while having pizza with friends. When you work, focus on your work and get it done. When you play, enjoy playing without having to think about work.

Take a Break

If you are overwhelmed with the task at hand, sometimes it is best to just take a break. If you're stuck on a computer program or a math problem, take a break and do something else. As a general rule, take a break of 10 minutes for each hour of study. During the break, do something totally different. It is a good idea to get up and move around. Get up and pet your cat or dog, observe your goldfish, or shoot a few baskets. If time is really at a premium, use your break time to accomplish other important tasks. Put your clothes in the dryer, empty the dishwasher, or pay a bill.

Study in the Library

If you are having difficulty with studying, try studying at school in the library. Libraries are designed for studying, and other people are studying there as well. It is hard to do something else in the library without annoying the librarian or other students. If you can complete your studying at school, you can go home and relax. This may be especially important if family, friends, or roommates at home easily distract you.

"Don't say you don't have enough time. You have exactly the same number of hours per day that were given to Helen Keller, Pasteur, Michelangelo, Mother Teresa, Leonardo da Vinci, Thomas Jefferson, and Albert Einstein."

H. Jackson Browne

Learn to Say No Sometimes

Learn to say no to tasks that you do not have time to do. Follow your statement with the reasons for saying no: you are going to college and need time to study. Most people will understand this answer and respect it. You may need to say no to yourself as well. Maybe you cannot go out on Wednesday night if you have a class early on Thursday morning. Maybe the best use of your time right now is to turn off the TV or get off the Internet and study for tomorrow's test. You are investing your time in your future.

Dealing with Time Bandits

Time bandits are the many things that keep us from spending time on the things we think are important. Another word for a time bandit is a time waster. In college, it is tempting to do many things other than studying. We are all victims of different kinds of bandits.

Here are some ideas for keeping time bandits under control:

- **Schedule time for other people.** Friends and family are important, so we do not want to get rid of them! Discuss your goal of a college education with your friends and family. People who care about you will respect your goals. You may need to use a Do Not Disturb sign at times. If you are a parent, remember that you are a role

ACTIVITY

Put a checkmark next to the items that waste your time. Add your own personal time wasters at the end of the list.

_____ TV	_____ Phone	_____ Sleeping in
_____ Other electronic devices	_____ Household chores	_____ Shopping
_____ Daydreaming	_____ Roommates	_____ Being easily distracted
_____ Social networking	_____ Video games	_____ Studying at a bad time
_____ Saying yes when you mean no	_____ Partying	_____ Reading magazines
_____ Friends	_____ Children	_____ Studying in a distracting place
_____ Internet	_____ iPod	
_____ Social time	_____ Waiting time	_____ Movies
_____ Family	_____ Girlfriend, boyfriend, spouse	_____ Commuting time (travel)

List some of your personal time bandits here.

_____

_____

model for your children. If they see you studying, they are more likely to value their own education. Plan to spend quality time with your children and the people who are important to you. Make sure they understand that you care about them.

- **Remember the rewards.** Many of the time bandits listed above make good rewards for completing your work. Put the time bandits to work for you by studying first and then enjoying a reward. Enjoy the TV, Internet, iPod, video games, or phone conversations after you have finished your studies. Aim for a balance of work, study, and leisure time.

- **Use your prime time wisely.** Prime time is when you are most awake and alert. Use this time for studying. Use non-prime time for the time bandits. When you are tired, do household chores and shopping. If you have little time for household chores, you might find faster ways to do them. If you don't have time for shopping, you will notice that you spend less and have a better chance of following your budget.

- **Remind yourself about your priorities.** When time bandits attack, remind yourself of why you are in college. Think about your personal goals for the future. Remember that college is not forever. By doing well in college, you will finish in the shortest time possible.

- **Use a schedule.** Using a schedule or a to-do list is helpful in keeping you on track. Make sure you have some slack time in your schedule to handle unexpected phone calls and deal with the unplanned events that happen in life. If you cannot stick to your schedule, just get back on track as soon as you can.

Journal Entry #3

Write a paragraph about how you will manage your time to accomplish your goal of a college education. Use any of these questions to guide your thinking:

- What are your priorities?
- How will you balance school, work, and family/friends?
- What are some time management tools you plan to use?
- How can you deal with time bandits?

Dealing with Procrastination

Procrastination means putting off things until later. We all use delaying tactics at times. Procrastination that is habitual, however, can be self-destructive. Understanding some possible reasons for procrastination can help you use time more effectively and be more successful in accomplishing goals.

Why Do We Procrastinate?

There are many psychological reasons for procrastinating. Just becoming aware of these may help you deal with procrastination. If you have serious difficulty managing your time for psychological reasons, visit the counseling center at your college or university. Do you recognize any of these reasons for procrastination in yourself or others?

- **Fear of failure.** Sometimes we procrastinate because we are afraid of failing. We see our performance as related to how much ability we have and how worthwhile we are as human beings. We may procrastinate in our college studies because of doubts about our ability to do the work. Success, however, comes from trying and learning from mistakes. There is a popular saying: falling down is not failure, but failing to get up or not even trying is failure.

- **Fear of success.** Most students are surprised to find out that one of the reasons for procrastination is fear of success. Success in college means moving on with your life, getting a job, leaving a familiar situation, accepting increased responsibility, and sometimes leaving friends behind. None of these tasks is easy. An example of fear of success is not taking the last step required to be successful. Students sometimes do not take the last class needed to graduate. Some good students do not show up for the final exam or do not turn in a major project. If you ever find yourself procrastinating on an important last step, ask yourself if you are afraid of success and what lies ahead in your future.

- **Perfectionism.** Some people who procrastinate do not realize that they are perfectionists. Perfectionists expect more from themselves than is realistic and more than others expect of themselves. There is often no other choice than to procrastinate because perfectionism is usually unattainable. Perfectionism generates anxiety that further hinders performance. Perfectionists need to understand that perfection is seldom possible. They need to set time limits on projects and do their best within those time limits.

- **Need for excitement.** Some students can only be motivated by waiting until the last minute to begin a project. These students are excited and motivated by playing a game of "Beat the Clock." They like living on the edge and the adrenaline rush of responding to a crisis. Playing this game provides motivation, but it does not leave enough time to achieve the best results. Inevitably, things happen at the last minute to make the game even more exciting and dangerous: the printer breaks, the computer crashes, the student gets ill, the car breaks down, or the dog eats the homework. These students need to start projects earlier to improve their chances of success. It is best to seek excitement elsewhere, in sports or other competitive activities.

- **Excellence without effort.** In this scenario, students believe that they are truly outstanding and can achieve success without effort. These students think that they can go to college without attending classes or reading the text. They believe that they can pass the test without studying. They often do not succeed in college the first semester, which puts them at risk of dropping out of school. They often return to college later and improve their performance by putting in the effort required.

- **Loss of control.** Some students fear loss of control over their lives and procrastinate to gain control. An example is students who attend college because others (such as parents) want them to attend. Procrastination becomes a way of gaining control over the situation by saying, "You can't make me do this." They attend college but accomplish nothing. Parents can support and encourage education, but students need to choose their own goals in life and attend college because it is an important personal goal.

Tips for Dealing with Procrastination

When you find yourself procrastinating on a certain task, think about the consequences. Will the procrastination lead to failing an exam or getting a low grade? Think about the rewards of doing the task. If you do well, you can take pride in yourself and celebrate your success. How will you feel when the task is completed? Will you be able to enjoy your leisure time without guilt about not doing your work? How does the task help you to achieve your lifetime goals?

Maybe the procrastination is a warning sign that you need to reconsider lifetime goals and change them to better suit your needs.

Procrastination Scenario

George is a college student who is on academic probation for having low grades. He is required to make a plan for improving his grades in order to remain in college. George tells the counselor that he is making poor grades because of his procrastination. He is an accounting major and puts off doing homework because he dislikes it and does not find it interesting. The counselor asks George why he had chosen accounting as a major. He replies that accounting is a major that is in demand and has a good salary. The counselor suggests that George consider a major that he would enjoy more. After some consideration, George changes his major to psychology. He becomes more interested in college studies and is able to raise his grades to stay in college.

Most of the time, you will reap benefits by avoiding procrastination and completing the task at hand. Jane Burka and Lenora Yuen suggest the following steps to deal with procrastination:

1. Select a goal.

2. Visualize your progress.

3. Be careful not to sabotage yourself.

4. Stick to a time limit.

5. Don't wait until you feel like it.

6. Follow through. Watch out for excuses and focus on one step at a time.

7. Reward yourself after you have made some progress.

8. Be flexible about your goal.

9. Remember that it does not have to be perfect.[5]

Time Management, Part II

Test what you have learned by selecting the correct answers to the following questions.

1. To get started on a challenging project,
   a. think of a small first step and complete it.
   b. wait until you have plenty of time to begin.
   c. wait until you are well rested and relaxed.

2. If you are completing a to-do list of 10 items, the 80/20 rule states that
   a. 80% of the value comes from completing most of the items on the list.
   b. 80% of the value comes from completing two of the most important items.
   c. 80% of the value comes from completing half of the items on the list.

3. It is suggested that students aim for
   a. perfection.
   b. excellence.
   c. passing.

4. Sometimes students procrastinate because of
   a. fear of failure.
   b. fear of success.
   c. all of the above.

5. Playing the game "Beat the Clock" when doing a term paper results in
   a. increased motivation and success.
   b. greater excitement and quality work.
   c. increased motivation and risk.

How did you do on the quiz? Check your answers: 1. a, 2. b, 3. b, 4. c, 5. c

Journal Entry #4

Write a paragraph about how you will avoid procrastination. Consider these ideas when thinking about procrastination: fear of failure, fear of success, perfectionism, need for excitement, excellence without effort, and loss of control. How will you complete your assignments on time?

Managing Your Money

To be successful in college and in life, you will need to manage not only time, but money. One of the top reasons that students drop out of college is that they cannot pay for their education or that they have to work so much that they do not have time for school. Take a look at your lifetime goals. Most students have a goal related to money, such as becoming financially secure or becoming wealthy. If financial security or wealth is one of your goals, you will need to begin to take some action to accomplish that goal. If you don't take action on a goal, it is merely a fantasy.

How to Become a Millionaire

Save regularly. Frances Leonard, author of *Time Is Money,* cites some statistics on how much money you need to save to become a millionaire.[6] You can retire with a million dollars by age 68 by saving the following amounts of money at various ages. These figures assume a 10 percent return on your investment.

At age 22, save $87 per month
At age 26, save $130 per month
At age 30, save $194 per month
At age 35, save $324 a month

Notice that the younger you start saving, the less money is required to reach the million-dollar goal. (And keep in mind that even a million dollars may not be enough money to save for retirement.) How can you start saving money when you are a student struggling to pay for college? The answer is to practice money management techniques and to begin a savings habit, even if the money you save is a small amount to buy your books for next semester. When you get that first good job, save 10 percent of the money. If you are serious about becoming financially secure, learn about investments such as real estate, stocks and bonds, and mutual funds. Learning how to save and invest your money can pay big dividends in the future.

Think thrifty. Money management begins with looking at your attitude toward money. Pay attention to how you spend your money so that you can accomplish your financial goals such as getting a college education, buying a house or car, or saving for the future. The following example shows how one woman accomplished her financial goals through being thrifty. Amy Dacyczyn, author of *The Tightwad Gazette,* says, "A lot of people get a thrill out of buying things. Frugal people get a rush from the very act of saving. Saving can actually be fun—we think of it almost as a sport."[7] She noticed that people were working harder and harder for less and less. Amy Dacyczyn had the goals of marriage, children, and a New England farmhouse to live in. She wanted to stay home and take care of her six children instead of working. In seven years, she was able to accomplish her goals with her husband's income of $30,000 a year. During this time, she saved $49,000 for the down payment on a rural farmhouse costing $125,000. She also paid cash for $38,000 worth of car, appliance, and furniture purchases while staying at home with her children. How did she do this? She says that she just started paying attention to how she was spending her money.

To save money, Amy Dacyczyn made breakfast from scratch. She made oatmeal, pancakes, and muffins instead of purchasing breakfast cereals. She saved $440 a year in this way. She purchased the family clothing at yard sales. She thought of so many ideas to save money that she began publishing *The Tightwad Gazette* to share her money-saving ideas with others. At $12 per subscription, she grosses a million dollars a year!

Challenge yourself to pay attention to how you spend your money, and make a goal of being thrifty in order to accomplish your financial goals. With good money management, you can work less and have more time for college and recreational activities.

Managing Your Money

- Monitor your spending
- Prepare a budget
- Beware of credit and interest
- Watch spending leaks

Budgeting: The Key to Money Management

It is important to control your money, rather than letting your money control you. One of the most important things that you can do to manage your money and begin saving is to use a budget. A budget helps you become aware of how you spend your money and will help you make a plan for how you would like to spend your money.

Monitor how you spend your money. The first step in establishing a workable budget is to monitor how you are actually spending your money at the present time. For one month, keep a list of purchases with the date and amount of money spent for each. You can do this on a sheet of paper, on your calendar, on index cards, or on a money management application for your phone. If you write checks for items, include the checks written as part of your money monitor. At the end of the month, group your purchases in categories such as food, gas, entertainment, and credit card payments, and add them up. Doing this will yield some surprising results. For example, you may not be aware of just how much it costs to eat at a fast-food restaurant or to buy lunch or coffee every day.

Prepare a budget. One of the best tools for managing your money is a budget. At the end of this chapter, you will find a simple budget sheet that you can use as a college student. After you finish college, update your budget and continue to use it. Follow these three steps to make a budget:

1. Write down your income for the month.
2. List your expenses. Include tuition, books, supplies, rent, telephone, utilities (gas, electric, water, cable TV), car payments, car insurance, car maintenance (oil, repairs), parking fees, food, personal grooming, clothes, entertainment, savings, credit card payments, loan payments, and other bills. Use your money monitor to discover how you are spending your money and include categories that are unique to you.
3. Subtract your total expenses from your total income. You cannot spend more than you have. Make adjustments as needed.

Beware of credit and interest. College students are often tempted to use credit cards to pay for college expenses. This type of borrowing is costly and difficult to repay. It is easy to pull out a plastic credit card and buy items that you need and want. Credit card companies earn a great deal of money from credit cards. Jane Bryant Quinn gives an example of the cost of credit cards.[8] She says that if you owe $3,000 at 18 percent interest and pay the minimum payment of $60 per month, it will take you 30 years and 10 months to get out of debt! Borrowing the $3,000 would cost about $22,320 over this time! If you use a credit card, make sure you can pay it off in one to three months. It is good to have a credit card in order to establish credit and to use in an emergency.

Watch those spending leaks. We all have spending problem areas. Often we spend small amounts of money each day that add up to large spending leaks over time. For example, if you spend $3 on coffee each weekday for a year, this adds up to $780 a year!

If you eat lunch out each weekday and spend $8 for lunch, this adds up to $2,080 a year. Here are some common areas for spending leaks:

- Fast food and restaurants
- Entertainment and vacations
- Clothing
- Miscellaneous cash
- Gifts

To identify your spending problem areas, write down all of your expenditures for one month. Place a three-by-five card in your wallet or use your phone to monitor your cash expenditures. At the end of the month, organize your expenditures into categories and total them up. Then ask yourself if this is how you want to spend your money.

Need More Money?

You may be tempted to work more hours to balance your budget. Remember that to be a full-time college student, it is recommended that you work no more than 20 hours per week. If you work more than 20 hours per week, you will probably need to decrease your course load. Before increasing your work hours, see if there is a way you can decrease your monthly expenses. Can you make your lunch instead of eating out? Can you get by without a car? Is the item you are purchasing a necessity, or do you just want to have it? These choices are yours.

1. **Check out financial aid.** All students can qualify for some type of financial aid. Visit the Financial Aid Office at your college for assistance. Depending on your income level, you may qualify for one or more of the following forms of aid.

   - **Loans.** A loan must be paid back. The interest rate and terms vary according to your financial need. With some loans, the federal government pays the interest while you are in school.

   - **Grants.** A grant does not need to be repaid. There are both state and federal grants based on need.

   - **Work/study.** You may qualify for a federally subsidized job depending on your financial need. These jobs are often on campus and provide valuable work experience for the future.

   The first step in applying for financial aid is to fill out the Free Application for Federal Student Aid (FAFSA). This form determines your eligibility for financial aid. You can obtain this form from your college's financial aid office or over the Internet at www.fafsa.ed.gov.

   Here are some other financial aid resources that you can obtain from your financial aid office or over the Internet.

   - **Student Guide.** The Student Guide, published by the U.S. Department of Education, describes in detail the kinds of financial aid available and eligibility requirements; it is available over the Internet at studentaid.ed.gov/students/publications/student_guide/index.html.

   - **How to apply for financial aid.** Learn how to apply for federal financial aid and scholarships at www.finaid.org.

   - **Student Gateway.** Visit the new Student Gateway to the U.S. Government, which has information about planning and paying for your education, at www.students.gov/STUGOVWebApp/index.jsp.

2. **Apply for a scholarship.** Applying for a scholarship is like having a part-time job, only the pay is often better, the hours are flexible, and you can be your own boss. For this part-time job, you will need to research scholarship opportunities and fill out applications. There are multitudes of scholarships available, and sometimes no one even applies for them. Some students do not apply for scholarships because they think that high grades and financial need are required. While many scholarships are based on grades and financial need, many are not. Any person or organization can offer a scholarship for any reason they want. For example, scholarships can be based on hobbies, parent's occupation, religious background, military service, and personal interests, to name a few.

   There are several ways to research a scholarship. As a first step, visit the financial aid office on your college campus. This office is staffed with persons knowledgeable about researching and applying for scholarships. Organizations or persons wishing to fund scholarships often contact this office to advertise opportunities.

   You can also research scholarships through your public or college library. Ask the reference librarian for assistance. You can use the Internet to research scholarships as well. Use a search engine such as yahoo.com and simply type in the keyword *scholarships*. The following websites index thousands of scholarships:

   - Federal Student Aid Scholarship Wizard at studentaid2.ed.gov/getmoney/ scholarship/scholarship_search_select.asp?13817
   - fastweb.com
   - princetonreview.com/college/finance
   - college-scholarships.com
   - guaranteed-scholarships.com
   - collegenet.com/mach25
   - studentscholarshipsearch.com
   - collegeboard.com/paying

   To apply for scholarships, start a file of useful material usually included in scholarship applications. You can use this same information to apply for many scholarships.

   - Three current letters of recommendation
   - A statement of your personal goals
   - A statement of your financial need
   - Copies of your transcripts
   - Copies of any scholarship applications you have filled out

   Be aware of scholarship scams. You do not need to pay money to apply for a scholarship. No one can guarantee that you will receive a scholarship. Use your college scholarship office and your own resources to research and apply for scholarships.

The Best Ideas for Becoming Financially Secure

Financial planners provide the following ideas as the best ways to build wealth and independence.[9] If you have financial security as your goal, plan to do the following:

1. **Use a simple budget to track income and expenses.** Do not spend more than you earn.

2. **Have a financial plan.** Include goals such as saving for retirement, purchasing a home, paying for college, or taking vacations.

3. **Save 10 percent of your income.** As a college student, you may not be able to save this much, but plan to do it as soon as you get your first good-paying job. If you cannot save 10 percent, save something to get in the habit of saving. Save to pay for your tuition and books.

4. **Don't take on too much debt.** Be especially careful about credit cards and consumer debt. Credit card companies often visit college campuses and offer high-interest credit cards to students. It is important to have a credit card, but pay off the balance each month. Consider student loans instead of paying college fees by credit card.

5. **Don't procrastinate.** The earlier you take these steps toward financial security, the better.

Tips for Managing Your Money

Keeping these guidelines in mind can help you to manage your money.

- Don't let friends pressure you into spending too much money. If you can't afford something, learn to say no.
- Keep your checking account balanced or use online banking so you will know how much money you have.
- Don't lend money to friends. If your friends cannot manage their money, your loan will not help them.
- Use comparison shopping to find the best prices on the products that you buy.
- Get a part-time job while in college. You will earn money and gain valuable job experience.
- Don't use shopping as a recreational activity. When you visit the mall, you will find things you never knew you needed and will wind up spending more money than intended.
- Make a budget and follow it. This is the best way to achieve your financial goals.

Do What Is Important First

The most important thing you can do to manage time and money is to spend it on what is most important. Manage time and money to help you live the life you want. How can you do this? Author Stephen Covey wrote a book titled *The Seven Habits of Highly Effective People.* One of the habits is "Put first things first." Covey suggests that in time management, the "challenge is not to manage our time but to manage ourselves."[10]

How can you manage yourself? Our first thoughts in answering this question often involve suggestions about willpower, restriction, and self-control. Schedules and budgets are seen as instruments for self-control. It seems that the human spirit resists attempts at control, even when we aim to control ourselves. Often the response to control is rebellion. With time and money management, we may not follow a schedule or budget. A better approach to begin managing yourself is to know your values. What is important in your life? Do you have a clear mental picture of what is important? Can you describe your values and make a list of what is important to you? With your values and goals in mind, you can begin to manage both your time and your money.

When you have given some thought to your values, you can begin to set goals. When you have established goals for your life, you can begin to think in terms of what is most important and establish your priorities. Knowing your values is essential in making decisions about how to invest your time and money. Schedules and budgets are merely tools for helping you accomplish what you have decided is important. Time and money management is not about restriction and control, but about making decisions regarding what is important in your life. If you know what is important, you can find the strength to say no to activities and expenditures that are less important.

As a counselor, I have the pleasure of working with many students who have recently explored and discovered their values and are highly motivated to succeed. They are willing to do what is important first. I recently worked with a young couple who came to enroll in college. They brought their young baby with them. The new father was interested in environmental engineering. He told me that in high school, he never saw a reason for school and did just the minimum needed to get by. He was working as a construction laborer and making a living, but did not see a future in the occupation. He had observed an environmental engineer who worked for the company and decided that was what he wanted for his future. As he looked at his new son, he told me that he needed to have a better future for himself and his family.

He and his wife decided to do what was important first. They were willing to make the sacrifice to attend school and invest the time needed to be successful. The father planned to work during the day and go to school at night. Later, he would go to school full-time and get a part-time job in the evening. His wife was willing to get a part-time job also, and they would share in taking care of the baby. They were willing to manage their money carefully to accomplish their goals. As they left, they added that their son would be going to college as well.

How do you get the energy to work all day, go to school at night, and raise a family? You can't do it by practicing self-control. You find the energy by having a clear idea of what you want in your life and focusing your time and resources on the goal. Finding what you want to do with your life is not easy either. Many times people find what they want to do when some significant event happens in their lives.

Begin to think about what you want out of life. Make a list of your important values and write down your lifetime goals. Don't forget about the people who are important to you, and include them in your priorities. Then you will be able to do what is important first.

> "Fathers send their sons to college either because they went to college or because they didn't."
> L. L. Henderson

Journal Entry #5

What is your plan for managing your money? Consider these ideas when thinking about your plan: monitoring how you spend your money, using a budget, applying for financial aid and scholarships, saving money, and spending money wisely.

JOURNAL ENTRIES

Managing Time and Money

Go to http://www.collegesuccess1.com/JournalEntries.htm for Word files of the Journal Entries

Success over the Internet

Visit the *College Success Website* at http://www.collegesuccess1.com/

The *College Success Website* is continually updated with new topics and links to the material presented in this chapter. Topics include:

- Suggestions for time management
- How to overcome procrastination
- How to deal with perfectionism
- Goal setting
- Goal setting in sports
- Goal setting and visualization
- Scholarship websites
- Recognizing scholarship scams
- Financial aid websites

Ask your instructor if you need any assistance in accessing the *College Success Website*.

Notes

1. Quoted in Rob Gilbert, ed., *Bits and Pieces,* November 4, 1999, 15.

2. Alan Lakein, *How to Get Control of Your Time and Your Life* (New York: Peter H. Wyden, 1973).

3. Ibid., 70–71.

4. Dave Ellis, *Becoming a Master Student* (Boston: Houghton Mifflin, 1998).

5. Jane Burka and Lenora Yuen, *Procrastination* (Reading, MA: Addison-Wesley, 1983).

6. Frances Leonard, *Time Is Money* (Addison-Wesley), cited in the *San Diego Union Tribune,* October 14, 1995.

7. Amy Dacyczyn, *The Tightwad Gazette II* (Villard Books), cited in the *San Diego Union Tribune,* February 20, 1995.

8. Jane Bryant Quinn, "Money Watch," *Good Housekeeping*, November 1996, 80.

9. Robert Hanley, "Breaking Bad Habits," *San Diego Union Tribune,* September 7, 1992.

10. Stephen R. Covey, *The Seven Habits of Highly Effective People* (New York: Simon and Schuster, 1990), 150.

My Lifetime Goals: Brainstorming Activity

Name _____ Date _____

1. Think about the goals that you would like to accomplish in your life. At the end of your life, you do not want to say, "I wish I would have _____." Set a timer for five minutes and write whatever comes to mind about what you would like to do and accomplish over your lifetime. Include goals in these areas: career, personal relationships, travel, and financial security or any area that is important to you. Write down all your ideas. The goal is to generate as many ideas as possible in five minutes. You can reflect on which ones are most important later. You may want to do this as part of a group activity in your class.

Look over the ideas you wrote above and highlight or underline the goals that are most important to you.

2. Ask yourself what you would like to accomplish in the next five years. Think about where you want to be in college, what you want to do in your career, and what you want to do in your personal life. Set a timer and write whatever comes to mind in five minutes. The goal is to write down as many ideas as possible.

Again, look over the ideas you wrote and highlight or underline the ideas that are most important to you.

3. What goals would you like to accomplish in the next year? What are some steps that you can begin now to accomplish your lifetime goals? Consider work, study, leisure, and social goals. Set your timer for five minutes and write down your goals for the next year.

Review what you wrote and highlight or underline the ideas that are most important to you. When writing your goals, include fun activities as well as taking care of others.

Looking at the items that you have highlighted or underlined, make a list of your lifetime goals using the form that follows. Make sure your goals are specific enough so that you can break them into steps you can achieve.

Name _____ Date _____

Using the ideas that you brainstormed in the previous exercise, make a list of your lifetime goals. Make sure your goals are specific and concrete. Begin with goals that you would like to accomplish over a lifetime. In the second section, think about the goals you can accomplish over the next one to three years.

Long-Term Goals (lifetime goals)

Short-Term Goals (one to three years)

What are some steps you can take now to accomplish intermediate and long-term goals?

Successful Goal Setting

Name _____ Date _____

Look at your list of lifetime goals. Which one is most important? Write the goal here:

Answer these questions about the goal you have listed above.

1. What skills, abilities, and resources do you have to achieve this goal? What skills, abilities, and resources will you need to develop to achieve this goal?

2. Do you believe you can achieve it? Write a brief positive statement about achieving this goal.

3. State your goal in specific terms that can be observed or counted. Rewrite your goal if necessary.

4. Write a brief statement about how this goal will give you personal satisfaction.

5. How will you motivate yourself to achieve this goal?

6. What are your personal values that match this goal?

7. List some steps that you will take to accomplish this goal.

8. When will you finish this goal?

9. What roadblocks will make this goal difficult to achieve?

10. How will you deal with these roadblocks?

Weekly College Schedule

Name _____ Date _____

Copy the following schedule to use in future weeks or design your own schedule. Fill in this schedule and try to follow it for at least one week. First, fill in scheduled commitments (classes, work, activities). Next, fill in the time you need for studying. Put in some tasks related to your lifetime goals. Leave some blank time as a shock absorber to handle unexpected activities.

Time	Monday	Tuesday	Wednesday	Thursday	Friday	Saturday	Sunday
7 A.M.							
8							
9							
10							
11							
Noon							
1 P.M.							
2							
3							
4							
5							
6							
7							
8							
9							
10							
11							

Weekly To-Do Chart

Name _____ Date _____

Using a to-do list is an easy way to remind yourself of important priorities each day. This chart is divided into three areas representing types of tasks that college students need to balance: academic, personal, and social.

Weekly To-Do List

	Monday	Tuesday	Wednesday	Thursday	Friday
Academic					
Personal					
Social					

Study Schedule Analysis

Name _____ Date _____

Before completing this analysis, use the schedule form to create a master schedule. A master schedule blocks out class and work times as well as any regularly scheduled activities. Looking at the remaining time, write in your planned study times. It is recommended that you have two hours of study time for each hour in class. For example, a three-unit class would require six hours of study time. A student with 12 units would require 24 hours of study time. You may need more or fewer hours, depending on your study skills, reading skills, and difficulty of courses.

1. How many units are you enrolled in?

2. How many hours of planned study time do you have?

3. How many hours do you work each week?

4. How many hours do you spend in relaxation/social activities?

5. Do you have time planned for exercise?

6. Do you get enough sleep?

7. What are some of your time bandits (things that take up your time and make it difficult to accomplish your goals)?

Write a few discovery statements about how you use your time.

8. Are you spending enough time to earn the grades you want to achieve? Do you need to spend more time studying to become successful?

9. Does your work schedule allow you enough time to study?

10. How can you deal with your time bandits?

11. How can you use your time more effectively to achieve your goals?

Name _____ Date _____

This circle represents 24 hours. Each piece is six hours. Draw a slice of pie to represent how much time you spend on each of these activities in a typical day: sleeping, attending classes, studying, work, family, friends, and other activities.

Thinking about your values is the first step in setting goals. How you spend your time determines whether you will accomplish these goals. Are you using your time to accomplish your goals? Make some intention statements for the future on how you want to spend your time.

I intend to:

The College Student's Tightwad Gazette

Name _____   Date _____

List five ideas for saving money that could be included in a publication called *The College Student's Tightwad Gazette*.

1. _____

2. _____

3. _____

4. _____

5. _____

Get together with other students in the class and come up with five additional ideas that college students can use to save money or increase income.

1. _____

2. _____

3. _____

4. _____

5. _____

List five ways that college students can have fun without spending much money.

1. _____

2. _____

3. _____

4. _____

5. _____

Name _____ Date _____

Before you complete this budget, monitor your expenses for one month. Write down all expenditures and then divide them into categories that have meaning for you. Then complete the following budget and try to follow it for at least two months. Do this exercise on your own, since it is likely to contain private information.

College Student Monthly Budget

Monthly income for _____ (month)	
Income from job _____	
Money from home _____	**Total Income** [ ]
Financial aid _____	
Other _____	

Budgeted Monthly Expenses:	**Actual Monthly Expenses:**
Total Budgeted [ ]	**Total Actual**

Total Income [   ]   **Minus Total Budgeted** [   ]   **Equals** [   ]

CHAPTER 5

Improving Memory and Reading

Learning Objectives

Read to answer these key questions:

- How does the memory work?

- Why do we forget?

- How can I remember what I study?

- What are some memory tricks?

- How can I apply memory techniques to reading?

- What is a reading system for college texts?

- What are some ways to improve reading speed and comprehension?

- Why is positive thinking a key to remembering and reading?

Name: Ally Bracken

Major: Early Childhood Education

Year: Junior

Hometown: Mattawan, MI

Involvement: Fall Welcome Ambassador, First-Year Seminar Student Instructor, 2014 First-Year Seminar Intern

Quote: "There is no passion to be found in settling for a life that is less than the one you are capable of living."—Nelson Mandela

Coming to Western Michigan University has easily been **one of the best choices I have made in my life.** Being a student at WMU has pushed me out of my comfort zone, led me to **countless opportunities**, and **provided me with the necessary challenges** to become a better student and leader.

I never considered myself a shy person, until I got to college. It seemed as though everybody knew their place here at WMU, and as a nervous first-year, I had no clue where my place was. It was scary and nerve-racking, but at the end of my first year, I was offered the opportunity to become a **First-Year Seminar student instructor.** And just like that, **I found my place here at WMU.** I have become a part of the First-Year Experience Programs, and it has truly been the best experience. FYE has led me to a better understanding of myself and of the strengths that I provide to those around me. There is a home away from home for everybody on campus; you just need to be willing to take risks and **put yourself out there.**

Being involved is one of the best ways to make the most of **your college experience.** It provides you with opportunities to **develop your leadership skills, enhance your works skills**, and **make new friends.** But, it is also very important to **take your academics seriously**, especially during your first year. It is easy to get caught up in the social aspects of college, but **you are here for a reason**, and it is to get an education. You need to know your limits and how to find a balance between your classes and your social life. That **balance will be the key to your success** at WMU. **Put your all into your time at WMU**, and I promise, you will be amazed at what opportunities this university will provide you with. **Go Broncos!**

Learning how to improve your memory and remember what you read will be a great asset in college, on the job, and in life in general. This chapter describes how memory works and provides some practical techniques for improving your memory. Once you understand how memory works, you can apply these techniques to remembering what you read. Positive thinking will help you be successful in remembering and reading effectively.

Improving Your Memory

How Does the Memory Work?

Understanding how the memory works provides the framework for effective study techniques. There are three stages of memory: **sensory register, short-term memory,** and **long-term memory.** Understanding these stages of memory will help you learn how to store information in your long-term memory, which lasts a lifetime.

- **Sensory register.** The first stage of memory is called sensory register. It is the initial moment of perception. This stage of memory lasts less than a second and is used to record sensory experience (what you see, hear, taste, touch, or do). It is like a quickly fading snapshot of what your senses perceive. The purpose of the sensory register is to allow the brain to process information and to focus on relevant information. To remember information for more than a second, it must be transferred to short-term memory.

- **Short-term memory (STM).** Paying attention to the information you have perceived in the sensory register transfers the information to STM. STM is temporary and limited, lasting only about half a minute. The information must be rehearsed or renewed for longer storage. STM records what we see, hear, feel, taste, or touch. Information is best stored in STM through recitation or mentally talking to ourselves. If the information is not repeated, it is very quickly lost. For example, when you meet a person for the first time, the person's name is often quickly forgotten because it is only stored in short-term memory. The purpose of STM is to ponder the significance of the stimuli we have received, detect patterns, and decide if the information is important enough to remember.

Grouping together or chunking bits of information can increase the limited capacity of STM. George Miller of Harvard University found that the optimum number of chunks or bits of information that we can hold in STM is five to nine.[1] For example, we remember telephone numbers of seven digits by using a hyphen to separate the numbers into two more easily remembered chunks. We divide our Social Security numbers into three chunks for easier recall.

According to George Miller's research, we often use the "Magical Number Seven" technique to remember material. It is much easier to remember material that is grouped in chunks of seven or less. You can find many examples of groups of seven used to enhance memory. There are seven days of the week and seven numbers in your driver's license and license plate. There are also seven dwarfs, seven deadly sins, and seven wonders of the world!

- **Long-term memory (LTM).** Long-term memory has a large capacity and is used to store information more permanently. You will want to use your LTM to store important information that you want to be able to recall at a later date. Most psychologists

How Does the Memory Work?

Sensory Register	**Initial moment of perception**	**Lasts less than a second**
STM Short Term Memory	**Temporary and limited**	**Lasts less than 30 seconds**
LTM Long Term Memory	**Permanent storage of information**	**Lasts forever, although you may lose access through disuse**

Figure 5.1 Short-Term Memory and Long-Term Memory

agree that once information is in LTM, it is there forever. Although the information is available, the problem becomes how to access it. Think of LTM as a library in which many available books are stored. If the books in the library are randomly stored, retrieval of information becomes extremely difficult. If the books are properly stored and indexed, we can find them more easily.

How are long-term memories formed? Short-term memories become long-term through repetition or meaningful association. Creating long-term memories takes some purposeful action. We are motivated to take some purposeful action to remember if the information has some survival value. When we touch a hot stove, this memory moves from sensory register to short-term memory and then is stored in long-term memory to avoid injury in the future. In an academic setting, we must convince ourselves of the survival value of what we are learning. Is the information needed to pass a test, to be successful in a career, or for personal reasons? If so, it is easier to take the action required to store information in long-term memory. Emotions such as fear, anger, or joy are also involved in the storing of memories. In the hot stove example, fear elevates the importance of the memory and helps us to store it in long-term memory. In the educational setting, an interest or joy in learning helps to store information in long-term memory.

It is interesting to note that computers are designed much like STM and LTM. The Random Access Memory (RAM) is the working and calculating part of the computer and can be compared to the STM. When the computer is turned off, the contents of RAM disappear, just as information quickly disappears in STM. The Read Only Memory (ROM) is the permanent storage component, similar to LTM.

In summary, when you are trying to store information in your memory, the first step is receiving information through the five senses to store in the sensory register, similar to entering data in a computer through the use of a keyboard. This takes less than a second. The next step involves paying attention to the sensory stimulus in order to transfer it to STM for the purpose of seeing patterns and judging significance or importance. Information only stays in STM for 30 seconds or less unless rehearsed or repeated. If you decide that the information is likely to be on a test and you need to remember it, you must organize the material in a meaningful way or repeat it to store the information in LTM. Information must be stored in LTM in order for you to remember it permanently. Effective techniques for storing information in LTM will be presented later in this chapter.

Why Do We Forget?

Is it true that we never forget? Material that is stored in the sensory register is forgotten in less than one second. Material stored in STM is forgotten in 30 seconds unless rehearsed or repeated. We do not forget material stored in LTM, but we can lose access to the information, similar to when a book is filed incorrectly in the library. The book is in the library, but we cannot find it.

Examining the following lists of items frequently forgotten or remembered can give us insight into why forgetting or losing access occurs.

We frequently forget these things:

- Unpleasant experiences
- Names of people, places, or things
- Numbers and dates
- What we have barely learned
- Material we do not fully understand
- What we try to remember when embarrassed, frustrated, tired, or ill
- Material we have learned by cramming
- Ideas or theories that conflict with our beliefs

We tend to remember these things:

- Pleasant experiences
- Material that is important to us
- What we have put an effort into learning
- What we have reviewed or thought about often
- Material that is interesting to us
- Muscular skills such as riding a bike
- What we had an important reason to remember
- Items we discuss with others
- Material that we understand
- Frequently used information

Theories of Forgetting

An understanding of theories of forgetting is also helpful in developing techniques for effective study and learning. There are many theories about why we forget or lose access to information stored in LTM.

1. **I forgot.** If you forget a name, number, or fact, you might just say, "I forgot." The information was stored in STM and never made it to LTM. Have you ever been introduced to a person and really not listened to his or her name? You didn't forget it. You never learned it.

2. **The mental blur.** If you are studying and don't understand the material, you will not remember it.

3. **The decay theory.** If you do not use information, you lose access to it, just as weeds grow over a path that is seldom used.

4. **Interference theory.** New memories interfere with old memories, and old memories interfere with new memories. Interference is especially likely when the memories are similar. For example, when I meet my students in the hallway, it is difficult to remember which class they are in because I have several similar classes.

5. **Reactive interference.** We tend not to remember ideas or subjects that we dislike.

6. **Reconstruction theory.** What we remember becomes distorted over time. Our personal biases affect what we remember.

7. **Motivated forgetting.** We choose to remember pleasant experiences and to forget unpleasant experiences.

Minimizing Forgetting

Herman Ebbinghaus (1850–1909), a German psychologist and pioneer in research on forgetting, described a curve of forgetting.[2] He invented nonsense syllables such as WUX, CAZ, BIJ, and ZOL. He chose these nonsense syllables so that there would be no meaning, associations, or organizations that could affect the memory of the words. He would learn these lists of words and measure forgetting over time. The following is a chart of time and forgetting of nonsense syllables.

Time	Percent Forgotten
After 20 minutes	47
After 1 day	62

"Just as iron rusts from disuse, even so does inaction spoil the intellect."

Leonardo da Vinci

Memorization Tips

- Meaningful organization
- Visualization
- Recitation
- Develop an interest
- See the big picture first
- Intend to remember
- Learn small amounts frequently
- Basic background
- Relax

> "Today I will do what others won't, so I can accomplish what others can't."
>
> Jerry Rice

After 2 days	69
After 15 days	75
After 31 days	78

We can draw three interesting conclusions from examining these figures. First, most of the forgetting occurs within the first 20 minutes. Immediate review, or at least review during the first 20 minutes, would prevent most of the forgetting. Second, forgetting slows down over time. The third conclusion is that forgetting is significant after 31 days. Fortunately, we do not need to memorize nonsense syllables. We can use meaning, associations, organization, and proper review to minimize forgetting.

Review is important in transferring information from short-term to long-term memory. You can also minimize forgetting over time through the proper use of review.[3] Let's assume that you spend 45 minutes studying and learning something new. The optimum schedule for review would look like this:

After 10 minutes	Review for 5 minutes
After 1 day	Review for 5 minutes
After 1 week	Review for 3 minutes
After 1 month	Review for 3 minutes
After 6 months	Review for 3 minutes

ACTIVITY

Magical Number Seven

Remember George Miller's Magical Number Seven Theory? It is more efficient to limit the number of categories to seven or less, although you can have subcategories. Examine the following list of words.

goat	horse	cow
carrot	cat	lettuce
banana	tomato	pig
celery	orange	peas
cherry	apple	strawberry

Look at the list for one minute. Then look away from the list and write down all the words you can recall. Record the number of words you remembered: _____

Note that the following lists are divided into categories: animals, crops, and tropical fruits.

animals	crops	tropical fruits
lion	wheat	banana
giraffe	beans	kiwi
kangaroo	corn	mango
coyote	hay	guava
bear	oats	orange

Look at the above list for one minute. Then look away from the list and write down the words you recall. Record the number of words you remembered: _____

You probably remembered more from the second list because the list is organized into categories. Notice that there are only five words in each category. Remember that it is easier to remember lists with seven items or less. If these words have some meaning for you, it is easier to remember them. A farmer from the Midwest would probably have an easier time remembering the crops. A person from Hawaii would probably remember the list of tropical fruits. We also tend to remember unusual items and the first and last items on the list. If you need to memorize a list, pay more attention to the mundane items and the items in the middle of the list.

By spending about 20 minutes in review time, you can remember 90 to 100 percent of the material. The short periods of review are much easier to accomplish than spending larger periods of review. Make good use of your time by having material for review immediately available. When you have three to five minutes available, review some material that you have learned previously. You will be improving access to material stored in long-term memory, and you will be able to easily recall the information for an exam or for future use in your career.

Improving Memory and Reading **Chapter 5** 149

How Can I Remember What I Study?

Based on the above theories of memory and forgetting, here are some practical suggestions for storing information in LTM. Information stored in LTM can be retrieved for tests in college and for success in your career and personal life.

Meaningful Organization

There is no better method of memory improvement than imposing your own form of personal organization on the material you are trying to remember. Psychologists have even suggested that your intelligence quotient (IQ) may be related to how well you have organized material you learned in the past. When learning new material, cluster facts and ideas into categories that are meaningful to you.

Visualization

Another very powerful memorization technique is visualization. The right side of the brain specializes in visual pictures and the left side in verbal functions. If you focus on the words only, you are using only half of your brain. If you can focus on the words and accompany them with pictures, you are using your brain in the most efficient way. Advertisers use pictures as powerful influences to motivate you to purchase their products. You can use the same power of visualization to enhance your studying. While you are studying history, picture what life would be like in that time period. In engineering, make pictures in your mind or on paper to illustrate scientific principles. Challenge yourself to see the pictures along with the words. Add movement to your pictures, as in a video. During a test, relax and recall the pictures.

Recitation

Although scientists are still researching and learning how the memory works and how information is stored, we do know that recitation, rehearsal, and reviewing the ideas are powerful techniques for learning. Memories exist in the brain in the form of a chemical neural trace. Some researchers think that it takes about four or five seconds for this neural trace to be established in LTM. It is through recitation that we keep the ideas in our mind long enough to store them in LTM. Often students say they cannot remember the material that they have just read. The reason for this problem is not a lack of intelligence, but rather a simple lack of rehearsal. If information obtained through reading is stored in STM, it is very quickly forgotten. Say aloud or to yourself the material you want to remember. This process takes about five seconds.

Applying the recitation technique can help you remember names. When you are introduced to someone, first pay attention to make sure that you have heard the name correctly. Ask the person to repeat their name if necessary. Repeat the name out loud or in your mind. Say something like, "Glad to meet you, *Lydia*." Say the name silently to yourself five times to establish the neural trace. If possible, make a visual connection with the name. If the person's name is Frank, you might picture a hot dog, for example. Thinking about the name or reviewing it will help to access the name in the future.

Remember that most of the forgetting occurs in the first 20 minutes after learning something. Reviewing the material within 20 minutes is the fastest and most effective way to remember it. You will also need to review the information you have stored in LTM periodically so it is more accessible. This periodic review can be done effectively in three to five minutes.

"Knowledge is power, but enthusiasm pulls the switch."

Ivern Ball

"The secret of a good memory is attention, and attention to a subject depends on interest in it. We rarely forget what makes a deep impression on our mind."

Tyron Edwards

Develop an Interest

We tend to remember what interests us. People often have phenomenal memories when it comes to sports, automobiles, music, stamp collecting, or anything they consider fun or pursue as a hobby. Find something interesting in your college studies. If you are not interested in what you are studying, look for something interesting or even pretend that you are interested. Reward yourself for studying by doing something enjoyable.

Attitude has a significant impact on memory. Approaching your studies with a positive attitude will help you to find something interesting and make it easier to remember. In addition, the more you learn about a topic, the more interesting it becomes. Often we judge a subject as boring because we know nothing about it.

Another way to make something interesting is to look for personal meaning. How can I use this information in my future career? Does the information relate to my personal experience in some way? How can I use this information? What is the importance of this information? And finally, is this information likely to be on the test?

See the Big Picture First

Imagine looking at a painting one inch at a time. It would be difficult to understand or appreciate a painting in this way. College students often approach reading a textbook in the same way. They focus on the small details without first getting an idea of the main points. By focusing on the details without looking at the main points, it is easy to get lost.

The first step in reading is to skim the chapter headings to form a mental outline of what you will be learning. Then read for detail. Think of the mind as a file cabinet or a computer. Major topics are like folders in which we file detailed information. When we need to find or access the information, we think of the major topic and look in the folder to find the details. If we put all of our papers into the file drawer without organization, it is difficult to find the information we need. Highlight or underline key ideas to focus on the main points and organize what you are learning.

Be selective and focus on key ideas to increase learning efficiency. Herman Ebbinghaus studied the length of time needed to remember series of six nonsense syllables and 12 nonsense syllables.[4] We might assume that it would take twice as long to remember 12 syllables as it would six syllables. Ebbinghaus found that it took 15 times longer to memorize 12 syllables. The Magic Number Seven Theory seems to apply to the number of items that can be memorized efficiently.

Does this mean that we should try to remember only seven or less ideas in studying a textbook chapter? No—it is most efficient to identify seven or fewer key ideas and then cluster less important ideas under major headings. In this way, you can remember the key ideas in the chapter you are studying. The critical thinking required by this process also helps in remembering ideas and information.

Intend to Remember

Tell yourself that you are going to remember. If you think you won't remember, you won't remember. This step also relates to positive thinking and self-confidence and will take some practice to apply. Once you have told yourself to remember, apply some of the above techniques such as organizing, visualizing, and reciting. If you intend to remember, you will pay attention, make an effort to understand, and use memory techniques to strengthen your memory.

One practical technique that involves intent to remember is the memory jogger. This involves doing something unusual to jog or trigger your memory. If you want to be sure to remember your books, place your car keys on the books. Since you cannot go anywhere without your keys, you will find them and remember the books too. Another application is putting your watch on your right hand to remember to do something. When you look at your left hand and notice that the watch is not there, the surprise will jog your memory for the item you wish to recall. You can be creative with this technique and come up with your own memory joggers.

Distribute the Practice

Learning small amounts of material and reviewing frequently are more effective than a marathon study session. One research study showed that a task that took 30 minutes to learn in one day could be learned in 22 minutes if spread over two days. This is almost a 30 percent increase in efficiency.[5]

If you have a list of vocabulary words or formulas to learn, break the material into small parts and frequently review each part for a short period of time. Consider putting these facts or figures on index cards to carry with you in your purse or pocket. Use small amounts of time to quickly review the cards. This technique works well because it prevents fatigue and helps to keep motivation high. One exception to the distributed practice rule is creative work such as writing a paper or doing an art project, where a longer time period is needed for creative inspiration and immediate follow-through.

A learning technique for distributed practice is summed up in the acronym **SAFMEDS**, which stands for Say All Fast for one Minute Each Day and Shuffle.[6] With this technique, you can easily and quickly learn 100 or more facts. To use this technique, prepare flash cards that contain the material to be learned (vocabulary, foreign language words, numbers, dates, places, names, formulas). For example, if you are learning Spanish, place the Spanish word on one side of the card and the English word on the other side. Just writing out the flash cards is an aid to learning and is often sufficient for learning the material. Once the cards are prepared, *say* the Spanish word and see if you can remember what it means in English. Look at the back of the card to see if your answer is correct. Do this with *all* of the cards as *fast* as you can for *one minute each day*. Then *shuffle* the cards and repeat the process the next day.

It is important that you do this activity quickly. Don't worry if you do not know the answer. Just flip each card over, quickly look at the answer, and put the cards that you missed into a separate pile. At the end of the minute, count the number of cards you answered correctly. You can learn even faster if you take the stack of cards you missed and practice them quickly one more time. Shuffling the cards helps you to remember the actual meanings of the words, instead of just the order in which they appear. In the case of the Spanish cards, turn the cards over and say each English word to see if you can remember the equivalent word in Spanish. Each day, the number of correct answers will increase, and you will have a concrete measure of your learning. Consider this activity as a fun and fast-moving game to challenge yourself.

Create a Basic Background

You remember information by connecting it to things you already know. The more you know, the easier it is to make connections that make remembering easier. You will even find that it is easier to remember material toward the end of a college class because you have established a basic background at the beginning of the semester. With this in mind, freshman-level courses will be the most difficult in college because they form the basic background for your college education. College does become easier as you establish this basic background and practice effective study techniques.

You can enhance your basic background by reading a variety of books. Making reading a habit also enhances vocabulary, writing, and spelling. College provides many opportunities for expanding your reading horizons and areas of basic knowledge.

Relax While Studying

The brain works much better when it is relaxed. As you become more confident in your study techniques, you can become more relaxed. Here are some suggestions to help you relax during study time.

- Use distributed practice to take away some of the pressure of learning; take breaks between periods of learning. Give yourself time to absorb the material.
- Plan ahead so that you do not have to cram. Waiting until the last minute to study produces anxiety that is counterproductive.
- If you are anxious, try a physical activity or relaxation exercise before study sessions. For example, imagine a warm, relaxing light beginning at the feet and moving slowly up the body to the top of the head. Feel each part of the body relax as the light makes contact with it. You will find other relaxation techniques in Chapter 12.
- If you are feeling frustrated, it is often a good idea to stop and come back to your studies later. You may gain insight into your studies while you are more relaxed and doing something else. You can often benefit from a fresh perspective.

Journal Entry #1

Review the memory techniques explained in this chapter: meaningful organization, visualization, recitation, develop an interest, see the big picture, intend to remember, distribute the practice, create a basic background, and relax while studying. List and briefly explain at least three techniques you are willing to try, and give examples of how you would use each of the three memory techniques you select.

Using Mnemonics and Other Memory Tricks

Memory tricks can be used to enhance your memory. These memory tricks include acrostics, acronyms, peg systems, and loci systems. These systems are called *mnemonics*, from the Greek word *mneme* which means "to remember."

Mnemonic devices are very effective. A research study by Gerald R. Miller found that students who used mnemonic devices improved their test scores by up to 77 percent.[7] Mnemonics are effective because they help to organize material. They have been used throughout history, in part as a way to entertain people with amazing memory feats.

Mnemonics are best used for memorizing facts. They are not helpful for understanding or thinking critically about the information. Be sure to memorize your mnemonics carefully and review them right before exam time. Forgetting the mnemonic or a part of it can cause major problems.

Memorization Tricks

- Acrostics
- Acronyms
- Peg systems
- Loci systems
- Visual clues
- Say it aloud
- Have a routine
- Write it down

Acrostics

Acrostics are creative rhymes, songs, poems, or sentences that help us to remember. Maybe you previously learned some of these in school.

- Continents: Eat an Aspirin after a Nighttime Snack (Europe, Antarctica, Asia, Africa, Australia, North America, South America)
- Directions of the compass: Never Eat Sour Watermelons (North, East, South, West)

- Geological ages: Practically Every Old Man Plays Poker Regularly (Paleocene, Eocene, Oligocene, Miocene, Pliocene, Pleistocene, Recent)
- Guitar Strings: Eat All Dead Gophers Before Easter (E, A, D, G, B, E)
- Oceans: I Am a Person (Indian, Arctic, Atlantic, Pacific)
- Metric system in order: King Henry Drinks Much Dark Chocolate Milk (Kilometer, hectometer, decameter, meter, decimeter, centimeter, millimeter
- Notes on the treble clef in music: Every Good Boy Does Fine (E, G, B, D, F)
- Classification in biology: Kings Play Cards on Fairly Good Soft Velvet (Kingdom, Phylum, Class, Order, Family, Genus, Species, Variety)

An effective way to invent your own acrostics is to first identify key ideas you need to remember, underline these key words or write them down as a list, and think of a word that starts with the first letter of each idea you want to remember. Rearrange the words if necessary to form a sentence. The more unusual the sentence, the easier it is to remember.

In addition to acrostics, there are many other creative memory aids:

- Days in each month: Thirty days hath September, April, June, and November. All the rest have 31, except February which has 28 until leap year gives it 29.
- Spelling rules: *i* before *e* except after *c*, or when sounding like *a* as in neighbor and weigh.
- Numbers: Can I remember the reciprocal? To remember the reciprocal of pi, count the letters in each word of the question above. The reciprocal of pi = .3 1 8 3 10

Mnemonics become more powerful when used with visualization. For example, if you are trying to remember the planets, use a mnemonic and then visualize Saturn as a hula-hoop dancer to remember that it has rings. Jupiter could be a king with a number of maids to represent its moons.

Acronyms

Acronyms are commonly used as shortcuts in our language. The military is especially fond of using acronyms. For example, NASA is the acronym for the National Aeronautics and Space Administration. You can invent your own acronyms as a memory trick. Here are some common ones that students have used:

- The colors of the spectrum: Roy G. Biv (red, orange, yellow, green, blue, indigo, violet)
- The Great Lakes: HOMES (Huron, Ontario, Michigan, Erie, Superior)
- The stages of cell division in biology: IPMAT (interphase, prophase, metaphase, and telophase)

To make your own acronym, list the items you wish to remember. Use the first letter of each word to make a new word. The word you make can be an actual word or an invented word.

Peg Systems

Peg systems start with numbers, typically 1 to 100. Each number is associated with an object. The object chosen to represent each number can be based on rhyme or on a logical association. The objects are memorized and used with a mental picture to recall a list.

There are entertainers who can have the audience call out a list of 100 objects and then repeat all of the objects through use of a peg system. Here is an example of a commonly used peg system based on rhyme:

One	Bun	Six	Sticks
Two	Shoe	Seven	Heaven
Three	Tree	Eight	Gate
Four	Door	Nine	Wine
Five	Hive	Ten	Hen

For example, if I want to remember a grocery list consisting of milk, eggs, carrots, and butter, I would make associations between the peg and the item I want to remember. The more unusual the association is, the better. I would start by making a visual connection between *bun*, my peg word, and *milk*, the first item on the list. I could picture dipping a bun into a glass of milk for a snack. Next I would make a connection between *shoe* and *eggs*. I could picture eggs being broken into my shoe as a joke. Next I would picture a *tree* with orange *carrots* hanging from it and then a *door* with *butter* dripping from the doorknob. The technique works because of the organization provided by the pegs and the power of visualization.

There are many variations of the peg system. One variation is using the letters of the alphabet instead of numbers. Another variation is to visualize objects and put them in a stack, one on top of the other, until you have a great tottering tower, like a totem pole telling a story. Still another variation is to use your body or your car as a peg system. Using our example of the grocery list above, visualize balancing the milk on your head, carrying eggs in your hands, having carrots tied around your waist and smearing butter on your feet. Remember that the more unusual the pictures, the easier they are to remember.

Loci Systems

Loci or location systems use a series of familiar places to aid the memory. The Roman orators often used this system to remember the outline of a speech. For example, the speaker might connect the entry of a house with the introduction, the living room with the first main point, and each part of the speech with a different room. Again, this technique works through organization and visualization.

Another example of using a loci system to remember a speech or dramatic production is to imagine a long hallway. Mentally draw a picture of each topic or section you need to remember, and then hang each picture on the wall. As you are giving your speech or acting out your part in the play, visualize walking down the hallway and looking at the pictures on the wall to remind yourself of the next topic. For multiple topics, you can place signs over several hallway entrances labeling the contents of each hallway.

Visual Clues

Visual clues are helpful memory devices. To remember your books, place them in front of the door so you will see them on your way to school. To remember to take your finished homework to school, put it in your car when you are done. To remember to fill a prescription, put the empty bottle on the front seat of your car. Tie a bright ribbon on your backpack to remind you to attend a meeting with your study group. When parking your car in the mall, look around and notice landmarks such as nearby stores or row numbers. When you enter a large department store, notice the items that are near the door you entered. Are you worried that you left the iron on? Tie a ribbon around the handle of the iron each time you turn it off or unplug it. To find out if you have all the items you need to go skiing, visualize yourself on the ski slope wearing all those items.

Say It Aloud

Some people are auditory learners and can remember items by repeating them out loud. For example, if you want to remember where you hid your diamond ring; say it out loud a few times. Then reinforce the memory by making a visual picture of where you have hidden the ring. You can also use your auditory memory by making a rhyme or song to remember something. Commercials use this technique all the time to try to get you to remember a product and purchase it.

Have a Routine

Do you have a difficult time trying to remember where you left your keys, wallet, or purse? Having a routine can greatly simplify your life and help you to remember. As you enter your house, hang your keys on a hook each time. Decide where you will place your wallet or purse and put it in the same place each time. When I leave for work, I have a mental checklist with four items: keys, purse, glasses, and cell phone.

Write It Down

One of the easiest and most effective memory techniques is to simply write something down. Make a grocery list or to-do list, send yourself an email, or tape a note to your bathroom mirror or the dashboard of your car.

Remembering Names

Many people have difficulty remembering names of other people in social or business situations. The reason we have difficulty in remembering names is that we do not take the time to store the name properly in our memories. When we first meet someone, we are often distracted or thinking about ourselves. We are trying to remember our own names or wondering what impression we are making on the other person.

To remember a name, first make sure you have heard the name correctly. If you have not heard the name, there is no way you can remember it. Ask the person to repeat his or her name or check to see if you have heard it correctly. Immediately use the name. For example, say "It is nice to meet you, *Nancy*." If you can mentally repeat the name about five times, you have a good chance of remembering it. You can improve the chances of remembering the name if you can make an association. For example, you might think, "She looks like my daughter's friend Nancy." Some people remember names by making a rhyme such as "fancy Nancy."

Journal Entry #2

Review the memory tricks explained in this chapter: acrostics, acronyms, peg systems, loci systems, visual clues, say it aloud, have a routine, write it down, and remembering names. List and briefly explain at least three memory tricks you are willing to try, and give examples of how you would use each of the three memory tricks you select.

Optimize Your Brain Power

The mind can be strengthened and remain healthy throughout life. Scientists have studied a group of nuns from Mankato, Minnesota, who have lived long lives and suffer less from dementia and brain diseases than the general population. These nuns have lived a long time because they do not drink to excess or smoke. They have kept their minds healthy into old age by staying mentally active. They keep active by discussing current events, playing cards, practicing math problems, and doing crossword puzzles. Arnold Scheibel, head of the UCLA Brain Institute, gives the following suggestions for strengthening your mind.

- Do jigsaw and crossword puzzles.
- Play a musical instrument.
- Fix something. The mental challenge stimulates the brain.
- Participate in the arts. Draw or paint something.
- Dance. Exercise and rhythm are good for the brain.
- Do aerobic exercise. This promotes blood flow to the brain.
- Meet and interact with interesting people.
- Read challenging books.
- Take a college class.[8]

Doing these kinds of activities can actually stimulate the development of neurons and nerve connections in the brain so that the brain functions more efficiently. The good news is that you can do this at any age.

Besides doing mental exercises to strengthen your brain, you can take other actions to keep your brain healthy. Here are some ideas:

1. **Do aerobic exercise.** Exercise improves the flow of oxygen to the brain. The brain needs oxygen to function. Researchers have just found that the human brain can grow new nerve cells by putting subjects on a three-month aerobic workout regimen. It was interesting to note that these new nerve cells could be generated at any age and are important in reversing the aging process and delaying the onset of Alzheimer's disease or other cognitive disorders.[9] For optimum health and learning, it is important to exercise the body as well as the mind.

2. **Get enough rest.** Nobel laureate Francis Crick, who studies the brain at the Salk Institute, proposes that the purpose of sleep is to allow the brain to "take out the trash." Sleep provides time for the brain to review the events of the day and to store what is needed and discard what is not worth remembering. During sleep, the brain sorts memories and stores significant ones in long-term memory. Studies have shown that when humans and lab animals are taught a new task and deprived of sleep, they do not perform the task the next day as well as non-sleep-deprived subjects.[10] Chronic lack of sleep can even lead to death.

3. **Eat a balanced, low-fat diet.** The brain needs nutrients, vitamins, and minerals to be healthy. Low-fat diets have been shown to improve mental performance.[11]

4. **Eat proteins and carbohydrates.** Proteins are the building blocks of neurotransmitters that increase mental activity. Carbohydrates provide energy and are the building blocks of neurotransmitters that have a calming effect.[12]

5. **Drink caffeine in moderation.** Caffeine can make you feel stressed, making it difficult to think.

6. **Don't abuse drugs or alcohol.** These substances kill brain cells and change brain chemistry.

7. **Use safety gear.** Wear a seat belt when driving and a helmet when biking or skating to reduce head injuries.

Improving Your Reading

Myths about Reading

Effective reading techniques are crucial to college success. The level and quantity of reading expected in college may be greatly increased over what you have experienced in the past. The following are some myths about reading that cause problems for many college students.

1. **"If I read a chapter, I should remember what I read."** Many students say that they read the chapter, but "it goes in one ear and out the other." After such a frustrating experience, students often conclude that they cannot read well or are not intelligent enough to succeed in college. If you just read the chapter, you have stored it in short-term memory, which lasts about 30 seconds. Reading a chapter takes a lot of effort. You want to make sure the effort you have invested pays off by storing the material in long-term memory. You can then retrieve the information in the future, as well as pass exams. Material is stored in long-term memory through rehearsal or review. Without review, you will not remember.

2. **"I do not need to read if I go to class."** The role of the college professor is to supplement material in the text and increase student understanding of the material. Some professors do not even cover topics contained in the text and consider it the student's responsibility to learn textbook material. If you do not read the text, you may miss out on important material that is not presented during class. Reading the text also helps you understand the material that the professor presents.

3. **"Practice makes perfect."** Students think that if they keep reading the way they are reading, their reading will get better. The truth is that "perfect practice makes perfect." If you are reading in a way that enhances memory, you will get better and better. Success in college reading may mean learning some new reading habits. You will learn about effective reading habits in this chapter.

4. **"Learn the facts that will be on the test."** Focusing on details without looking at the big picture can slow down learning and lead to frustration. If you start with the big picture or outline, then it is easier to learn the details.

A Study System for Reading a College Text: SQ4R

There are many systems for reading a college textbook. All successful systems involve ways to store information in long-term memory: recognizing major points, organizing material to be learned, reviewing, intending to remember, and critical thinking about reading. The crucial step in transferring information to long-term memory is rehearsal, reviewing, or reciting. You need to keep information in your mind for five to 15 seconds in order for it to be stored in long-term memory. The **SQ4R system (Survey, Question, Read, Recite, Review, Reflect)** is a simple and effective way to store information in long-term memory. This system was derived from an information-processing theory developed by Francis P. Robinson in 1941 for use by military personnel attending college during World War II. Since that time, the system has been used by many colleges to teach students effective study skills. The system can be broken down into three steps.

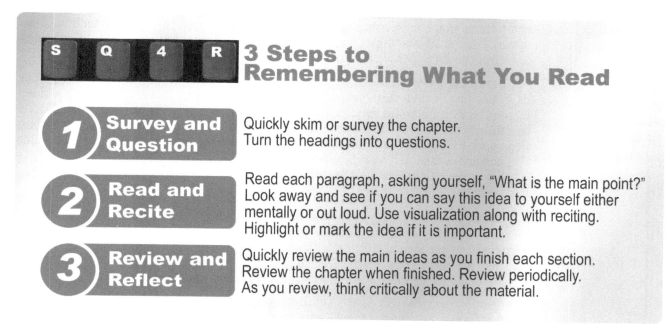

3 Steps to Remembering What You Read

1 Survey and Question
Quickly skim or survey the chapter.
Turn the headings into questions.

2 Read and Recite
Read each paragraph, asking yourself, "What is the main point?" Look away and see if you can say this idea to yourself either mentally or out loud. Use visualization along with reciting. Highlight or mark the idea if it is important.

3 Review and Reflect
Quickly review the main ideas as you finish each section. Review the chapter when finished. Review periodically. As you review, think critically about the material.

Figure 5.2 The SQ4R System for reading a college textbook.

Step 1: Survey and Question. The first step is to survey and question the chapter before you begin reading. Read the title and first paragraph or introduction to the chapter and then look quickly through the chapter, letting your eyes glide across bold headings, diagrams, illustrations, and photos. Read the last paragraph or summary of the chapter. This process should take five minutes or less for a typical chapter in a college textbook.

While you are surveying the chapter, ask yourself questions. Take each major heading in the chapter and turn it into a question. For example, in this section of the book you might ask: What is a system for reading a college text? Why do I need a system? What is SQ4R? What is the first step of SQ4R? You can also ask some general questions as you survey the chapter: What is the main point? What will I learn? Do I know something about this? Can I find something that interests me? How can I use this? Does this relate to something said in class? What does this mean? Is this a possible test question? Asking questions will help you to become an active reader and to find some personal meaning in the content that will help you remember it. If you at least survey and question the relevant textbook material before you go to class, you will have the advantage of being familiar with some of the key ideas to be discussed.

There are several benefits to taking this first step:

- This is the first step in rehearsal for storage of information into long-term memory.
- The quick survey is a warmup for the brain, similar to an athlete's warmup before exercise.
- A survey step is also good practice for improving your reading speed.
- Reading to answer questions increases comprehension, sparks interest, and has the added bonus of keeping you awake while reading.

If you want to be able to read faster, improve your reading comprehension, and increase retention of your reading material, practice the survey and question step before you begin your detailed reading.

Step 2: Read and recite. The second step in reading a text is to read and recite. Read each paragraph and look for the most important point or topic sentence. If the point is important, highlight or underline it. You might use different colors to organize the ideas. You can also make a notation or outline in the margin of the text if the point is especially significant, meaningful, useful, or likely to appear on an exam. A picture, diagram, or chart drawn in the margin is a great way to use visualization to improve retention of the material. If you are reading online, take notes on the important points or use cut and paste to collect the main ideas in a separate document.

Next, look away and see if you can say the main point to yourself either silently or out loud. Reciting is even more powerful if you combine it with visualization. Make a video in your head to illustrate what you are learning. Include color, movement, and sound if possible. Reciting is crucial to long-term memory storage. It will also keep you awake. Beginning college students will find this step a challenge, but practice makes it a habit that becomes easier and easier.

If you read a paragraph or section and do not understand the main point, try these techniques:

1. **Notice any vocabulary or technical terms that are unfamiliar.** Look up these words in a dictionary or in the glossary at the back of the book. Use index cards; write the words on one side and the definition on the other side. Use the SAFMEDS technique (Say All Fast in one Minute Each Day Shuffle) discussed earlier in this chapter. You are likely to see these vocabulary words on quizzes and exams.

2. **Read the paragraph again.** Until you get into the habit of searching for the main point, you may need to reread a paragraph until you understand. If this does not work, reread the paragraphs before and after the one you do not understand.

3. **Write a question in the margin and ask your instructor or tutor to explain.** College instructors have office hours set aside to assist students with questions, and faculty are generally favorably impressed with students who care enough to ask questions. Most colleges offer tutoring free of charge.

4. **If you are really frustrated, put your reading away and come back to it later.** You may be able to relax and gain some insight about the material.

5. **Make sure you have the proper background for the course.** Take the introductory course first.

6. **Assess your reading skills.** Colleges offer reading assessments, and counselors can help you understand your skill level and suggest appropriate courses. Most colleges offer reading courses that can help you to be successful in college.

7. **If you have always had a problem with reading, you may have a learning disability.** A person with a learning disability is of average or higher-than-average intelligence, but has a problem that interferes with learning. Most colleges offer assessment that can help you understand your learning disability and tutoring that is designed to help you to compensate for the disability.

Step 3: Review and reflect. The last step in reading is to review and reflect. After each section, quickly review what you have highlighted or underlined. Again, ask questions. How can I use this information? How does it relate to what I already know? What is most important? What is likely to be on the exam? Is it true? Learn to think critically about the material you have learned.

When you finish the chapter, quickly (in a couple of minutes) look over the highlights again. This last step, review and reflect, is another opportunity for rehearsal. At this point, you have stored the information in long-term memory and want to make sure that you can access the information again in the future. Think of this last step as a creative step in which you put the pieces together, gain an understanding, and begin to think of how you can apply your new knowledge to your personal life. This is the true reward of studying.

Review is faster, easier, and more effective if done immediately. As discussed previously in this chapter, most forgetting occurs in the first 20 minutes after exposure to new information. If you wait 24 hours to review, you will probably have forgotten 80 percent of the material and will have to spend a longer time in review. Review periodically to make sure that you can access the material easily in the future, and review again right before the test.

As you read about the above steps, you may think that this process takes a lot of time. Remember that it is not how much you read, but how you read that is important. In reality, the SQ4R technique is a time-saver in that you do not have to reread all the material before the test. You just need to quickly review information that is stored in long-term memory. Rereading can be purely mechanical and consume your time with little payoff. Rather than rereading, spend your time reciting the important points. With proper review, you can remember 80 to 90 percent of the material.

In his book *Accelerated Learning*, Colin Rose states that you can retain 88 percent of the material you study using the following review schedule.[13] He also notes that the rate of retention using this schedule is four times better than the expected curve of forgetting.

1. Review immediately within 30 seconds.
2. Review after a few minutes.
3. Review after one hour.
4. Review a day later after an overnight rest.
5. Review after a week.
6. Review after one month.

Suggestions for review schedules vary, but the key point is that review is most effective when it is done in short sessions spaced out over time.

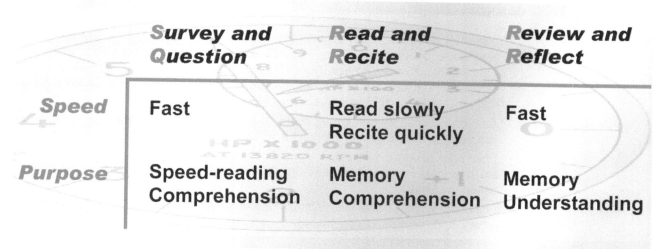

	Survey and Question	Read and Recite	Review and Reflect
Speed	Fast	Read slowly Recite quickly	Fast
Purpose	Speed-reading Comprehension	Memory Comprehension	Memory Understanding

Figure 5.3 This chart summarizes the speed and purpose of each SQ4R step.

Online Reading Strategies

To read efficiently, you will need some reading strategies for the vast amount of online material you will use in college and in everyday life. First, determine your purpose for reading. If you are reading for entertainment, to interact with others, or to find needed information, quickly scan the material to see if it meets your needs. Look for bulleted lists, menu bars, highlighted words, and headers; read only what suits your purpose. Avoid getting lost on your search by using browser tools such as favorites/bookmarks or the history, which is a list of the pages you have visited before. Use multiple browser windows to compare or synthesize information. To avoid eyestrain while reading online, be sure to take breaks and look away from the screen. It is important to get up and stretch periodically. If you are study reading for an online course, first scan the material for key words. Then carefully read each section and summarize what you have learned. If you cannot do this, reread the section. If you are an auditory learner, you can repeat to yourself what you have learned, either silently or aloud. If you are a kinesthetic learner who learns by the hands-on approach, take notes on the important points. You can save time by opening a separate document in a new window and cutting and pasting the important points into your notes. Be sure to include the source of the material, so that you can use it in writing papers or find the material again. As in reading print material, use some techniques to assure good comprehension: as you read each section, visualize what you are reading, ask questions, and think critically about the material.

Journal Entry #4

Describe a system for college reading. Include these ideas: survey, question, read, recite, review, and reflect.

Guidelines for Marking Your Textbook

Marking your textbook can help you pick out what is important, save time, and review the material. It is a great way to reinforce your memory and help you access the material you have learned. In high school, you were given the command, "Thou shalt not mark in thy book!" College is different. You have paid for the book and need to use it as a tool. Even if you plan to sell your book, you can still mark it up. Here are some guidelines for marking your book:

- Underline or mark the key ideas in your text. You don't have to underline complete sentences; just underline enough to make sense when you review your markings. This technique works especially well for kinesthetics or tactile learners. If reading online, use the highlighter tool to mark the main points and then cut and paste the main points into a separate document.

- Aim for marking or highlighting about 20 percent of the most important material. If you mark too much of your reading, it will be difficult to review the main points.

- Read each paragraph first. Ask yourself, "What is the main point?" Highlight or mark the main point if it is important. Not every paragraph has a main point that needs to be marked.

- Use other marks to help you organize what you have read. Write in numbers or letters and use different colors to help you organize ideas.

- Most college texts have wide margins. Use these margins to write down questions, outlines, or key points to remember.
- Learn to be brief, fast, and neat in your marking or highlighting.
- If you are tempted to mark too much, use the double system of first underlining with a pencil as much as you want and then using a highlighter to pick out the most important 20 percent of the material in the chapter.
- Use different kinds of marks and symbols, such as the following:
  - Single or double underlines
  - Brackets around an important paragraph
  - Numbers or letters to organize points
  - Circles or squares to make important words stand out
  - An asterisk or star in the margin for a very important idea
  - A question mark next to something you do not understand
  - "DEF" in the margin to point out a definition
  - Use your imagination to come up with your own symbols
- Learn to recognize organizing patterns in your reading. These patterns will help you to pick out and mark the important ideas.
  - **The listing pattern.** Identify and mark the items in the list. Use numbers and letters to identify the parts of a list.
  - **The sequence pattern.** This pattern presents a list in a certain order. Note the items in the list and the order by using numbers or letters.
  - **The definition pattern.** Circle the word being defined. Underline the definition.
  - **The comparison/contrast pattern.** This pattern explains similarities or differences. Underline or mark these.
  - **The cause/effect pattern.** This pattern describes the reasons things happen. Underline or mark the cause and the effect.
- Quickly review the important points after you have marked each section. Quickly review again when you have finished the chapter. If you review within 20 minutes, the review will be faster and easier.

Improving Reading

Test what you have learned by circling the letters of the correct answers to the following questions.

1. If you have read the chapter and can't remember what you have read,

    a. read the chapter again.
    b. remember to select important points and review them.
    c. the material is stored in long-term memory.

2. When you start reading a new textbook,

    a. begin with chapter one.
    b. focus on the details you will need to remember.
    c. skim over the text to get a general idea of what you will be reading.

3. The first step in reading a chapter in a college textbook is to

    a. survey and question.
    b. read and recite.
    c. review and reflect.

4. As you are reading each paragraph in a college textbook, it is most important to

    a. read quickly.
    b. identify the main point and recite it.
    c. focus on the details first.

5. When marking a college textbook, it is recommended to mark about

    a. 50%.
    b. 30%.
    c. 20%.

How did you do on the quiz? Check your answers: 1. b, 2. c, 3. a, 4. b, 5. c

Reading for Speed and Comprehension

In *How to Read for Speed and Comprehension*, Gordon Wainwright suggests using different gears, or speeds, when reading for different purposes.[14] Understanding these four gears can be helpful for college students.

1. **Studying.** In this gear, the maximum reading speed is about 200 words per minute. It is used for material that is difficult or unfamiliar, such as a college textbook. For this material, a high quality of retention is required. It involves the steps described in SQ4R.

2. **Slow reading.** In this gear, reading speed ranges from 150 to 300 wpm. It is used for material that is fairly difficult when a good quality of retention is desired.

3. **Rapid reading.** In rapid reading, speeds range from 300 to 800 wpm. It is used for average or easy material. Use this gear for review of familiar material.

4. **Skimming.** Skimming is a type of very fast reading, done at 800 to 1000 wpm. With practice, it is possible to skim at 2000 to 3000 wpm. Using this technique, the eyes glide quickly down the page looking for specific information. Not every group of words or line is read. The eyes focus quickly on key ideas, bold headings, and titles. The purpose is to get a quick overview of the important ideas in the material.

Different reading speeds are used for different purposes. In college reading, it is more important to have good comprehension and retention than speed. However, we all live busy lives, and many college students today try to combine study, work, family, and social life. Learning to read faster is important to survival. You can learn to read faster by practicing skimming as a first step in reading. The next step is to slow down, look for the major points, and rehearse them so that they are stored in long-term memory. Using the SQ4R study technique described above will guide you through the process so that you can remember what you read.

What to Do If Your Reading Goes in One Ear and Out the Other

1. **Silence your inner critic.**
   If you have always told yourself that you are a poor reader or hate reading, these thoughts make it difficult to read. Think positively and tell yourself that with some effort, you can read and understand. Focus on what you can do, rather than what you can't do.

2. Look for the key ideas and underline them.

3. **Try visualization.**
   Make a mental picture or video with the material you are reading.

4. **Look for personal meaning.**
   Can you relate the material to your life in any way?

5. Do a quick scan of the material to find some major points and then reread the material closely.

6. Try talking to the text as you read it. Ask questions. Why is this important? Do you know anything about this? Do you agree or disagree? Do you think it is a good or bad idea? Can you use this information in the future? Can you find something interesting in the text? Challenge the material and think critically about it. Make humorous remarks. Imagine yourself in the situation. What would it be like and what would you do? You can write your comments in the text or do this silently in your head.

Improving Reading Concentration

Hank Aaron said that what separates the superstar from the average ballplayer is that the superstar concentrates just a little longer. Athletes are very aware of the power of concentration in improving athletic performance. Coaches remind athletes to focus on the ball and to develop good powers of concentration and visualization. Being able to concentrate on your reading helps you to study more efficiently.

It is important to have a regular place for studying that has all the needed materials. You will need a table or desk with space for a computer, space for writing, and a comfortable chair. Keep a good supply of writing materials, computer supplies, and reference materials. To minimize fatigue and eyestrain, good lighting is essential. It is best to have an overhead light and a lamp. Place the lamp to your left if you are right-handed. In this way, you will not be writing in a shadow. Do the reverse if you are left-handed. If you have space, use two lamps with one placed on each side. Eliminate glare by using a lampshade. Study lamps often come with a deflector on the bottom of the lampshade that further eliminates glare. Lighter colors on your desk and wall also help to eliminate glare and fatigue.

In setting up your regular place for studying, keep in mind your environmental preferences as identified by your PEPS learning style inventory. Consider these factors:

- Do you need a quiet environment to focus on your studies?
- Do you prefer bright or dim light?

Improving Reading
Concentration

1. Become an active
   reader
2. Remember your
   purpose
3. Use daydreaming to
   relax
5. Plan to deal with
   worry
6. Break tasks into small
   parts

- Do you prefer a warm or cool environment?
- Do you prefer learning by yourself or with others?
- Do you study best in the morning or the afternoon?

Having and using a well-equipped and comfortable study place reduces external distractions. Internal distractions are many and varied and may be more difficult to manage. Internal distractions include being hungry, tired, or ill. It is a good idea to eat and be well rested before reading any course material. If you are ill, rest and get well. Study when you feel better. Many internal distractions are mental, such as personal problems, worrying about grades, lack of interest or motivation, frustration, or just daydreaming.

Here are some ideas for dealing with internal mental distractions while reading.

1. **Become an active reader.** Read to answer questions. Search for the main idea. Recite or re-say the main idea in your mind. Reflect and think critically about the material you are reading. Mark or highlight the text. Visualize what you are reading.

2. **Remind yourself of your purpose for reading.** Think of your future college and career goals.

3. **Give yourself permission to daydream.** If you like to daydream, give yourself permission to daydream as a break from your studies. Come back to your studies with a more relaxed attitude.

4. **Plan to deal with worry.** Worry is not a very good motivator and it interferes with memory. Take some positive action to deal with problems that cause you to worry. If you are worried about your grades, what can you do right now to improve your chances of making better grades? See a college counselor if worrying about personal problems interferes with studying.

5. **Break the task into small parts.** If the task seems overwhelming, break it into small parts and do the first part. If you have 400 pages to read in 10 days, read 40 pages each day. Make a schedule that allows time to read each day until you have accomplished your goal. Use distributed practice in your studies. Study for a short time each day rather than holding a marathon study session before the test.

Reading Strategies for Different Subjects

While the SQ4R technique is a good general strategy for reading textbook material, there are steps that you will need to add depending on the subject area you are studying.

Math

1. Make sure you have the proper prerequisites or background courses before you begin your math class.

2. When skimming a math book, keep in mind that many of the topics will be unfamiliar to you. You should be able to understand the first few pages and build your knowledge from there. If all the concepts are familiar to you, you may be taking a class that you do not need.

3. It is not enough to read and understand mathematical concepts. Make sure that you add practice to your study system when studying math. Practice gives you the self-confidence to relax when working with math.

4. It is helpful to read over your math book before you go to class so that you will know what areas need special attention.

Reading Speed, Comprehension, and Concentration

Test what you have learned by circling the letters of the correct answers to the following questions.

1. A friend is have difficulties with reading in college and has stated that he is frustrated because the reading "goes in one ear and out the other." What is the best advice that you could give your friend?

   a. Don't worry. It will get better with practice.
   b. Question the material and search for personal meaning.
   c. Search for the details and memorize them.

2. Learn to increase your reading speed by

   a. applying all steps of SQ4R.
   b. starting with skimming.
   c. learning to concentrate.

3. Improve reading comprehension by

   a. applying the steps of SQ4R.
   b. reading as quickly as possible.
   c. worrying about what you will remember.

4. Improve reading concentration by

   a. reading a large amount of material at one time.
   b. reading without questioning.
   c. having a regular place for studying with needed materials.

5. To deal with mental distractions that interfere with reading,

   a. practice "Be Here Now."
   b. ignore personal problems.
   c. never daydream while reading.

How did you do on the quiz? Check your answers: 1. b, 2. b, 3. a, 4. c, 5. a

5. Focus on understanding the math problems and concepts rather than on memorizing problems.

6. Do not get behind in your math studies. You need to understand the first step before you can go on to the next.

7. Ask for help as soon as you have difficulties.

Science

1. In science classes, the scientific method is used to describe the world. The scientific method relies on questioning, observing, hypothesizing, researching, and analyzing. You will learn about theories and scientific principles. Highlight or mark theories, names of scientists, definitions, concepts, and procedures.

2. Understand the scientific principles and use flash cards to remember details and formulas.

3. Study the charts, diagrams, tables, and graphs. Draw your own pictures and graphs to get a visual picture of the material.

4. Use lab time as an opportunity to practice the theories and principles that you have learned.

Social and Behavioral Sciences

1. Social and behavioral scientists focus on principles of behavior, theories, and research. Notice that there are different theories that explain the same phenomena. Highlight, underline, and summarize these theories in your own words.

2. When looking at the research, ask yourself what the point of the research was, who conducted the research, when the research was completed, what data was collected, and what conclusions were drawn.

3. Think of practical applications of theories.

4. Use flash cards to remember details.

Literature Courses

When taking a course in literature, you will be asked to understand, appreciate, interpret, evaluate, and write about the literature.

1. Underline the names of characters and write plot summaries.

2. Write notes about your evaluation of literary works.

3. Make flash cards to remember literary terms.

4. Write down important quotes or note page numbers on a separate piece of paper so that you don't have to go back and find them later when you are writing about a work.

Foreign Language Courses

Foreign language courses require memorization and practice.

1. Distribute the practice. Practice a small amount each day. It is not possible to learn everything at once.

2. Complete the exercises as a way to practice and remember.

3. Study out loud.

4. Practice speaking the language with others.

5. Use flash cards to remember vocabulary.

6. Make charts to practice verb conjugations.

7. Ask for help if you do not understand.

8. Learn to think in the foreign language. Translating from English causes confusion because the structures of languages are different.

> "Whatever the mind of man can conceive and believe, it can achieve."
> Napoleon Hill

Positive Thinking

You can improve your memory and your reading (as well as your life) by using positive thinking. Positive thinking involves two aspects: thinking about yourself and thinking about the world around you. When you think positively about yourself, you develop confidence in your abilities and become more capable of whatever you are attempting to do. When you think positively about the world around you, you look for possibilities and find interest in what you are doing.

Golfer Arnold Palmer has won many trophies, but places high value on a plaque on his wall with a poem by C.W. Longenecker:

If you think you are beaten, you are.
If you think you dare not, you don't.
If you like to win but think you can't,
It's almost certain that you won't.

Life's battles don't always go
To the stronger woman or man,
But sooner or later, those who win
Are those who think they can.[15]

Success in athletics, school, or any other endeavor begins with positive thinking. To remember anything, you first have to believe that you can remember. Trust in your abilities. Then apply memory techniques to help you to remember. If you think that you cannot remember, you will not even try. To be a good reader, you need to think that you can become a good reader and then work toward learning, applying, and practicing good reading techniques.

The second part of positive thinking involves thinking about the world around you. If you can convince yourself that the world and your college studies are full of interesting possibilities, you can start on a journey of adventure to discover new ideas. It is easier to remember and to read if you can find the subject interesting. If the topic is interesting, you will learn more about it. The more you learn about a topic, the more interesting it becomes, and you are well on your way in your journey of discovery. If you tell yourself that the task is boring, you will struggle and find the task difficult. You will also find it difficult to continue.

You can improve your reading through positive thinking. Read with the intent to remember and use reading techniques that work for you. We remember what interests us, and having a positive attitude helps us to find something interesting. To find something interesting, look for personal meaning. How can I use this information? Does it relate to something I know? Will this information be useful in my future career? Why is this information important? Write down your personal goals and remind yourself of your purpose for attending college. You are not just completing an assignment: you are on a path to discovery.

To be successful in college and to remember what you read, start with the belief that you can be successful. Anticipate that the journey will be interesting and full of possibilities. Enjoy the journey!

Journal Entry #5

How can you use positive thinking to improve memory, reading, and success in college? Use any of these questions to guide your thinking:

- How can I think positively about myself?
- How can I think positively about my college experience?
- What is the connection between belief and success?
- How can positive thinking make college more fun?

Improving Memory and Reading

Go to http://www.collegesuccess1.com/JournalEntries.htm for Word files of the Journal Entries

Success over the Internet

Visit the *College Success Website* at http://www.collegesuccess1.com/

The *College Success Website* is continually updated with new topics and links to the material presented in this chapter. Topics include:

- Memory techniques
- Reading strategies
- How to concentrate
- How to highlight a textbook
- Speed reading
- How to study science
- Study groups
- Examples of mnemonics

Contact your instructor if you need assistance in accessing the *College Success Website.*

Notes

1. G. A. Miller, "The Magical Number Seven, Plus or Minus Two: Some Limits on Our Capacity for Processing Information," *Psychological Review* 63 (March 1956): 81–97.
2. Colin Rose, *Accelerated Learning* (New York: Dell Publishing, 1985), 33–36.
3. Ibid., 50–51.
4. Walter Pauk, *How to Study in College* (Boston: Houghton Mifflin, 1989), 96–97.
5. Rose, *Accelerated Learning*, 34.
6. Adapted from Paul Chance, *Learning and Behavior* (Pacific Grove, CA: Brooks/Cole, 1979), 301.
7. Pauk, *How to Study in College,* 108.
8. Daniel Golden, "Building a Better Brain," *Life Magazine,* July 1994, 63–70.
9. Mary Carmichael, "Stronger, Faster, Smarter," *Newsweek,* March 26, 2007, 38–46.
10. Scott LaFee, "A Chronic Lack of Sleep Can Lead to the Big Sleep," *San Diego Union Tribune,* October 8, 1997.

11. Randy Blaun, "How to Eat Smart," *Psychology Today,* May/June 1996, 35.

12. Ibid.

13. Rose, *Accelerated Learning*, 51.

14. Gordon R. Wainwright, *How to Read for Speed and Comprehension* (NJ: Prentice-Hall, 1977), 100–101.

15. Rob Gilbert, ed., *Bits and Pieces* (Fairfield, NJ: The Economics Press, 1998), Vol. R, No. 40, p. 12.

Name _____ Date _____

Review the main ideas on improving memory and reading. Based on these ideas, how would you be successful in the following situations? You may want to do this as a group activity in your class.

1. You just read the assigned chapter in economics and cannot remember what you read. It went in one ear and out the other.

2. In your anatomy and physiology class, you are required to remember the scientific names for 100 different muscles in the body.

3. You signed up for a philosophy class because it meets general education requirements. You are not interested in the class at all.

4. You have a midterm in your literature class and have to read 400 pages in one month.

5. You must take American history to graduate from college. You think that history is boring.

6. You have been introduced to an important business contact and would like to remember his/her name.

7. You are enrolled in an algebra class. You continually remind yourself that you have never been good at math. You don't think that you will pass this class.

8. You have noticed that your grandmother is becoming very forgetful. You want to do whatever is possible to keep your mind healthy as you age.

Memory Test

Name _____ Date _____

Part 1. Your professor will read a list of 15 items. Do not write them down. After listening to this list, see how many you can remember and write them here.

1.   6.   11.

2.   7.   12.

3.   8.   13.

4.   9.   14.

5.   10.   15.

After your professor has given you the answers, write the number of words you remembered: _____

Part 2. Your professor will discuss memory techniques that you can use to improve your test scores and then will read another list. Again, do not write the words down, but try to apply the recommended techniques. Write as many words as you can remember.

1.   6.   11.

2.   7.   12.

3.   8.   13.

4.   9.   14.

5.   10.   15.

How many words did you remember this time? _____

Practice with Mnemonics

Name _____ Date _____

Join with a group of students in your class to invent some acrostics and acronyms.

Acrostics

Acrostics are creative rhymes, songs, poems, or sentences that help us to remember. To write an acrostic, think of a word that starts with the same letter as each idea you want to remember. Sometimes you can rearrange the words if necessary to form a sentence. At other times, it is necessary to keep the words in order. The more unusual the sentence, the easier it is to remember.

> **Example:** Classification in biology: Kings Play Cards on Fairly Good Soft Velvet (Kingdom, Phylum, Class, Order, Family, Genus, Species, Variety)

Create an acrostic for the planets in the solar system. Keep the words in the same order as the planets from closest to the sun to farthest from the sun.

Mercury, Venus, Earth, Mars, Jupiter, Saturn, Uranus, Neptune, Pluto

_____

_____

_____

Acronyms

To make your own acronym, list the items you wish to remember. Use the first letter of each word to make a new word. The new word you invented can be an actual word or an invented word.

> **Example:** The Great Lakes: HOMES (Huron, Ontario, Michigan, Erie, and Superior)

The following are the excretory organs of the body. Make an acronym to remember them. Rearrange the words if necessary.

intestines, liver, lungs, kidneys, skin

_____

_____

_____

Write down any acrostics or acronyms that you know. Share them with your group.

Check Your Textbook Reading Skills

Name _____ Date _____

As you read each of the following statements, mark your response using this key:

1   I seldom or never do this.

2   I occasionally do this, depending on the class.

3   I almost always or always do this.

_____   **1.**   Before I read the chapter, I quickly skim through it to get main ideas.

_____   **2.**   As I skim through the chapter, I form questions based on the bold printed section headings.

_____   **3.**   I read with a positive attitude and look for something interesting.

_____   **4.**   I read the introductory and summary paragraphs in the chapter before I begin reading.

_____   **5.**   As I read each paragraph, I look for the main idea.

_____   **6.**   I recite the main idea so I can remember it.

_____   **7.**   I underline, highlight, or take notes on the main ideas.

_____   **8.**   I write notes or outlines in the margin of the text.

_____   **9.**   After reading each section, I do a quick review.

_____   **10.**   I quickly review the chapter immediately after reading it.

_____   **11.**   During or after reading, I reflect on how the material is useful or meaningful to me.

_____   **12.**   I read or at least skim the assigned chapter before I come to class.

_____   **13.**   I have planned reading time in my weekly schedule.

_____   **14.**   I generally think positively about my reading assignments.

_____   **Total points**

Check your score.
42–36   You have excellent college reading skills.
35–30   You have good skills, but can improve.
29–24   Some changes are needed.
23–14   Major changes are needed.

Becoming an Efficient College Reader

Name _____ Date _____

1. Based on your responses to the reading skills checklist on the previous page, list some of your good reading habits.

2. Based on this same checklist, what are some areas you need to improve?

3. Review the material on SQ4R and reading for speed and comprehension. Write five intention statements about how you plan to improve your reading. I intend to . . .

4. Review the material on how to concentrate while reading. List some ideas that you can use.

Surveying and Questioning a Chapter

Name _____ Date _____

Using the *next chapter* assigned in this class or any other class, answer these questions. Again, challenge yourself to do this activity quickly. Can you finish the exercise in five to seven minutes? Notice your beginning and end times.

1. What is the title of the chapter? Write the title in the form of a question. For example, the title of this chapter is "Improving Memory and Reading." A good question would be, "How can I improve my memory and reading?"

2. Briefly list one key idea mentioned in the introduction or first paragraph.

3. Write five questions you asked yourself while surveying this chapter. Read the bold section headings in the chapter and turn them into questions. For example, one heading in this chapter is "Myths about Reading." This heading might prompt you to ask, "What are some myths about reading? Do I believe in some of these myths?"

4. List three topics that interest you.

5. Briefly write one key idea from the last paragraph or chapter summary.

6. How long did it take you to do this exercise? Write your time here.

7. What did you think of this exercise on surveying and questioning a chapter?

Taking Notes, Writing, and Speaking

Learning Objectives

Read to answer these key questions:

- Why is it important to take notes?

- What are some good listening techniques?

- What are some tips for taking good lecture notes?

- What are some note-taking systems?

- What is the best way to review my notes for the test?

- What is power writing?

- How can I make a good speech?

Knowing how to listen and take good notes can make your college life easier and may help you in your future career as well. Professionals in many occupations take notes as a way of recording key ideas for later use. Whether you become a journalist, attorney, architect, engineer, or other professional, listening and taking good notes can help you to get ahead in your career.

Good writing and speaking skills are important to your success in college and in your career. In college, you will be asked to write term papers and complete other writing assignments. The writing skills you learn in college will be used later in jobs involving high responsibility and good pay; on the job, you will write reports, memos, and proposals. In college, you will probably take a speech class and give oral reports in other classes; on the job, you will present your ideas orally to your colleagues and business associates.

Why Take Notes?

The most important reason for taking notes is to remember important material for tests or for future use in your career. If you just attend class without taking notes, you will forget most of the material by the next day.

How does taking notes enhance memory?

- In college, the lecture is a way of supplementing the written material in the textbook. Without good notes, an important part of the course is missing. Note taking provides material to rehearse or recite, so that it can be stored in long-term memory.
- When you take notes and impose your own organization on them, the notes become more personally meaningful. If they are meaningful, they are easier to remember.
- Taking notes helps you to make new connections. New material is remembered by connecting it to what you already know.
- For kinesthetic and tactile learners, the physical act of writing the material is helpful in learning and remembering it.
- For visual learners, notes provide a visual map of the material to be learned.
- For auditory learners, taking notes is a way to listen carefully and record information to be stored in the memory.
- Note taking helps students to concentrate, maintain focus, and stay awake.
- Attending the lectures and taking notes helps you to understand what the professor thinks is important and to know what to study for the exam.

The College Lecture

You will experience many different types of lectures while in college. At larger universities, many of the beginning-level courses are taught in large lecture halls with 300 people or more. More advanced courses tend to have fewer students. In large lecture situations, it is not always possible or appropriate to ask questions. Under these circumstances, the large lecture is often supplemented by smaller discussion sessions where you can ask questions and review the lecture material. Although attendance may not be checked, it is important to attend both the lectures and the discussion sessions.

A formal college lecture is divided into four parts. Understanding these parts will help you to be a good listener and take good notes.

1. **Introduction.** The professor uses the introduction to set the stage and to introduce the topic of the lecture. Often an overview or outline of the lecture is presented. Use the introduction as a way to begin thinking about the organization of your notes and the key ideas you will need to write down.

2. **Thesis.** The thesis is the key idea in the lecture. In a one-hour lecture, there is usually one thesis statement. Listen carefully for the thesis statement and write it down in your notes. Review the thesis statement and related ideas for the exam.

3. **Body.** The body of the lecture usually consists of five or six main ideas with discussion and clarification of each idea. As a note taker, your job is to identify the main ideas, write them in your notes, and put in enough of the explanation or examples to understand the key ideas.

4. **Conclusion.** In the conclusion, the professor summarizes the key points of the lecture and sometimes asks for questions. Use the conclusion as an opportunity to check your understanding of the lecture and to ask questions to clarify the key points.

> "Education is not a problem. It is an opportunity."
> Lyndon B. Johnson

How to Be a Good Listener

Effective note taking begins with good listening. What is good listening? Sometimes students confuse listening with hearing. Hearing is done with the ears. Listening is a more active process done with the ears and the brain engaged. Good listening requires attention and concentration. Practice these ideas for good listening:

- **Be physically ready.** It is difficult to listen to a lecture if you are tired, hungry, or ill. Get enough sleep so that you can stay awake. Eat a balanced diet without too much caffeine or sugar. Take care of your health and participate in an exercise program so that you feel your best.

- **Prepare a mental framework.** Look at the course syllabus to become familiar with the topic of the lecture. Use your textbook to read, or at least survey, the material to be covered in the lecture. If you are familiar with the key concepts from the textbook, you will be able to understand the lecture and know what to write down in your notes. If the material is in your book, there is no need to write it down in your notes.

  The more complex the topic, the more important it is for you to read the text first. If you go to the lecture and have no idea what is being discussed, you may be overwhelmed and find it difficult to take notes on material that is totally new to you. Remember that it is easier to remember material if you can connect it to material you already know.

- **Find a good place to sit.** Arrive early to get a good seat. The best seats in the classroom are in the front and center of the room. If you were buying concert tickets, these would be the best and most expensive seats. Find a seat that will help you to hear and focus on the speaker. You may need to find a seat away from your friends to avoid distractions.

- **Have a positive mental attitude.** Convince yourself that the speaker has something important to say and be open to new ideas. This may require you to focus on your goals and to look past some distractions. Maybe the lecturer doesn't have the best speaking voice or you don't like his or her appearance. Focus on what you can learn from the professor rather than outward appearances.

- **Listen actively to identify the main points.** As you are listening to the lecture, ask yourself, "What is the main idea?" In your own words, write the main points down in your notes. Do not try to write down everything the professor says. This will be impossible and unnecessary. Imagine that your mind is a filter and you are actively sorting through the material to find the key ideas and write them down in your notes. Try to identify the key points that will be on the test and write them in your notes.

- **Stay awake and engaged in learning.** The best way to stay awake and focused is to listen actively and take notes. Have a mental debate with the professor. Listen for the main points and the logical connection between ideas. The physical act of writing the notes will help to keep you awake.

Tips for Good Note Taking

Here are some suggestions for taking good notes:

1. Attend all of the lectures. Because many professors do not take attendance, students are often tempted to miss class. If you do not attend the lectures, however, you will not know what the professor thinks is important and what to study for the test. There will be important points covered in the lectures that are not in the book.

2. Have the proper materials. A three-ring notebook and notebook paper are recommended. Organize notes chronologically and include any handouts given in class. You can have a small notebook for each class or a single large notebook with dividers for each class. Just take the notebook paper to class and later file it in your notebook at home. Use your laptop as an alternative to a paper notebook.

3. Begin your notes by writing the date of the lecture, so you can keep your notes in order.

4. Write notes on the front side only of each piece of paper. This will allow you to spread the pages out and see the big picture or pattern in the lectures when you are reviewing.

5. Write notes neatly and legibly so you can read and review them easily.

6. Do not waste time recopying or typing your notes. Your time would be better spent reviewing your notes.

7. As a general rule, do not rely on a tape recorder for taking notes. With a tape recorder, you will have to listen to the lecture again on tape. For a semester course, this would be about 45 hours of tape! It is much faster to review carefully written notes.

8. Copy down everything written on the board and the main points from PowerPoint or other visual presentations. If it is important enough for the professor to write on the board, it is important enough to be on the test.

9. Use key words and phrases in your notes. Leave out unimportant words and don't worry about grammar.

10. Use abbreviations as long as you can read them. Entire sentences or paragraphs are not necessary and you may not have time to write them.

11. Don't loan your whole notebook to someone else because you may not get it back. If you want to share your notes, make copies.

12. If the professor talks too fast, listen carefully for the key ideas and write them down. Leave spaces in your notes to fill in later. You may be able to find the information in the text or get the information from another student.

13. Explore new uses of technology for note taking. Students are taking notes and sharing them on Facebook and GradeGuru, for example.

Listening and Note Taking

Test what you have learned by selecting the correct answers to the following questions.

1. When taking notes on a college lecture, it is most important to

    a. write down everything you hear.
    b. write down the main ideas and enough explanation to understand them.
    c. write down names, dates, places, and numbers.

2. To be a good listener,

    a. read or skim over the material before you attend the lecture.
    b. attend the lecture first and then read the text.
    c. remember that listening is more important than note taking.

3. To stay awake during the lecture,

    a. drink lots of coffee.
    b. sit near your friends so you can make some comments on the lecture.
    c. listen actively by taking notes.

4. Since attendance is not always checked in college classes,

    a. it is not necessary to attend class if you read the textbook.
    b. it is acceptable to miss lectures as long as you show up for the exams.
    c. it is up to you to attend every class.

5. When taking notes, be sure to

    a. use complete sentences and good grammar.
    b. write down whatever is written on the board or the visual presentations.
    c. write the notes quickly without worrying about neatness.

How did you do on the quiz? Check your answers: 1. b, 2. a, 3. c, 4. c, 5. b

Journal Entry #1

Write one paragraph giving advice to a new student about taking notes in college. Use any of these questions to guide your thinking:

- Why is note taking necessary in college?
- How can you be a good listener?
- What are some tips for taking good notes?
- What are some ideas that don't work?

Note-Taking Systems

There are several systems for taking notes. How you take notes will depend on your learning style and the lecturer's speaking style. Experiment with these systems and use what works best for you.

The Cornell Format

The Cornell format is an efficient method of taking notes and reviewing them. It appeals to students who are logical, orderly, and organized and have lectures that fit into this pattern. The Cornell format is especially helpful for thinking about key points as you review your notes.

Step 1: Prepare. To use the Cornell format, you will need a three-ring notebook with looseleaf paper. Draw or fold a vertical line 2½ inches from the left side of the paper. This is the recall column that can be used to write key ideas when reviewing. Use the remaining section of the paper for your notes. Write the date and title of the lecture at the top of the page.

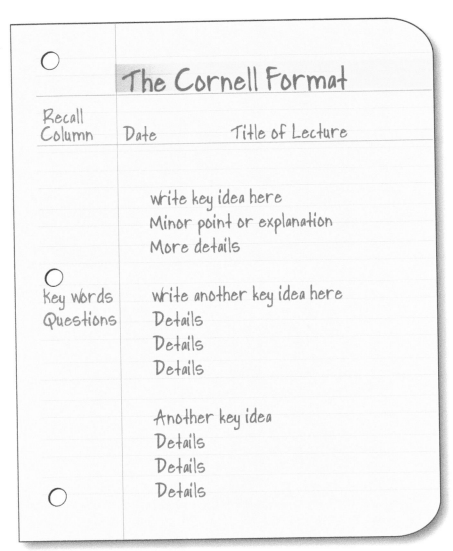

Figure 6.1 The Cornell format is an efficient way of organizing notes and reviewing them.

Step 2: Take notes. Use the large area to the right of the recall column to take notes. Listen for key ideas and write them just to the right of the recall column line, as in the diagram above. Indent your notes for minor points and illustrative details. Then skip a space and write the next key idea. Don't worry about using numbers or letters as in an outline format. Just use the indentations and spacing to highlight and separate key ideas. Use short phrases, key words, and abbreviations. Complete sentences are not necessary, but write legibly so you can read your notes later.

Step 3: Use the recall column for review. Read over your notes and write down key words or ideas from the lecture in the recall column. Ask yourself, "What is this about?" Cover up the notes on the right-hand side and recite the key ideas of the lecture. Another variation is to write questions in the margin. Find the key ideas and then write possible exam questions in the recall column. Cover your notes and see if you can answer the questions.

The Outline Method

If the lecture is well organized, some students just take notes in outline format. Sometimes lecturers will show their outline as they speak.

- Use Roman numerals to label main topics. Then use capital letters for main ideas and Arabic numerals for related details or examples.

- You can make a free-form outline using just indentation to separate main ideas and supporting details.

- Leave spaces to fill in material later.

- Use a highlighter to review your notes as soon as possible after the lecture.

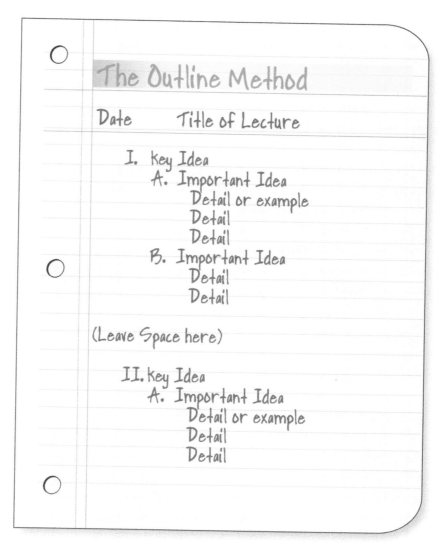

Figure 6.2 If a lecture is well organized, the outline format of taking notes works well.

The Mind Map

A mind map shows the relationship between ideas in a visual way. It is much easier to remember items that are organized and linked together in a personally meaningful way. As a result, recall and review is quicker and more effective. Mind maps have appeal to visual learners and those who do not want to be limited by a set structure, as in the outline formats. They can also be used for lectures that are not highly structured. Here are some suggestions for using the mind-mapping technique:

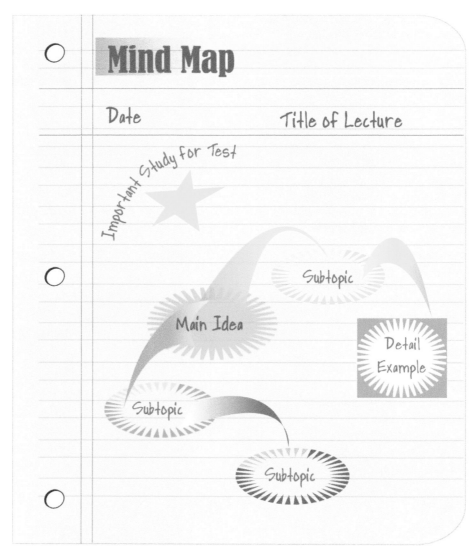

Figure 6.3 The mind map format of taking notes shows the relationship between ideas in a visual way.

- Turn your paper sideways to give you more space. Use standard-size notebook paper or consider larger sheets if possible.
- Write the main idea in the center of the page and circle it.
- Arrange ideas so that more important ideas are closer to the center and less important ideas are farther out.
- Show the relationship of the minor points to the main ideas using lines, circles, boxes, charts, and other visual devices. Here is where you can use your creativity and imagination to make a visual picture of the key ideas in the lecture.

- Use symbols and drawings.
- Use different colors to separate main ideas.
- When the lecturer moves to another main idea, start a new mind map.
- When you are done with the lecture, quickly review your mind maps. Add any written material that will be helpful in understanding the map later.
- A mind map can also be used as:
  - a review tool for remembering and relating the key ideas in the textbook;
  - a preparation tool for essay exams in which remembering main ideas and relationships is important; and
  - the first step in organizing ideas for a term paper.

Improving Note-Taking Efficiency

Improve note-taking efficiency by listening for key words that signal the main ideas and supporting details. Learn to write faster by using telegraphic sentences, abbreviations, and symbols.

Signal Words

Signal words are clues to understanding the structure and content of a lecture. Recognizing signal words can help you identify key ideas and organize them in your notes. The table on the following page lists some common signal words and their meaning.

Telegraphic Sentences

Telegraphic sentences are short, abbreviated sentences used in note taking. They are very similar to the text messages sent on a cell phone. There are four rules for telegraphic sentences:

1. Write key words only.

2. Omit unnecessary words (*a, an, the*).

3. Ignore rules of grammar.

4. Use abbreviations and symbols.

Here is an example of a small part of a lecture followed by a student's telegraphic notes:

Heavy drinking of alcoholic beverages causes students to miss class and to fall behind in schoolwork. College students who are considered binge drinkers are at risk for many alcohol-related problems. Binge drinking is simply drinking too much alcohol at one time. Binge drinking is defined by researchers as drinking five or more drinks in a row for men or four or more drinks in a row for women. Researchers estimate that two out of five college students (40 percent) are binge drinkers.

Binge drinking—too much alcohol at one time
    Men = 5 in row
    Women = 4
    2 out of 5 (40%) college students binge

Signal Words

Type	Examples	Meaning
Main idea words	And most important A major development The basic concept is Remember that The main idea is We will focus on The key is	Introduce the key points that need to be written in your notes.
Example words	To illustrate For example For instance	Clarify and illustrate the main ideas in the lecture. Write these examples in your notes after the main idea. If multiple examples are given, write down the ones you have time for or the ones that you understand the best.
Addition words	In addition Also Furthermore	Add more important information. Write these points down in your notes.
Enumeration words	The five steps First, second, third Next	Signal a list. Write down the list in your notes and number the items.
Time words	Before, after Formerly Subsequently Prior Meanwhile	Signal the order of events. Write down the events in the correct order in your notes.
Cause and effect words	Therefore As a result If . . ., then	Signal important concepts that might be on the exam. When you hear these words, label them "cause" and "effect" in your notes and review these ideas for the exam.
Definition words	In other words It simply means That is In essence	Provide the meanings of words or simplify complex ideas. Write these definitions or clarifications in your notes.
Swivel words	However Nevertheless Yes, but Still	Provide exceptions, qualifications, or further clarification. Write down qualifying comments in your notes.
Compare and contrast words	Similarly Likewise In contrast	Present similarities or differences. Write these similarities and differences in your notes and label them.
Summary words	In conclusion To sum up In a nutshell	Restate the important ideas of the lecture. Write the summaries in your notes.
Test words	This is important. Remember this. You'll see this again. You might want to study this for the test.	Provide a clue that the material will be on the test. Write these down in your notes and mark them in a way that stands out. Put a star or asterisk next to these items or highlight them. Each professor has his or her own test clue words.

Abbreviations

If you have time, write out words in their entirety for ease of reading. If you are short on time, use any abbreviation as long as you can read it. Here are some ideas:

1. Use the first syllable of the word.

democracy	dem
education	ed
politics	pol
different	diff
moderate	mod
characteristic	char
develop	dev

2. Use just enough of the word so that you can recognize it.

republican	repub
prescription	prescrip
introduction	intro
intelligence	intell
association	assoc

3. Abbreviate or write out the word the first time, then use an acronym. For example, for the United States Department of Agriculture, abbreviate it as "US Dept of Ag" and then write it as USDA in subsequent references. Other examples:

| short-term memory | STM |
| as soon as possible | ASAP |

4. Omit vowels.

background	bkgrnd
problem	prblm
government	gvt

5. Use g in place of ing.

| checking | ckg |
| decreasing | decrg |

6. Write your notes in text message format.

Symbols

Use common symbols or invent your own to speed up the note-taking process.

Common Symbols Used in Note Taking

Symbol	Meaning	Symbol	Meaning
&	and	B4	before
w	with	BC	because
wo	without	esp	especially
wi	within	diff	difference
<	less than	min	minimum
>	more than	gov	government
@	at	ex	example
/	per	↑	increasing
2	to, two, too	↓	decreasing
∴	therefore	=	equal
vs	versus, against	≠	not equal

How to Review Your Notes

Immediate review. Review your notes as soon as possible after the lecture. The most effective review is done immediately or at least within 20 minutes. If you wait until the next day to review, you may already have forgotten much of the information. During the immediate review, fill in any missing or incomplete information. Say the important points to yourself. This begins the process of rehearsal for storing the information in long-term memory.

There are various methods for review depending on your note-taking system:

- For the Cornell format, use the recall column to write in key words or questions. Cover your notes and see if you can recall the main ideas. Place checkmarks by the items you have mastered. Don't worry about mastering all the key points from the beginning. With each review, it will be easier to remember the information.
- For the outline format, use a highlighter to mark the key ideas as you repeat them silently to yourself.
- For mind maps, look over the information and think about the key ideas and their relationships. Fill in additional information or clarification. Highlight important points or relationships with color.

Intermediate review. Set up some time each week for short reviews of your notes and the key points in your textbook from previous weeks. Quickly look over the notes and recite the key points in your mind. These intermediate reviews will help you to master the material and avoid test anxiety.

Test review. Complete a major review as part of your test preparation strategy. As you look through your notes, turn the key ideas into possible test questions and answer them.

Final review. The final review occurs after you have received the results of your test. Ask yourself these questions:

- What percentage of the test questions came from the lecture notes?
- Were you prepared for the exam? Is so, congratulate yourself on a job well done. If not, how can you improve next time?
- Were your notes adequate? If not, what needs to be added or changed?

QUIZ

Note-Taking Efficiency

Test what you have learned by selecting the correct answers to the following questions.

1. Recognizing signal words will help you to
   a. know when the lecture is about to end.
   b. identify the key ideas and organize them in your notes.
   c. know when to pay attention.

2. When taking notes, be sure to
   a. write your notes in complete sentences.
   b. use correct grammar.
   c. use telegraphic sentences.

3. The best time to review your notes is
   a. as soon as possible after the lecture.
   b. within 24 hours.
   c. within one week.

4. Using abbreviations in note taking is
   a. not a good idea.
   b. a good idea as long as you can read them.
   c. makes review difficult.

5. To avoid test anxiety,
   a. review your notes just before the test.
   b. review your notes the week before the test.
   c. review your notes periodically throughout the semester.

How did you do on the quiz? Check your answers: 1. b, 2. c, 3. a, 4. b, 5. c

Journal Entry #2

Write five intention statements about improving your note-taking skills. Consider your note-taking system, how to take notes more efficiently, and the best way to review your notes. I intend to . . .

Power Writing

Power Writing

- Prepare
- Organize
- Write
- Edit
- Revise

Effective writing will help you in school, on the job, and in your personal life. Good writing will help you to create quality term papers. The writing skills that you learn in college will be used later in jobs involving high responsibility and good pay. You can become an excellent writer by learning about the steps in POWER writing: prepare, organize, write, edit, and revise.

Prepare

Plan your time. The first step in writing is to plan your time so that the project can be completed by the due date. Picture this scene: It is the day that the term paper is due. A few students proudly hand in their term papers and are ready to celebrate their accomplishments. Many of the students in the class are absent, and some will never return to the class. Some of the students look as though they haven't slept the night before. They look stressed and weary. At the front of the class is a line of students wanting to talk with the instructor. The instructor has heard it all before:

- I had my paper all completed and my printer jammed.
- My hard drive crashed and I lost my paper.
- I was driving to school and my paper flew off my motorcycle.
- I had the flu.
- My children were sick.
- I had to take my dog to the vet.
- My dog ate my paper.
- My car broke down and I could not get to the library.
- My grandmother died and I had to go to the funeral.
- My roommate accidentally took my backpack to school.
- I spilled salad dressing on my paper, so I put it in the microwave to dry it out and the writing disappeared!

To avoid being in this uncomfortable and stressful situation, plan ahead. Plan to complete your project at least one week ahead of time so that you can deal with life's emergencies. Life does not always go as planned. You or your children may get sick, or your dog may do strange things to your homework. Your computer may malfunction, leading you to believe it senses stress and malfunctions just to frustrate you even more.

To avoid stress and do your best work, start with the date that the project is due and then think about the steps needed to finish. Write these dates on your calendar or on your list of things to do. Consider all these components:

Project due date:

To do	By when?
1. Brainstorm ideas.	_____
2. Choose a topic.	_____
3. Gather information.	_____
4. Write a thesis statement.	_____
5. Write an outline.	_____
6. Write the introduction.	_____

"The most valuable of all education is the ability to make yourself do the thing you have to do, when it has to be done, whether you like it or not."

Aldous Huxley

Prepare

- Plan your time
- Find space and time
- Choose general topic
- Gather information
- Write thesis statement

7. Write the first draft. _____

8. Prepare the bibliography. _____

9. Edit. _____

10. Revise. _____

11. Print and assemble. _____

Find a space and time. Find a space where you can work. Gather the materials that you will need to write. Generally, writing is best done in longer blocks of time. Determine when you will work on your paper and write the time on your schedule. Start right away to avoid panic later.

Choose a general topic. This task will be easy if your topic is already clearly defined by your instructor or your boss at work. Make sure that you have a clear idea of what is required, such as length, format, purpose, and method of citing references and topic. Many times the choice of a topic is left to you. Begin by doing some brainstorming. Think about topics that interest you. Write them down. You may want to focus your attention on brainstorming ideas for five or 10 minutes, and then put the project aside and come back to it later. Once you have started the process of thinking about the ideas, your mind will continue to work and you may have some creative inspiration. If inspiration does not come, repeat the brainstorming process.

Gather information. Go to your college library and use the Internet to gather your information. As you begin, you can see what is available, what is interesting to you, and what the current thinking is on your topic. Note the major topics of interest that might be useful to you. Once you have found some interesting material, you will feel motivated to continue your project. As you find information relevant to your topic, make sure to write down the sources of your information to use in your bibliography. The bibliography contains information about where you found your material. Write down the author, the title of the publication, the publisher, and the place and date of publication. For Internet resources, list the address of the website and the date accessed.

Write the thesis statement. The thesis statement is the key idea in your paper. It provides a direction for you to follow. It is the first step in organizing your work. To write a thesis statement, review the material you have gathered and then ask these questions:

- What is the most important idea?
- What question would I like to ask about it?
- What is my answer?

For example, if I decide to write a paper for my health class on the harmful effects of smoking, I would look at current references on the topic. I might become interested in how the tobacco companies misled the public on the dangers of smoking. I would think about my thesis statement and answer the questions stated above.

- **What is the most important idea?** Smoking is harmful to your health.
- **What question would I like to ask about it?** Did the tobacco companies mislead the public about the health hazards of smoking?
- **What is my answer?** The tobacco companies misled the public about the hazards of smoking in order to protect their business interests.
- **My thesis statement:** Tobacco companies knew that smoking was hazardous to health, but to protect their business interests, they deliberately misled the public.

The thesis statement helps to narrow the topic and provide direction for the paper. I can now focus on reference material related to my topic: research on health effects of smoking, congressional testimony relating to regulation of the tobacco industry, and how advertising influences people to smoke.

Organize

At this point you have many ideas about what to include in your paper, and you have a central focus, your thesis statement. Start to organize your paper by listing the topics that are related to your thesis statement. Here is a list of topics related to my thesis statement about smoking:

> **Organize**
> * List related topics
> * Arrange in logical order
> * Have an organizational structure

* Tobacco companies' awareness that nicotine is addictive
* Minimizing health hazards in tobacco advertisements
* How advertisements encourage people to smoke
* Money earned by the tobacco industry
* Health problems caused by smoking
* Statistics on numbers of people who have health problems or die from smoking
* Regulation of the tobacco industry
* Advertisements aimed at children

Think about the topics and arrange them in logical order. Use an outline, a mind map, a flowchart, or a drawing to think about how you will organize the important topics. Keep in mind that you will need an introduction, a body, and a conclusion. Having an organizational structure will make it easier for you to write because you will not need to wonder what comes next.

Write

Write the First Sentence
Begin with the main idea.

> **Write**
> * First sentence
> * Introduction
> * Body
> * Conclusion
> * References

Write the Introduction
This is the road map for the rest of the paper. The introduction includes your thesis statement and establishes the foundation of the paper. It introduces topics that will be discussed in the body of the paper. The introduction should include some interesting points that provide a "hook" to motivate the audience to read your paper. For example, for a paper on the hazards of smoking, you might begin with statistics on how many people suffer from smoking-related illnesses and premature death. Note the large profits earned by the tobacco industry. Then introduce other topics: deception, advertisements, and regulation. The introduction provides a guide or outline of what will follow in the paper.

Write the Body of the Paper
The body of the paper is divided into paragraphs that discuss the topics that you have introduced. As you write each paragraph, include the main idea and then explain it and give examples. Here are some good tips for writing:

1. Good writing reflects clear thinking. Think about what you want to say and write about it so the reader can understand your point of view.

2. Use clear and concise language. Avoid using too many words or scholarly-sounding words that might get in the way of understanding.

3. Don't assume that the audience knows what you are writing about. Provide complete information.

4. Provide examples, stories, and quotes to support your main points. Include your own ideas and experiences.

5. Beware of plagiarism. Plagiarism is copying the work of others without giving them credit. It is illegal and can cause you to receive a failing grade on your project or even get you into legal trouble. Faculty regularly uses software programs that identify plagiarized material in student papers. You can avoid plagiarism by using quotation marks around an author's words and providing a reference indicating where you found the material. Another way to avoid plagiarism is by carefully reading your source material while using critical thinking to evaluate it. Then look away from the source and write about the ideas in your own words, including your critical thinking about the subject. Don't forget to include a reference for the source material in your bibliography.

Write the Conclusion

The conclusion summarizes the topics in the paper and presents your point of view. It makes reference to the introduction and answers the question posed in your thesis statement. It often makes the reader think about the significance of your point and the implications for the future. Make your conclusion interesting and powerful.

Include References

No college paper is complete without references. References may be given in footnotes, endnotes, a list of works cited, or a bibliography. You can use your computer to insert these references. There are various styles for citing references depending on your subject area. There are computer programs that put your information into the correct style. Ask your instructor which style to use for your particular class or project. Three frequently used styles for citing references are APA, Chicago, and MLA.

1. The American Psychological Association (APA) style is used in psychology and other behavioral sciences. Consult the *Publication Manual of the American Psychological Association*, 6th ed. (Washington, DC: American Psychological Association, 2010). You can find this source online at www.apastyle.org.

2. Chicago style is used by many professional writers in a variety of fields. Consult the *Chicago Manual of Style*, 16th ed. (Chicago: University of Chicago Press, 2010). You can find this source online at www.chicagomanualofstyle.org/home.html.

3. The Modern Language Association (MLA) style is used in English, classical languages, and the humanities. Consult the *MLA Handbook for Writers of Research Papers*, 7th ed. (New York: Modern Language Association, 2009). This source is available online at www.mla.org/style.

Each of these styles uses a different format for listing sources, but all include the same information. Make sure you write down this information as you collect your reference material. If you forget this step, it is very time-consuming and difficult to find later.

- Author's name
- Title of the book or article
- Journal name
- Publisher

- City where book was published
- Publication date
- Page number (and volume and issue numbers, if available)

Here are some examples of citations in the APA style:

- **Book.** Include author, date of publication, title, city of publication, and publisher.
  Fralick, M. (2011). *College and career success* (5th ed.). Dubuque, IA: Kendall Hunt.
- **Journal article.** Include author, date, title, name of journal, volume and issue numbers, pages.
  Fralick, M. (1993). College success: A study of positive and negative attrition. *Community College Review, 20*(5), 29–36.
- **Website.** Include author, date listed or updated, document title or name of website, URL or website address, and date accessed. Include as many of the above items as possible. Methods of citing information from the Internet are still evolving.
  Fralick, M. (2011, January). *Note taking*. Retrieved January 2011 from College Success 1 at http://www.collegesuccess1.com/

Save Your Work

As soon as you have written the first paragraph, save it on your computer. Save your work in two places: on your hard drive and on a flash drive or external hard drive. At the end of each section, save your work again to both of these places. When you are finished, print your work and save a paper copy. Then, if your hard drive crashes, you will still have your work at another location. If your file becomes corrupted, you will still have the paper copy. Following these procedures can save you a lot of headaches. Any writer can tell you stories of lost work because of computer problems, lightning storms, power outages, and other unpredictable events.

Put It Away for a While

The last step in writing the first draft is easy. Put it away for a while and come back to it later. In this way, you can relax and gain some perspective on your work. You will be able to take a more objective look at your work to begin the process of editing and revising.

Writer's Block

Many people who are anxious about writing experience "writer's block." You have writer's block if you find yourself staring at that blank piece of paper or computer screen not knowing how to begin or what to write. Here are some tips for avoiding writer's block.

- **Write freely.** Just write anything about your topic that comes to mind. Don't worry about organization or perfection at this point. Don't censure your ideas. You can always go back to organize and edit later. Free-writing helps you to overcome one of the main causes of writer's block: you think it has to be perfect from the beginning. This expectation of perfection causes anxiety. You freeze up and become unable to write. Perhaps you have past memories of writing where the teacher made many corrections on your paper. Maybe you lack confidence in your writing skills. The only way you will become a better writer is to keep writing and perfecting your writing skills, so to start the writing process, just write what comes to mind. Don't worry how great it is. You can fix it later. Just begin.

- **Use brainstorming if you get stuck.** For five minutes, focus your attention on the topic and write whatever comes to mind. You don't even need to write full sentences; just jot down ideas. If you are really stuck, try working on a different topic or take a break and come back to it later.

- **Realize that it is only the first draft.** It is not the finished product and it does not have to be perfect. Just write some ideas on paper; you can revise them later.

- **Read through your reference materials.** The ideas you find can get your mind working. Also, reading can make you a better writer.

- **Break the assignment up into small parts.** If you find writing difficult, write for five minutes at a time. Do this consistently and you can get used to writing and can complete your paper.

- **Find a good place for writing.** If you are an introvert, look for a quiet place for concentration. If you are an extrovert, go to a restaurant or coffee shop and start your writing.

- **Beware of procrastination.** The more you put off writing, the more anxious you will become and the more difficult the task will be. Make a schedule and stick to it.

Edit and Revise

The editing and revising stage allows you to take a critical look at what you have written. It takes some courage to do this step. Once people see their ideas in writing, they become attached to them. With careful editing and revising, you can turn in your best work and be proud of your accomplishments. Here are some tips for editing and revising:

1. **Read your paper as if you were the audience.** Pretend that you are the instructor or another person reading your paper. Does every sentence make sense? Did you say what you meant to say? Read what you have written, and the result will be a more effective paper.

2. **Read paragraph by paragraph.** Does each paragraph have a main idea and supporting details? Do the paragraphs fit logically together? Use the cut-and-paste feature on your computer to move sentences and paragraphs around if needed.

3. **Check your grammar and spelling.** Use the spell check and grammar check on your computer. These tools are helpful, but they are not thorough enough. The spell check will pick up only misspelled words. It will skip words that are spelled correctly but not the intended word—for example, if you use "of" instead of "on" or "their" instead of "there." To find such errors, you need to read your paper after doing a spell check.

4. **Check for language that is biased in terms of gender, disability, or ethnic group.** Use words that are gender neutral. If a book or paper uses only the pronoun "he" or "she," half of the population is left out. You can often avoid sexist language by using the plural forms of nouns:

   (singular)   The successful student knows *his* values and sets goals for the future.

   (plural)   Successful students know *their* values and set goals for the future.

After all, we are trying to make the world a better place, with opportunity for all. Here are some examples of biased language and better alternatives.

Biased Language	***Better Alternatives***
policeman	police officer
chairman	chair
fireman	firefighter

draftsman	drafter
mankind	humanity
manmade	handcrafted
housewife	homemaker
crippled and disabled persons	persons with disabilities

Tips for Editing and Revising

1. Read your paper objectively
2. Read paragraph by paragraph
3. Check grammar and spelling
4. Check for biased language
5. Have someone else read your paper
6. Review the introduction and conclusion
7. Prepare final copy
8. Prepare title page

5. **Have someone else read your paper.** Ask your reader to check for clarity and meaning. After you have read your paper many times, you do not really see it anymore. If you need assistance in writing, colleges offer tutoring or writing labs where you can get help with editing and revising.

6. **Review your introduction and conclusion.** They should be clear, interesting, and concise. The introduction and conclusion are the most powerful parts of your paper.

7. **Prepare the final copy.** Check your instructor's instructions on the format required. If there are no instructions, use the following format:

   • Use double-spacing.

   • Use 10- or 12-point font.

   • Use one-inch margins on all sides.

   • Use a three-inch top margin on the first page.

   • Single-space footnotes and endnotes.

   • Number your pages.

8. **Prepare the title page.** Center the title of your paper and place it one third of the page from the top. On the bottom third of the page, center your name, the professor's name, the name of the class, and the date.

Final Steps

Make sure you follow instructions about using a folder or cover for your paper. Generally professors dislike bulky folders or notebooks because they are difficult to carry. Imagine your professor trying to carry 50 notebooks to his or her office! Unless asked to do so, do not use plastic page protectors. Professors like to write comments on papers, and it is extremely difficult to write on papers with page protectors.

Turning your paper in on time is very important. Some professors do not accept late papers. Others subtract points if your paper is late. Put your paper in the car or someplace where you will have to see it before you go to class. **Then reward yourself for a job well done!**

Journal Entry #3

Write five intention statements about improving your writing. While thinking about your statements, consider the steps of POWER writing: prepare, organize, write, edit, and revise. Do you need to work on problems such as writer's block or getting your writing done on time? I intend to . . .

Effective Public Speaking

You may need to take a speech class in order to graduate from college, and many of your classes will require oral presentations. Being a good speaker can contribute to your success on the job as well. A study done at Stanford University showed that one of the top predictors of success in professional positions was the ability to be a good public speaker.[1] You will need to present information to your boss, your colleagues, and your customers or clients.

Learn to Relax

Whenever I tell students that they will need to take a speech class or make an oral presentation, I see a look of panic on their faces. Good preparation can help you to feel confident about your oral presentation. Professional speaker Lilly Walters believes that you can deal with 75 percent of your anxiety by being well prepared.[2] You can deal with the remaining 25 percent by using some relaxation techniques.

- If you are anxious, admit to yourself that you are anxious. If it is appropriate, as in a beginning speech class, you can even admit to the audience that you are anxious. Once you have admitted that you are anxious, visualize yourself confidently making the speech.

- You do not have to be perfect; it is okay to make mistakes. Making mistakes just shows you are human like the rest of us.

- If you are anxious before your speech, take three to five deep breaths. Breathe in slowly and hold your breath for five seconds, and then breathe out slowly. Focus your mind on your breathing rather than your speech.

- Use positive self-talk to help you to relax. Instead of saying to yourself, "I will look like a fool up there giving the speech," tell yourself, "I can do this" or "It will be okay."

- Once you start speaking, anxiety will generally decline.

- With experience, you will gain confidence in your speaking ability and will be able to relax more easily.

Preparing and Delivering Your Speech

Write the Beginning of the Speech

The beginning includes a statement of your objective and what your speech will be about. It should prepare the audience for what comes next. You can begin your speech with a personal experience, a quote, a news article, or a joke. Jokes can be effective, but they are risky. Try out your joke with your friends to make sure that it is funny. Do not tell jokes that put down other people or groups.

Write the Main Body of the Speech

The main body of the speech consists of four or five main points. Just as in your term paper, state your main points and then provide details, examples, or stories that illustrate them. As you present the main points of your speech, consider your audience. Your speech will be different depending on whether it is made to a group of high school students, your college classmates, or a group of professionals. You can add interest to your speech by using props, pictures, charts, PowerPoint, music, or video clips. College students today are increasingly using PowerPoint software to make classroom presentations. If you are planning to enter a professional career, learning how to make PowerPoint presentations will be an asset.

> "Let us think of education as the means of developing our greatest abilities, because in each of us there is a private hope and dream which, fulfilled, can be translated into greater benefit for everyone and greater strength for our nation."
> John F. Kennedy

Write the Conclusion

In your conclusion, summarize and review the key points of your speech. The conclusion is like the icing on a cake. It should be strong, persuasive, and interesting. Invest some time in your ending statement. It can be a call to action, a recommendation for the future, a quote, or a story.

Practice Your Speech

Practice your speech until you feel comfortable with it. Prepare a memory system or notes to help you deliver your speech. You will want to make eye contact with your audience, which is difficult if you are trying to read your speech. A memory system useful for delivering speeches is the loci system. Visualize a house, for example: the entryway is the introduction, and each room represents a main point in the speech. Visualize walking into each room and what you will say in each room. Each room can have items that remind you of what you are going to say. At the conclusion, you say good-bye at the door. Another technique is to prepare brief notes or outlines on index cards or sheets of paper. When you are practicing your speech, time it to see how long it is. Keep your speech within the time allowed. Most people tend to speak longer than necessary.

QUIZ

Writing and Speaking

Test what you have learned by selecting the correct answers to the following questions.

1. To make sure to get your paper done on time,

   a. have someone remind you of the deadline.
   b. write the due date on your calendar and the date for completion of each step.
   c. write your paper just before the due date to increase motivation.

2. The thesis statement is the

   a. most important sentence in each paragraph.
   b. key idea in the paper.
   c. summary of the paper.

3. If you have writer's block, it is helpful to

   a. delay writing your paper until you feel relaxed.
   b. make sure that your writing is perfect from the beginning.
   c. begin with brainstorming or free writing.

4. No college paper is complete without

   a. the references.
   b. a professional-looking cover.
   c. printing on quality paper.

5. You can deal with most of your anxiety about public speaking by

   a. striving for perfection.
   b. visualizing your anxiety.
   c. being well prepared.

How did you do on the quiz? Check your answers: 1. b, 2. b, 3. c, 4. a, 5. c

Review the Setup

If you are using props, make sure that you have them ready. If you are using equipment, make sure it is available and in working condition. Make arrangements in advance for the equipment you need and, if possible, check to see that it is running properly right before your presentation.

Deliver the Speech

Wear clothes that make you feel comfortable, but not out of place. Remember to smile and make eye contact with members of the audience. Take a few deep breaths if you are nervous. You will probably be less nervous once you begin. If you make a mistake, keep your sense of humor. I recall the famous chef Julia Child doing a live television production on how to cook a turkey. As she took the turkey out of the oven, it slipped and landed on the floor right in front of the television cameras. She calmly picked it up and said, "And remember that you are the only one that really knows what goes on in the kitchen." It was one of the shows that made her famous.

Journal Entry #4

Write one paragraph giving advice to a new college student on how to make a speech. Use any of these questions to guide your thinking:

- What are some ways to deal with anxiety about public speaking?
- How can you make your speech interesting?
- What are some steps in preparing a speech?
- What are some ideas that don't work?

Be Selective

Psychologist and philosopher William James said, "The essence of genius is knowing what to overlook."[3] This saying has a variety of meanings. In reading, note taking, marking a college textbook, and writing, it is important to be able to pick out the main points first and then identify the supporting details. Imagine you are trying to put together a jigsaw puzzle. You bought the puzzle at a garage sale and all the pieces are there, but the lid to the box with the picture of the puzzle is missing. It will be very difficult, if not impossible, to put this puzzle together. Reading, note taking, marking, and writing are very much like putting a puzzle together. First you will need an understanding of the main ideas (the big picture) and then you can focus on the details.

How can you get the overall picture? When reading, you can get the overall picture by skimming the text. As you skim the text, you get a general outline of what the chapter contains and what you will learn. In note taking, actively listen for the main ideas and write them down in your notes. In marking your text, try to pick out about 20 percent of the most important material and underline or highlight it. In writing, think about what is most important, write your thesis statement, and then provide the supporting details. To select what is most important, be courageous, think, and analyze.

Does this mean that you should forget about the details? No, you will need to know some details too. The supporting details help you to understand and assess the value of the main idea. They help you to understand the relationship between ideas. Being selective means getting the general idea first, and then the details will make sense to you and you will be able to remember them. The main ideas are like scaffolding or a net that holds the details in some kind of framework so you can remember them. If you focus on the details first, you will have no framework or point of reference for remembering them.

Experiment with the idea of being selective in your personal life. If your schedule is impossibly busy, be selective and choose to do the most important or most valuable activities. This takes some thinking and courage too. If your desk drawer is stuffed with odds and ends and you can never find what you are looking for, take everything out and only put back what you need. Recycle, give away, or throw away surplus items around the house. You can take steps toward being a genius by being selective and taking steps to simplify and organize your life and your work.

Journal Entry #5

How can being selective help you achieve success in college and in life? Use any of these questions to guide your thinking:

- How can being selective help you to be a better note taker, writer, or speaker?
- How can being selective help you to manage your time and your life?
- What is the meaning of this quote by William James: "The essence of genius is knowing what to overlook?"

Taking Notes, Writing, and Speaking

Go to http://www.collegesuccess1.com/JournalEntries.htm for Word files of the Journal Entries

Success over the Internet

Visit the *College Success Website* at http://www.collegesuccess1.com/

The *College Success Website* is continually updated with new topics and links to the material presented in this chapter. Topics include:

- Note taking
- Mind maps
- Memory and note taking
- Telegraphic sentences
- Signal words
- Listening to lectures
- Grammar and style
- Quotes to use in speeches and papers
- The virtual public speaking assistant
- Researching, organizing, and delivering a speech
- Best speeches in history

Contact your instructor if you have any problems accessing the *College Success Website*.

Notes

1. T. Allesandra and P. Hunsaker, *Communicating at Work* (New York: Fireside, 1993), 169.

2. Lilly Walters, *Secrets of Successful Speakers: How You Can Motivate, Captivate, and Persuade* (New York: McGraw-Hill, 1993), 203.

3. Quoted in Rob Gilbert, ed., *Bits and Pieces*, August 12, 1999, 15.

Note-Taking Checklist

Name _____ Date _____

Place a checkmark next to the note-taking skills you have now.

_____ I attend every (or almost every) lecture in all my classes.

_____ I check the syllabus to find out what is being covered before I go to class.

_____ I read or at least skim through the reading assignment before attending the lecture.

_____ I attend lectures with a positive attitude about learning as much as possible.

_____ I am well rested so that I can focus on the lecture.

_____ I eat a light, nutritious meal before going to class.

_____ I sit in a location where I can see and hear easily.

_____ I have a laptop or a three-ring binder, looseleaf paper, and a pen for taking notes.

_____ I avoid external distractions (friends, sitting by the door).

_____ I am alert and able to concentrate on the lecture.

_____ I have a system for taking notes that works for me.

_____ I am able to determine the key ideas of the lecture and write them down in my notes.

_____ I can identify signal words that help to understand key points and organize my notes.

_____ I can write quickly using telegraphic sentences, abbreviations, and symbols.

_____ If I don't understand something in the lecture, I ask a question and get help.

_____ I write down everything written on the board or on visual materials used in the class.

_____ I review my notes immediately after class.

_____ I have intermediate review sessions to review previous notes.

_____ I use my notes to predict questions for the exam.

_____ I have clear and complete notes that help me to prepare adequately for exams.

Evaluate Your Note-Taking Skills

Name _____   Date _____

Use the note-taking checklist on the previous page to answer these questions.

1. Look at the items that you checked. What are your strengths in note taking?

2. What are some areas that you need to improve?

3. Write at least three intention statements about improving your listening and note-taking skills.

Assess Your College Writing Skills

Name _____ Date _____

Read the following statements and rate how true they are for you at the present time. Use the following scale:

5 Definitely true
4 Mostly true
3 Somewhat true
2 Seldom true
1 Never true

_____ I am generally confident in my writing skills.

_____ I have a system for reminding myself of due dates for writing projects.

_____ I start writing projects early so that I am not stressed by finishing them at the last minute.

_____ I have the proper materials and a space to write comfortably.

_____ I know how to use the library and the Internet to gather information for a term paper.

_____ I can write a thesis statement for a term paper.

_____ I know how to organize a term paper.

_____ I know how to write the introduction, body, and conclusion of a paper.

_____ I can cite references in the appropriate style for my subject.

_____ I know where to find information about citing material in APA, MLA, or Chicago style.

_____ I know what plagiarism is and know how to avoid it.

_____ I can deal with "writer's block" and get started on my writing project.

_____ I know how to edit and revise a paper.

_____ I know where I can get help with my writing.

_____ **Total**

60–70   You have excellent writing skills, but can always learn new ideas.

50–59   You have good writing skills, but there is room for improvement.

Below 50   You need to improve writing skills. The skills presented in this chapter will help. Consider taking a writing class early in your college studies.

Thinking about Writing

Name _____ Date _____

List 10 suggestions from this chapter that could help you improve your writing skills.

1.

2.

3.

4.

5.

6.

7.

8.

9.

10.

Name _____   Date _____

John is a new college student who needs help with college success skills. Using what you have learned in this chapter, give John some advice on how to take notes in class. This exercise can be done individually or as a group exercise in class.

> John is a new college student who has just graduated from high school. He is not sure what he wants to do with his life, but his parents want him to go to college. He misses the first class in Psychology 101 because he thinks nothing important happens on the first day. On the second day of class, John walks into class and finds some friends from high school. He takes a seat near them and starts a lively conversation. He has no books, paper, or pencil.

> The lecture is on the biological foundations of behavior. The topic is new for John and he is unfamiliar with the terms and concepts used in the lecture. He notices that the professor is wearing a tie that he must have purchased in 1970 and has an irritating habit of scratching his head. In addition, he is boring and speaks in a dull and monotonous way. John finds it difficult to concentrate. He becomes sleepy and starts to doze off during the lecture. At the end of the lecture, John realizes that he is going to have problems with psychology. For the next class, John brings a tape recorder and records the class. Again he finds it difficult to stay awake during the lecture. He works late at night and has scheduled this class for 8:00 in the morning.

What are the five most important suggestions you could make to help John take notes and be successful in this class?

1.

2.

3.

4.

5.

CHAPTER 7

Test Taking

Learning Objectives

Read to answer these key questions:

- What are some test preparation techniques?

- How should I review the material?

- How can I predict the test questions?

- What are some emergency test preparation techniques?

- How can I deal with test anxiety?

- How can I study math and deal with math anxiety?

- What are some tips for taking math tests?

- What are some tips for taking objective tests?

- How can I write a good essay?

Name: Britney Weizeorick
Major: Nursing
Hometown: Lisle, IL
Involvements: Alternative Spring Break, First-Year Seminar Co-Instructor (FYS), Fall Welcome Ambassador, Intramural Soccer, Bronson School of Nursing Program
Favorite Quote: "The best way to capture moments is to pay attention. This is how we cultivate mindfulness. Mindfulness means being awake. It means knowing what you are doing."—Jon Kabat-Zinn

You are in **charge of making all your own choices and decisions**; which means being more independent and having more responsibilities. I've learned to do not just what needs to be done but also what makes me happy, whether I'm doing it by myself or with friends. It is important to **find a balance that suits your lifestyle** and make time for the things that keep you going. **Western has many opportunities** and new experiences to offer. You may be surprised to **find enjoyment in classes** you never thought you would, and relationships in people you never would have expected. The only way to find out is to **try new things, and** continue to **be open to meeting new people**.

From being in college I have **become more in charge and interested in my own education**. I have had some **amazing experiences** but with that come uncomfortable and sometimes difficult ones as well. I feel these negative experiences are just as important as the amazing ones; they both shape us into **who we are** and force us to **face situations head on. College has given me more control of my life** and has helped me to **make better life choices.**

An important skill for survival in college is the ability to take tests. Passing tests is also important in careers that require licenses, certificates, or continuing education. Knowing how to prepare for and take tests with confidence will help you to accomplish your educational and career goals while maintaining your good mental health. Once you have learned some basic test-taking and relaxation techniques, you can turn your test anxiety into motivation and good test results.

Preparing for Tests

Attend Every Class

The most significant factor in poor performance in college is lack of attendance. Students who attend the lectures and complete their assignments have the best chance for success in college. Attending the lectures help you to be involved in learning and to know what to expect on the test. College professors know that students who miss three classes in a row are not likely to return, and some professors drop students after three absences. After three absences, students can fall behind in their schoolwork and become overwhelmed with makeup work.

Distribute the Practice

The key to successful test preparation is to begin early and do a little at a time. Test preparation begins the first day of class. During the first class, the professor gives an overview of the course content, requirements, tests, and grading. These items are described in writing in the class calendar and syllabus. It is very important to attend the first class to obtain this essential information. If you have to miss the first class, make sure to ask the professor for the syllabus and calendar and read it carefully.

Early test preparation helps you to take advantage of the powerful memory technique called distributed practice. In distributed practice, the material learned is broken up into small parts and reviewed frequently. Using this method can enable you to learn a large quantity of material without becoming overwhelmed. Here are some examples of using distributed practice:

- If you have a test on 50 Spanish vocabulary words in two weeks, don't wait until the day before the test to try to learn all 50 words. Waiting until the day before the test will result in difficulty remembering the words, test anxiety, and a dislike of studying Spanish. If you have 50 Spanish vocabulary words to learn in two weeks, learn five words each day and quickly review the words you learned previously. For example, on Monday you would learn five words, and on Tuesday, you would learn five new words and review the ones learned on Monday. Give yourself the weekends off as a reward for planning ahead.

- If you have to read a history book with 400 pages, divide that number by the number of days in the semester or quarter. If there are 80 days in the semester, you will only have to read five pages per day or 10 pages every other day. This is a much easier and more efficient way to master a long assignment.

- Don't wait until the last minute to study for a midterm or final exam. Keep up with the class each week. As you read each chapter, quickly review a previous chapter. In this way you can comfortably master the material. Just before a major test, you can review the material that you already know and feel confident about your ability to get a good grade on the test.

Schedule a Time and a Place for Studying

To take advantage of distributed practice, you will need to develop a study schedule. Write down your work time and school time and other scheduled activities. Identify times that can be used for studying each day. Get in the habit of using these available times for studying each week. As a general rule, you need two hours of study time for each hour spent in a college classroom. If you cannot find enough time for studying, consider either reducing your course load or reducing work hours.

Use your study schedule or calendar to note the due dates of major projects and all test dates. Schedule enough time to complete projects and to finish major reviews for exams. Look at each due date and write in reminders to begin work or review well in advance of the due date. Give yourself plenty of time to meet the deadlines. It seems that around exam time, students are often ill or have problems that prevent them from being successful. Having some extra time scheduled will help you to cope with the many unexpected events that happen in everyday life.

Try to schedule your study sessions during your prime time, when you are awake and refreshed. For many people, one hour of study during the daylight hours is worth one and a half hours at night. Trying to study late at night may not be the best idea, because it is difficult to motivate yourself to study when you are tired. Save the time at the end of the day for relaxing or doing routine chores.

Find a place to study. This can be an area of your home where you have a desk, computer, and all the necessary supplies for studying. As a general rule, do not study at the kitchen table, in front of the television, or in your bed. These places provide powerful cues for eating, watching television, or sleeping instead of studying. If you cannot find an appropriate place at home, use the college library as a place to study. The library is usually quiet and others are studying, so there are not too many distractions.

Test Review Tools

There are a variety of tools you can use to review for tests. Choose the tools according to your learning style and what works for you. Learning styles include visual, auditory,

Review Tools

- Flash cards
- Summary sheets
- Mind maps
- Study groups

kinesthetic, and tactile modes of learning. **Visual learners** find it easy to make mental pictures of the material to be learned. **Auditory learners** prefer listening and reciting material out loud. **Kinesthetic learners** benefit from moving around or acting out material to be learned. **Tactile learners** benefit from physical activities such as writing down items to be remembered.

- **Flash cards.** Flash cards are an effective way to learn facts and details for objective tests such as true-false, multiple-choice, matching, and fill-in-the-blank. For example, if you have 100 vocabulary words to learn in biology, put each word on one side of a card and the definition on the other side. First, look at each definition and see if you can recall the word. If you are a visual learner, look at the word and see if you can recall the definition. If you are an auditory learner, say the words and definitions. If you are a tactile or kinesthetic learner, carry the cards with you and briefly look at them as you are going about your daily activities. Make a game of studying by sorting the cards into stacks of information you know and information you still have to practice. Work with flash cards frequently and review them quickly. Don't worry about learning all the items at once. Each day that you practice, you will recall the items more easily. Check http://www.collegesuccess1.com/Links6Tests.htm for online tools for making flash cards.

- **Summary sheets.** Summary sheets are used to record the key ideas from your lecture notes or textbook. It is important to be selective; write only the most important ideas on the summary sheets. At the end of the semester, you might have approximately 10 pages of summary sheets from the text and 10 pages from your notes. If you are a kinesthetic learner, writing down the items you wish to remember will help you learn them. If you are a visual learner, the summary sheet becomes a picture of the ideas you need to remember. If you are an auditory learner, recite aloud the important ideas on the summary sheets.

- **Mind maps.** A mind map is a visual picture of the items you wish to remember. Start in the center of the page with a key idea and then surround it with related topics. You can use drawings, lines, circles, or colors to link and group the ideas. A mind map will help you to learn material in an organized way that will be useful when writing essay exams.

- **Study groups.** A study group is helpful in motivating yourself to learn through discussions of the material with other people. For the study group, select three to seven people who are motivated to be successful in class and can coordinate schedules. Study groups are often used in math and science classes. Groups of students work problems together and help each other understand the material. The study group is also useful in studying for exams. Give each member a part of the material to be studied. Have each person predict test questions and quiz the study group. Teaching the material to the study group can be the best way to learn it.

"I can accept failure. Everyone fails at something. But I can't accept not trying."
Michael Jordan

Reviewing Effectively

Begin your review early and break it into small parts. Remember that repetition is one of the effective ways to store information in long-term memory. Here are some types of review that help you to store information in long-term memory:

- **Immediate review.** This type of review is fast and powerful and helps to minimize forgetting. It is the first step in storing information in long-term memory. Begin the process by turning each bold-faced heading in the text into a question. Read each section to answer the question you have asked. Read your college texts with a highlighter in hand so that you can mark the key ideas for review. Some students use a variety of colors to distinguish main ideas, supporting points, and key examples, for instance. When you are finished using the highlighter, quickly review the items you have marked. As you complete each section, quickly review the main points. When you finish the chapter, immediately review the key points in the entire chapter again. As soon as you finish taking your lecture notes, take a few minutes to review them. To be most effective, immediate review needs to occur as soon as possible or at least within the first 20 minutes of learning something.

- **Intermediate review.** After you have finished reading and reviewing a new chapter in your textbook, spend a few minutes reviewing an earlier one. This step will help you to master the material and to recall it easily for the midterm or final exam. Another way to do intermediate review is to set up time periodically in your study schedule for reviewing previous chapters and classroom notes. Doing intermediate reviews helps to access the materials you have stored in long-term memory.

- **Final review.** Before a major exam, organize your notes, materials, and assignments. Estimate how long it will take you to review the material. Break the material into manageable chunks. For an essay exam, use mind maps or summary sheets to write down the main points that you need to remember and recite these ideas frequently. For objective tests, use flash cards or lists to remember details and concepts that you expect to be on the test. Here is a sample seven-day plan for reviewing 10 chapters for a final exam:

Day 1   Gather materials and study Chapters 1 and 2 by writing key points on summary sheets or mind maps. Make flash cards of details you need to remember. Review and highlight lecture notes and handouts on these chapters.

Day 2   Review Chapters 1 and 2. Study Chapters 3 and 4 and the corresponding lecture notes.

Day 3   Review Chapters 1 to 4. Study Chapters 5 and 6 and the corresponding lecture notes.

Day 4   Review Chapters 1 to 6. Study Chapters 7 and 8 along with the corresponding lecture notes.

Day 5   Review Chapters 1 to 8. Study Chapters 9 and 10 along with corresponding lecture notes.

Day 6   Review notes, summary sheets, mind maps, and flash cards for Chapters 1 to 10. Relax and get a good night's sleep. You are well prepared.

Day 7   Do one last quick review of Chapters 1 to 10 and walk into the test with the confidence that you will be successful on the exam.

Predicting Test Questions

There are many ways to predict the questions that will be on the test. Here are some ideas that might be helpful:

- Look for clues from the professor about what will be on the test. Many times professors put information about the tests on the course syllabus. During lectures, they often give hints about what will be important to know. If a professor repeats something more than once, make note of it as a possible test question. Anything written on the board is likely to be on the test. Sometimes the professor will even say, "This will be on the test." Write these important points in your notes and review them.

- College textbooks are usually written in short sections with bold headings. Turn each bold-faced heading into a question and read to answer the question. Understand and review the main idea in each section. The test questions will generally address the main ideas in the text.

- Don't forget to study and review the handouts that the professor distributes to the class. If the professor has taken the time and effort to provide extra material, it is probably important and may be on the test.

"The will to win is not nearly as important as the will to prepare to win."
Bobby Knight

- Form a study group and divide up the material to be reviewed. Have each member of the group write some test questions based on the important points in each main section of the text. When the study group meets, take turns asking likely test questions and providing the answers.
- When the professor announces the test, make sure to ask what material is to be covered on the test and what kind of test it is. If necessary, ask the professor which concepts are most important. Know what kinds of test questions will be asked (essay, true-false, multiple-choice, matching, or short-answer). Some professors may provide sample exams or math problems.
- Use the first test to understand what is expected and how to study for future tests.

Preparing for an Open-Book Test

In college, you may have some open-book tests. Open-book tests are often used in very technical subjects where specific material from the book is needed to answer questions. For example, in an engineering course, tables and formulas in the book may be needed to solve engineering problems on an exam. To study for an open-book test, focus on understanding the material and being able to locate key information for the exam. Consider making index tabs for your book so that you can locate needed information quickly. Be sure to bring your book, calculator, and other needed material to the exam.

Journal Entry # 1

Write one paragraph about the ideal way to prepare for a major exam such as a midterm or final. Consider these factors while thinking about your answer: attendance, distribute the practice, time management, review tools, predicting test questions and the most efficient way to review.

Emergency Procedures

If it is a day or two before the test and you have not followed the above procedures, it is time for the college practice known as "cramming." There are two main problems that result from this practice. First, you cannot take advantage of distributed practice, so it will be difficult to remember large amounts of material. Second, it is not fun, and if done often will result in anxiety and a dislike of education. Because of these problems, some students who rely on cramming wrongly conclude that they are not capable of finishing their education.

If you must cram for a test, here are some emergency procedures that may be helpful in getting the best grade possible under difficult circumstances:

- When cramming, *it is most important to be selective*. Try to identify the main points and recite and review them.
- Focus on reviewing and reciting the lecture notes. In this way, you will cover the main ideas the professor thinks are important.
- If you have not read the text, skim and search each chapter looking for the main points. Highlight and review these main points. Read the chapter summaries. In a math textbook, practice sample problems.
- Make summary sheets containing the main ideas from the notes and the text. Recite and review the summary sheets.

- For objective tests, focus on learning new terms and vocabulary related to the subject. These terms are likely to be on the test. Flash cards are helpful.
- For essay tests, develop an outline of major topics and review the outline so you can write an essay.
- Get enough rest. Staying up all night to review for the test can result in confusion, reduced mental ability, and test anxiety.
- Hope for the best.
- Plan ahead next time so that you can get a better grade.

If you have very little time to review for a test, you will probably experience information overload. One strategy for dealing with this problem is based on the work of George Miller of Harvard University. He found that the optimum number of chunks of information we can remember is seven plus or minus two (or five to nine chunks of information).[1] This is also known as the Magical Number Seven Theory. For this last-minute review technique, start with five sheets of paper. Next, identify five key concepts that are likely to be on the test. Write one concept on the top of each sheet of paper. Then check your notes and text to write an explanation, definition, or answer for each of these topics. If you have more time, find two to four more concepts and research them, writing the information on additional sheets. You should have no more than nine sheets of paper. Arrange the sheets in order of importance. Review and recite the key ideas on these sheets. Get a regular night's sleep before the test and do some relaxation exercises right before the test.

Ideas That Don't Work

Some students do poorly on tests for the following reasons.

- Attending a party or social event the evening before a major test rather than doing the final review will adversely affect your test score. Study in advance and reward yourself with the party after the test.
- Skipping the major review before the test may cause you to forget some important material.
- Taking drugs or drinking alcohol before a test may give you the impression that you are relaxed and doing well on the test, but the results are disastrous to your success on the exam and your good health.
- Not knowing the date of the test can cause you to get a low grade because you are not prepared.
- Not checking or knowing about the final exam schedule can cause you to miss the final.
- Missing the final exam can result in a lower grade or failing the class.
- Arriving late for the exam puts you at a disadvantage if you don't have time to finish or have to rush through the test.
- Deciding not to buy or read the textbook will cause low performance or failure.
- Having a fight, disagreement, or argument with parents, friends, or significant others before the test will make it difficult to focus on the exam.
- Sacrificing sleep, exercise, or food to prepare for the exam makes it difficult to do your best.
- Cheating on an exam can cause embarrassment, a lower grade, or failure. It can even lead to expulsion from college.
- Missing the exam because you are not prepared and asking the professor to let you make up the exam later is a tactic that many students try. Most professors will not permit you to take an exam late.

"Failure is simply the opportunity to begin again more intelligently."
Henry Ford

- Inventing a creative excuse for missing an exam is so common that some professors have a collection of these stories that they share with colleagues. Creative excuses don't work with most professors.
- Arriving at the exam without the proper materials such as a pencil, Scantron, paper, calculator, or book (for open-book exams) can cause you to miss the exam or start the exam late.

QUIZ

Test Preparation

Test what you have learned by selecting the correct answers to the following questions.

1. In test preparation, it is important to use this memory technique:

   a. Distribute the practice.
   b. Read every chapter just before the test.
   c. Do most of the review right before the test to minimize forgetting.

2. Schedule your study sessions

   a. late at night.
   b. during your prime time, which is generally earlier in the day.
   c. after all other activities are done.

3. Effective tools to learn facts and details are

   a. mind maps.
   b. summary sheets.
   c. flash cards.

4. The best way to review is

   a. to start early and break it into small parts.
   b. immediately before the test.
   c. in large blocks of time.

5. If you have to cram for an exam, it is most important to

   a. stay up all night studying for the exam
   b. focus on the lecture notes and forget about reading the text
   c. be selective and review and recite the main points

How did you do on the quiz? Check your answers: 1. a, 2. b, 3. c, 4. a, 5. c

Ten Rules for Success

Here are 10 rules for success on any test. Are there any new ideas you can put into practice?

1. **Make sure to set your alarm,** and consider having a backup in case your alarm doesn't go off. Set a second alarm or have someone call to make sure you are awake on time.

2. **Arrive a little early for your exam.** If you are taking a standardized test like the Scholastic Aptitude Test (SAT) or Graduate Record Exam (GRE), familiarize yourself with the location of the exam. If you arrive early, you can take a quick walk around the building to relax or spend a few minutes doing a review so that your brain will be tuned up and ready.

3. **Eat a light breakfast including some carbohydrates and protein.** Be careful about eating sugar and caffeine before a test, because this can contribute to greater anxiety and low blood sugar by the time you take the test. The worst breakfast would be something like a doughnut and coffee or a soda and candy bar. Examples of good breakfasts are eggs, toast, and juice or cereal with milk and fruit.

4. **Think positively about the exam.** Tell yourself that you are well prepared and the exam is an opportunity to show what you know.

5. **Make sure you have the proper materials:** Scantrons, paper, pencil or pen, calculator, books and notes (for open-book exams).

6. **Manage your time.** Know how long you have for the test and then scan the test to make a time management plan. For example, if you have one hour and there are 50 objective questions, you have about a minute for each question. Halfway through the time, you should have completed 25 questions. If there are three essay questions in an hour, you have less than 20 minutes for each question. Save some time to look over the test and make corrections.

7. **Neatness is important.** If your paper looks neat, the professor is more likely to have a positive attitude about the paper before it is even read. If the paper is hard to read, the professor will start reading your paper with a negative attitude, possibly resulting in a lower grade.

8. **Read the test directions carefully.** On essay exams, it is common for the professor to give you a choice of questions to answer. If you do not read the directions, you may try to answer all of the questions and then run out of time or give incomplete answers to them.

9. **If you get stuck on a difficult question, don't worry about it.** Just mark it and find an easier question. You may find clues on the rest of the test that will aid your recall, or you may be more relaxed later on and think of the answer.

10. **Be careful not to give any impression that you might be cheating.** Keep your eyes on your own paper. If you have memory aids or outlines memorized, write them directly on the test paper rather than a separate sheet so that you are not suspected of using cheat notes.

Journal Entry #2

Write one paragraph about the most common mistakes students make while getting ready for an exam.

Dealing with Test Anxiety

Some anxiety is a good thing. It can provide motivation to study and prepare for exams. However, it is common for college students to suffer from test anxiety. Too much anxiety can lower your performance on tests. Some symptoms of test anxiety include:

- Fear of failing a test even though you are well prepared
- Physical symptoms such as perspiring, increased heart rate, shortness of breath, upset stomach, tense muscles, or headache
- Negative thoughts about the test and your grade
- Mental blocking of material you know and remembering it once you leave the exam

You can minimize your test anxiety by being well prepared and by applying the memory strategies described in earlier chapters. Prepare for your exams by attending every class, keeping up with your reading assignments, and reviewing during the semester. These steps will help increase your self-confidence and reduce anxiety. Apply the principles of memory improvement to your studying. As you are reading, find the important points and highlight them. Review these points so that they are stored in your long-term memory. Use distributed practice and spread out learning over time rather than trying to learn it all at once. Visualize and organize what you need to remember. Trust in your abilities and intend to remember what you have studied.

If you find that you are anxious, here are some ideas you can try to cope with the anxiety. Experiment with these techniques to see which ones work best for you.

Tips to Minimize Anxiety

- Exercise
- Sleep
- Take deep breaths
- Visualize success
- Acknowledge anxiety
- Easy questions first
- Yell, "Stop!"
- Daydream
- Practice perspective
- Give yourself time
- Get help

- **Do some physical exercise.** Physical exercise helps to use up stress hormones. Make physical activity a part of your daily routine. Arrive for your test a little early and walk briskly around campus for about 20 minutes. This exercise will help you to feel relaxed and energized.

- **Get a good night's sleep before the test.** Lack of sleep can interfere with memory and cause irritability, anxiety, and confusion.

- **Take deep breaths.** Immediately before the test, take a few deep breaths; hold them for three to five seconds and let them out slowly. These deep breaths will help you to relax and keep a sufficient supply of oxygen in your blood. Oxygen is needed for proper brain function.

- **Visualize and rehearse your success.** Begin by getting as comfortable and relaxed as possible in your favorite chair or lying down in bed. Visualize yourself walking into the exam room. Try to imagine the room in as much detail as possible. If possible, visit the exam room before the test so that you can get a good picture of it. See yourself taking the exam calmly and confidently. You know most of the answers. If you find a question you do not know, see yourself circling it and coming back to it later. Imagine that you find a clue on the test that triggers your recall of the answers to the difficult questions. Picture yourself handing in the exam with a good feeling about doing well on the test. Then imagine you are getting the test back and you get a good grade on the test. You congratulate yourself for a job well done. If you suffer from test anxiety, you may need to rehearse this scene several times. When you enter the exam room, the visual picture that you have rehearsed will help you to relax.

- **Acknowledge your anxiety.** The first step in dealing with anxiety is to admit that you are anxious rather than trying to fight it or deny it. Say to yourself, "I am feeling anxious." Take a few deep breaths and then focus your attention on the test.

- **Do the easy questions first and mark the ones that may be difficult.** This will help you to relax. Once you are relaxed, the difficult questions become more manageable.

- **Yell, "Stop!"** Negative and frightening thoughts can cause anxiety. Here are some examples of negative thoughts:

> I'm going to fail this test.
>
> I don't know the answer to number 10!
>
> I never do well on tests.
>
> Essays! I have a hard time with those.
>
> I'll never make it through college.
>
> I was never any good in math!

These types of thoughts don't help you do better on the test, so stop saying them. They cause you to become anxious and to freeze up during the test. If you find yourself with similar thoughts, yell, "Stop!" to yourself. This will cause you to interrupt your train of thought so that you can think about the task at hand rather than becoming more anxious. Replace negative thoughts with more positive ones such as these:

> I'm doing the best I can.
>
> I am well prepared and know most of the answers.
>
> I don't know the answer to number 10, so I'll just circle it and come back to it later.
>
> I'll make an outline in the margin for the essay question.
>
> College is difficult, but I'll make it!
>
> Math is a challenge, but I can do it!

- **Daydream.** Think about being in your favorite place. Take time to think about the details. Allow yourself to be there for a while until you feel more relaxed.
- **Practice perspective.** Remember, one poor grade is not the end of the world. It does not define who you are. If you do not do well, think about how you can improve your preparation and performance the next time.
- **Give yourself time.** Test anxiety develops over a period of time. It will take some time to get over it. Learn the best ways to prepare for the exam and practice saying positive thoughts to yourself.
- **Get help.** If these techniques do not work for you, seek help from your college health or counseling center.

Journal Entry #3

You have a friend who prepares for exams, but suffers from test anxiety. Review the section on test anxiety and write a one paragraph e-mail to your friend with some ideas on dealing with test anxiety. Consider both physical and mental preparation as well as some relaxation techniques that can be helpful.

I am taking a college success course and the book has some ideas on dealing with test anxiety. The book suggests . . .

Studying Math and Dealing with Math Anxiety

When I mention to students that they need to take math, I often see a look of fear on their faces. Everyone needs to take math. Most colleges require math classes and demonstrated math competency in order to graduate. Math is essential for many high-paying technical and professional occupations. Being afraid of math and avoiding it will limit your career possibilities.

Begin your study of math with some positive thinking. You may have had difficulty with math in the past, but with a positive attitude and the proper study techniques, you can meet the challenge. The first step to success in math is to put in the effort required. Attend class, do your homework, and get help if needed. If you put in the effort and hard work, you will gain experience in math. If you gain experience with math, you will become more confident in your ability to do math. If you have confidence, you will gain satisfaction in doing math. You may even learn to like it! If you like the subject, you can gain competence. The process looks like this:

$$\text{Hard work} \rightarrow \text{Experience} \rightarrow \text{Confidence} \rightarrow \text{Satisfaction} \rightarrow \text{Competence}$$

Although you may have had difficulty with math in the past, you can become successful by following these steps. Your reward is self-satisfaction and increased opportunity in technical and professional careers.

- **Don't delay taking math.** You may need a sequence of math courses in order to graduate. If you delay taking math, you may delay your graduation from college.

- **Think positively about your ability to succeed in math.** You may have had difficulties in math classes before. Think about your educational history. Can you recall having difficulties in the past? These past difficulties cause a fear of math. You may have a picture of failure in your mind. You need to replace it with a picture of success. Acknowledge that you are afraid because of past experiences with math. Acknowledge that the future can be different, and spend the time and effort needed to be successful.

- **Start at the beginning.** Assess where your math skills are at the present time. If you have not taken math classes for some time, you may need to review. Take the college math assessment test, read the college catalog, and speak to a counselor about where you should start.

- **Ask questions in class.** Students are often afraid to ask questions in math classes because they are afraid other students will think they are not smart. It is more likely that other students are wishing that someone would ask a question because they don't understand either. Ask your questions early, as soon as you find something you don't understand.

- **Get help early.** If you are having difficulties, get tutoring right away. If you are confused, you will not understand the next step either.

- **Don't miss your math classes.** It is difficult to catch up if you miss class.

- **Do your math homework regularly.** Math skills depend on practice. Make sure you understand the examples given in the textbook. Practice as many questions as you can until you feel comfortable solving the problems. Assign yourself extra problems if necessary. It is difficult to cram for a math test.

- **Use a study group.** Work with groups of students to study math. Get the phone numbers of other students in the study group. If you do not understand, other students may be able to help.

- **Study for the math test.** Start early so that you will have time to go over each topic in the book and practice doing problems from each section. Check your work against the solutions given in the text.

- **Do the easiest problems first on a math test.** In this way, you can gain confidence and relax. Then focus on the problems that are worth the most points. Don't be distracted by problems that you do not know and that use up test time.
- **Solve problems systematically.** First make sure you understand the problem. Write out the given facts and equations you may need to use before working out the problem. Then make a plan for solving it. What have you learned in class that will help you to solve the problem? Carry out the plan. Then check your answer. Does the answer make sense? Check your calculator work over again at the end of the test.
- **Check for careless errors.** Go over your math test to see if you have made any careless errors. Forgetting a plus or minus sign or adding or subtracting incorrectly can have a big impact on your grade. Save at least five minutes to read over your test.
- **Get enough sleep before the math test.** If you are mentally sharp, the test will be easier.

Math Tests

Taking a math test involves some different strategies:

1. Some instructors will let you write down formulas on an index card or a small crib sheet. Prepare these notes carefully, writing down the key formulas you will need for the exam.

2. If you have to memorize formulas, review them right before the test and write them on the test immediately.

3. As a first step, quickly look over the test. Find a problem you can solve easily and do this problem first.

4. Manage your time. Find out how many problems you have to solve and how much time is available for each problem. Do the problems worth the most points first. Stay on track.

5. Try this four-step process:
   a. Understand the problem.
   b. Devise a plan to solve the problem. Write down the information that is given. Think about the skills and techniques you have learned in class that can help you to solve the problem.
   c. Carry out the plan.
   d. Look back to see if your answer is reasonable.

6. If you cannot work a problem, go on to the next question. Come back later when you are more relaxed. If you spend too much time on a problem you cannot work, you will not have time for the problems that you can work.

7. Even if you think an answer is wrong, turn it in. You may get partial credit.

8. Show all the steps in your work and label your answer. On long and complex problems, it is helpful to use short sentences to explain your steps in solving the problem.

9. Estimate your answer and see if it makes sense or is logical.

10. Write your numbers as neatly as possible to avoid mistakes and to make them legible for the professor.

11. Leave space between your answers in case you need to add to them later.

12. If you have time left over at the end, recheck your answers.

Tips for Avoiding Common Math Errors[2]

- Any quantity multiplied by zero is zero
- Any quantity raised to the zero power is one
- Any fraction multiplied by its reciprocal is one
- Only like algebraic terms may be combined
- Break down to the simplest form in algebra
- In algebra, multiply and divide before adding and subtracting
- If an algebraic expression has more than one set of parentheses, get rid of the inner parenthesis first and work outward
- Any operation performed on one side of the equation must be performed on the other side

Taking Tests

True-False Tests

Many professors use objective tests such as true-false and multiple-choice because they are easy to grade. The best way to prepare for these types of tests is to study the key points in the textbook, lecture notes, and class handouts. In the textbook, take each bold-faced topic and turn it into a question. If you can answer the questions, you will be successful on objective tests.

In addition to studying for the test, it is helpful to understand some basic test-taking techniques that will help you to determine the correct answer. Many of the techniques used to determine whether a statement is true or false can also be used to eliminate wrong answers on multiple-choice tests.

To develop strategies for success on true-false exams, it is important to understand how a teacher writes the questions. For a true-false question, the teacher identifies a key point in the book or lecture notes. Then he or she has two choices. For a true statement, the key idea is often written exactly as it appears in the text or notes. For a false statement, the key idea is changed in some way to make it false.

One way to make a statement false is to add a **qualifier** to the statement. Qualifiers that are **absolute** or extreme are generally, but not always, found in false statements. **General** qualifiers are often found in true statements.

Absolute Qualifiers (false)		General Qualifiers (true)	
all	none	usually	frequently
always	never	often	sometimes
only	nobody	some	seldom
invariably	no one	many	much
best	worst	most	generally
everybody	everyone	few	ordinarily
absolutely	absolutely not	probably	a majority
certainly	certainly not	might	a few
no	every	may	apt to

Seven Tips for Success on True-False Tests

1. **Identify the key ideas in the text and class notes and review them.**

2. **Accept the question at face value.** Don't overanalyze or create wild exceptions in your mind.

3. **If you don't know the answer, assume it is true.** There are generally more true statements because we all like the truth (especially teachers) and true questions are easier to write. However, some teachers like to test students by writing all false statements.

4. **If any part of a true-false statement is false, the whole statement is false.** Carefully read each statement to determine if any part of it is false. Students sometimes assume a statement is true if most of it is true. This is not correct.

    Example: Good relaxation techniques include deep breathing, exercise, and visualizing your failure on the exam.

    This statement is false because visualizing failure can lead to test anxiety and failure.

5. **Notice any absolute or general qualifiers.** Remember that absolute qualifiers often make a statement false. General qualifiers often make a statement true.

    Example: The student who crams **always** does poorly on the exam.

    This statement is false because **some** students are successful at cramming for an exam.

    Be careful with this rule. Sometimes the answer can be absolute.

    Example: The grade point average is always calculated by dividing the number of units attempted by the grade points. (true)

6. **Notice words such as** *because, therefore, consequently,* **and** *as a result.* They may connect two things that are true but result in a false statement.

    Example: Martha does not have test anxiety. (true)

    Martha makes good grades on tests. (true)
    Martha does not have test anxiety and therefore makes good grades on tests.

    This statement is false because she also has to prepare for the exam. Not having test anxiety could even cause her to lack motivation to study and do poorly on a test.

7. **Watch for double negatives.** Two nos equal a yes. If you see two negatives in a sentence, read them as a positive. Be careful with negative prefixes such as un-, im-, mis-, dis-, il-, and ir-. For example, the phrase "not uncommon" actually means "common." Notice that the word "not" and the prefix "un-" when used together form a double negative that equals a positive.

ACTIVITY

Practice True-False Test

Answer the following questions by applying the tips for success in the previous section. Place a T or an F in the blanks.

_____ 1. If a statement has an absolute qualifier, it is always false..

_____ 2. Statements with general qualifiers are frequently true.

_____ 3. If you don't know the answer, you should guess true.

_____ 4. Studying the key points for true-false tests is not unimportant.

_____ 5. Good test-taking strategies include eating a light breakfast that includes carbohydrates and protein and drinking plenty of coffee to stay alert.

_____ 6. Ryan attended every class this semester and therefore earned an A in the class.

How did you do on the test? Answers: 1. F, 2. T, 3. T, 4. T, 5. F, 6. F

Example: **Not** being **un**prepared for the test is the best way to earn good grades.

The above sentence is confusing. To make it clearer, change both of the negatives into a positive:

Being prepared for the test is the best way to earn good grades.

Multiple-Choice Tests

College exams often include multiple-choice questions rather than true-false questions because it is more difficult to guess the correct answer. On a true-false question, the student has a 50 percent chance of guessing the correct answer, while on a multiple-choice question, the odds of guessing correctly are only 25 percent. You can think of a multiple-choice question as four true-false questions in a row. First, read the question and try to answer it without looking at the options. This will help you to focus on the question and determine the correct answer. Look at each option and determine if it is true or false. Then choose the **best** answer.

To choose the best option, it is helpful to understand how a teacher writes a multiple-choice question. Here are the steps a teacher uses to write a multiple-choice exam:

1. Find an important point in the lecture notes, text, or handouts.

2. Write a **stem**. This is an incomplete statement or a question.

3. Write the correct answer as one of the options.

4. Write three or four plausible but incorrect options that might be chosen by students who are not prepared. These incorrect options are called **decoys**. Here is an example:

   Stem: If you are anxious about taking math tests, it is helpful to:

   a. Stay up the night before the test to review thoroughly. (**decoy**)

   b. Visualize yourself doing poorly on the test so you will be motivated to study. (**decoy**)

   c. Practice math problems regularly during the semester. (**correct answer**)

   d. Do the most difficult problem first. (**decoy**)

Learn to Recognize a Decoy
A Decoy Is an Incorrect Answer

1. Decoys are all true or all false
2. Decoys contain absolute qualifiers
3. Decoys can be partly true
4. Decoys have conjunctions that make them false
5. Decoys have double negatives
6. Decoys can be foolish
7. Decoys are high or low numbers
8. Decoys can look like the correct answer
9. Decoys are often the shorter answer
10. Decoys may be grammatically incorrect
11. Decoys may be an opposite
12. Decoys may be the same as another answer

Being well prepared for the test is the most reliable way of recognizing the correct answer and the decoys. In addition, becoming familiar with the following rules for recognizing decoys can help you determine the correct answer or improve your chances of guessing the correct answer on an exam. If you can at least eliminate some of the wrong answers, you will improve your odds of selecting the correct answer.

Rules for recognizing a decoy or wrong answer:

1. **The decoys are all true or all false statements.** Read each option and determine which options are false and which statements are true. This will help you to find the correct answer.

   Example: To manage your time on a test, it is important to:
   a. Skip the directions and work as quickly as possible. (false)
   b. Skim through the test to see how much time you have for each section. (true)
   c. Do the most difficult sections first. (false)
   d. Just start writing as quickly as possible. (false)

   Read the stem carefully, because sometimes you will be asked to identify one false statement in a group of true statements.

2. **The decoy may contain an absolute qualifier.** The option with the absolute qualifier (e.g., always, only, every) is likely to be false because few things in life are absolute. There are generally exceptions to any rule.

3. **The decoy can be partly true.** However, if one part of the statement is false, the whole statement is false and an incorrect answer.

   Example: Memory techniques include visualization, organization, and telling yourself you won't remember.

   In this example, the first two techniques are true and the last part is false, which makes the whole statement false.

4. **The decoy may have a conjunction or other linking words that makes it false.** Watch for words and phrases such as *because, consequently, therefore,* and *as a result.*

5. **The decoy may have a double negative.** Having two negatives in a sentence makes it difficult to understand. Read the two negatives as a positive.

6. **The decoy may be a foolish option.** Writing multiple decoys is difficult, so test writers sometimes throw in foolish or humorous options.

   Example: In a multiple-choice test, a decoy is:
   a. a type of duck.
   b. an incorrect answer.
   c. a type of missile used in air defense.
   d. a type of fish.

   The correct answer is b. Sometimes students are tempted by the foolish answers.

7. **The decoy is often a low or high number.** If you have a multiple-choice question with numbers, and you are not sure of the correct answer, choose the number in the middle range. It is often more likely to be correct.

   Example: George Miller of Harvard University theorized that the optimum number of chunks of material that we can remember is:
   a. 1–2 (This low number is a decoy.)
   b. 5–9 (This is the correct answer.)
   c. 10–12 (This is close to the correct answer.)
   d. 20–25 (This high number is a decoy.)

   There is an exception to this rule when the number is much higher or lower than the average person thinks is possible.

8. **The decoy may look like the correct answer.** When two options look alike, one is incorrect and the other may be the correct answer. Test writers often use words that look alike as decoys.

   Example: In false statements, the qualifier is often:
   a. absolute.
   b. resolute.
   c. general.
   d. exaggerated.

   The correct answer is a. Answer b is an incorrect look-alike option.

9. **Decoys are often shorter than the correct answer.** Longer answers are more likely to be correct because they are more complete. Avoid choosing the first answer that seems to be correct. There may be a better and more complete answer.

   Example: Good test preparation involves:
   a. doing the proper review for the test.
   b. good time management.
   c. a positive attitude.
   d. having good attendance, studying and reviewing regularly, being able to deal with test anxiety, and having a positive mental attitude.

   Option d is correct because it is the most complete and thus the best answer.

10. **Decoys may be grammatically incorrect.** The correct answer will fit the grammar of the stem. A stem ending with "a" will match an answer beginning with a consonant; stems ending with "an" will match a word beginning with a vowel. The answer will agree in gender, number, and person with the stem.

    Example: In test taking, a decoy is an:
    a. incorrect answer.
    b. correct answer.
    c. false answer.
    d. true answer.

    The correct answer is A. It is also the only answer that grammatically fits with the stem. Also note that decoys can be all true or all false. In standardized tests, the grammar is usually correct. On teacher-made tests, the grammar can be a clue to the correct answer.

11. **A decoy is sometimes an opposite.** When two options are opposites, one is incorrect and the other is sometimes, but not always, correct.

    Example: A decoy is:
    a. a right answer.
    b. a wrong answer.
    c. a general qualifier.
    d. a true statement.

    The two opposites are answers a and b. The correct answer is b.

12. **A decoy may be the same as another answer.** If two answers say the same thing in different ways, they are both decoys and incorrect.

    Example: A true statement is likely to have this type of qualifier:
    a. extreme
    b. absolute

c. general

d. factual

Notice that answers a and b are the same and are incorrect. The correct answer is c.

Example: How much does a gallon of water weigh?

a. 8.34 pounds

b. 5.5 pounds

c. 5 pounds 8 ounces

d. 20 pounds

B and c are the same and are therefore incorrect answers. Answer d is a high number. The correct answer is a.

If you are unable to identify any decoys, these suggestions may be helpful:

- Mark the question and come back to it later. You may find the answer elsewhere on the test, or some words that help you remember the answer. After answering some easier questions, you may be able to relax and remember the answer.
- Trust your intuition and choose something that sounds familiar.
- Do not change your first answer unless you have misread the question or are sure that the answer is incorrect. Sometimes students overanalyze a question and then choose the wrong answer.
- The option "All of the above" is often correct because it is easier to write true statements rather than false ones. Options like A and B, B and D, or other combinations are also likely to be correct for the same reason.
- If you have no idea about the correct answer, guess option B or C. Most correct answers are in the middle.

Practice Multiple-Choice Test

Circle the letters of the correct answers. Then check your answers using the key at the end of this section.

1. The correct answer in a multiple-choice question is likely to be
   a. the shortest answer.
   b. the longest and most complete answer.
   c. the answer with an absolute qualifier.
   d. the answer that has some truth in it.

2. When guessing on a question involving numbers, it is generally best to
   a. choose the highest number.
   b. choose the lowest number.
   c. choose the mid-range number.
   d. always choose the first option.

3. If you have test anxiety, what questions should you answer first on the test?
   a. The most difficult questions
   b. The easiest questions
   c. The questions at the beginning
   d. The questions worth the least number of points

4. When taking a multiple-choice test, you should
   a. pick the first choice that is true.
   b. read all the choices and select the best one.
   c. pick the first choice that is false.
   d. choose the extreme answer.

5. A good method for guessing is to
   a. identify which choices are true and false.
   b. use the process of elimination.
   c. notice absolute qualifiers and conjunctions.
   d. all of the above.

6. The key to success when taking a multiple-choice test is
   a. cheating.
   b. good preparation.
   c. knowing how to guess.
   d. being able to recognize a qualifier.

7. The following rule about decoys is correct:
   a. A decoy is always absolute.
   b. A decoy can be partly true.
   c. Every decoy has a qualifier.
   d. Decoys are invariably false statements.

8. An example of an absolute qualifier is
   a. generally.
   b. never.
   c. sometimes.
   d. frequently.

9. Statements with absolute qualifiers are generally
   a. true.
   b. false.
   c. irrelevant.
   d. confusing.

10. If two multiple-choice options are the same or very similar, they are most likely
   a. a decoy and a correct answer.
   b. a correct answer.
   c. a true answer.
   d. a mistake on the test.

11. It is generally not a good idea to change your answer unless
   a. you are very anxious about the test.
   b. you do not have good intuition.
   c. you notice that your intelligent friend has a different answer.
   d. you have misread the question and you are sure that the answer is incorrect.

How did you do on the quiz? Check your answers: 1. b, 2. c, 3. b, 4. b, 5. d, 6. b, 7. b (Notice the absolute qualifiers in the decoys), 8. b, 9. b (Notice the opposites), 10. a (Notice the grammar), 11. d

Matching Tests

A matching test involves two lists of facts or definitions that must be matched together. Here are some tips to help you successfully complete a matching exam:

1. Read through both lists to discover the pattern or relationship between the lists. The lists might give words and definitions, people and accomplishments, or other paired facts.

2. Count the items on the list of answers to see if there is only one match for each item or if there are some extra answer choices.

3. Start with one list and match the items that you know. In this way, you have a better chance of guessing on the items that you do not know.

4. If you have difficulty with some of the items, leave them blank and return later. You may find the answers or clues on the rest of the test.

ACTIVITY

Practice Matching Test

Match the items in the first column with the items in the second column. Write the letter of the matching item in the blank at the left.

_____ 1. Meaningful organization

_____ 2. Visualization

_____ 3. Recitation

_____ 4. Develop an interest

_____ 5. See the big picture

_____ 6. Intend to remember

_____ 7. Distribute the practice

_____ 8. Create a basic background

A. Learn small amounts and review frequently.

B. The more you know, the easier it is to remember.

C. Tell yourself you will remember.

D. Pretend you like it.

E. Make a mental picture.

F. Rehearse and review.

G. Focus on the main points first.

H. Personal organization.

Answers: 1. H,   2. E,   3. F,   4. D,   5. G,   6. C,   7. A,   8. B

Sentence-Completion or Fill-in-the-Blank Tests

Fill-in-the-blank and sentence-completion tests are more difficult than true-false or multiple-choice tests because they require the **recall** of specific information rather than the **recognition** of the correct answer. To prepare for this type of test, focus on facts such as definitions, names, dates, and places. Using flash cards to prepare can be helpful. For example, to memorize names, place each name on one side of a card and some identifying words on the other side. Practice looking at the names on one side of the card and then recalling the identifying words on the other side of the card. Then turn the cards over and look at the identifying words to recall the names.

Sometimes the test has clues that will help you to fill in the blank. Clues can include the length of the blanks and the number of blanks. Find an answer that makes sense in the sentence and matches the grammar of the sentence. If you cannot think of an answer, write a general description and you may get partial credit. Look for clues on the rest of the test that may trigger your recall.

ACTIVITY

Practice Fill-in-the-Blank Test

Complete each sentence with the appropriate word or words.

1. Fill-in-the-blank tests are more difficult because they depend on the _____ of specific information.

2. On a true-false test, a statement is likely to be false if it contains an _____ qualifier.

3. Test review tools include _____, _____, and _____.

4. When studying for tests, visualize your _____.

Answers: 1. recall, 2. absolute, 3. flash cards, summary sheets, and mind maps (also study groups and highlighters), 4. success

Essay Tests

Many professors choose essay questions because they are the best way to show what you have learned in the class. Essay questions can be challenging because you not only have to know the material, but must be able to organize it and use good writing techniques in your answer.

Essay questions contain key words that will guide you in writing your answer. One of the keys to success in writing answers to essay questions is to note these key words and then structure your essay accordingly. As you read through an essay question, look for these words:

Analyze	Break into separate parts and discuss, examine, or interpret each part.
Argue	State an opinion and give reasons for the opinion.
Comment	Give your opinion.
Compare	Identify two or more ideas and identify similarities and differences.
Contrast	Show how the components are the same or different.
Criticize	Give your opinion and make judgments.
Defend	State reasons.
Define	Give the meaning of the word or concept as used within the course of study.
Describe	Give a detailed account or provide information.
Demonstrate	Provide evidence.
Diagram	Make a drawing, chart, graph, sketch, or plan.
Differentiate	Tell how the ideas are the same and how they are different.
Describe	Make a picture with words. List the characteristics, qualities, and parts.
Discuss	Describe the pros and cons of the issues. Compare and contrast.
Enumerate	Make a list of ideas, events, qualities, reasons, and so on.
Explain	Make an idea clear. Show how and why.
Evaluate	Describe it and give your opinion about something.
Illustrate	Give concrete examples and explain them. Draw a diagram.
Interpret	Say what something means. Describe and then evaluate.
Justify	Prove a point. Give the reasons why.
Outline	Describe the main ideas.
Prove	Support with facts. Give evidence or reasons.
Relate	Show the connections between ideas or events.
State	Explain precisely. Provide the main points.
Summarize	Give a brief, condensed account. Draw a conclusion.
Trace	Show the order of events.

Here are some tips on writing essays:

1. To prepare for an essay test, use a mind map or summary sheet to summarize the main ideas. Organize the material in the form of an outline or mental pictures that you can use in writing.

2. The first step in writing an essay is to quickly survey the test and read the directions carefully. Many times you are offered a choice of which and how many questions to answer.

3. Manage your time. Note how many questions need to be answered and how many points each question is worth. For example, if you have three questions to answer in one hour, you will have less than 20 minutes for each question. Save some time to check over your work.

If the questions are worth different numbers of points, divide up your time proportionately. In the above example with three questions, if one question is worth 50 points and the other two are worth 25 points, spend half the time on the 50-point question (less than 30 minutes) and divide the remaining time between the 25-point questions (less than 15 minutes each).

4. If you are anxious about the test, start with an easy question in order to relax and build your confidence. If you are confident in your test-taking abilities, start with the question that is worth the most points.

5. Get organized. Write a brief outline in the margin of your test paper. Do not write your outline on a separate sheet of paper because you may be accused of using cheat notes.

6. In the first sentence of your essay, rephrase the question and provide a direct answer. Rephrasing the question keeps you on track and a direct answer becomes the thesis statement or main idea of the essay.

   Example: (Question:) Describe a system for reading a college textbook.
   (Answer:) A system for reading a college textbook is Survey, Question, Read, Review, Recite, and Reflect (SQ4R). (Then you would go on to expand on each part of the topic.)

7. Use the principles of good composition. Start with a thesis statement or main idea. Provide supporting ideas and examples to support your thesis. Provide a brief summary at the end.

8. Write your answer clearly and neatly so it is easy to grade. Grading an essay involves an element of subjectivity. If your paper looks neat and is easy to read, the professor is likely to read your essay with a positive attitude. If your paper is difficult to read, the professor will probably read your paper with a negative attitude.

9. Determine the length of your essay by the number of points it is worth. For example, a five-point essay might be a paragraph with five key points. A 25-point essay would probably be a five-paragraph essay with at least 25 key points.

10. Save some time at the end to read over your essays. Make corrections, make sure your answers make sense, and add any key information you may have forgotten to include.

What to Do When Your Test Is Returned

When your test is returned, use it as feedback for future test preparation in the course. Look at your errors and try to determine how to prevent these errors in the future.

- Did you study correctly?
- Did you study the proper materials?
- Did you use the proper test-taking techniques?
- Was the test more difficult than you expected?
- Did you run out of time to take the test?
- Was the test focused on details and facts or on general ideas and principles?
- Did you have problems with test anxiety?

Analyzing your test performance can help you to do better in the future.

Of course it is a good idea to be well prepared for exams, but there are times when you will have to figure out the answer or even make a guess on the correct answer. Review the section on "Taking Tests" and list five ideas for guessing that you can try in the future.

KEYS TO SUCCESS   Be Prepared

The key idea in this chapter is to be prepared. Good preparation is essential for success in test taking as well as in many other areas of life. Being successful begins with having a vision of the future and then taking steps to achieve your dream.

Sometimes people think of success in terms of good luck. Thomas Jefferson said, "I'm a great

> "The secret of getting ahead is getting started. The secret of getting started is breaking your complex, overwhelming tasks into small manageable tasks, and then starting on the first one."
>
> Mark Twain

believer in luck, and I find the harder I work, the more I have of it." Don't depend on good luck. Work to create your success.

You can reach your dream of attaining a college education through preparation and hard work. Use the ideas in this chapter to ensure your success. Remember that preparation begins on the first day of class: it does not begin when the professor announces a test. On the first day of class, the professor provides an overview, or outline, of what you will learn. Attend every class. The main points covered in the class will be on the test. Read your assignments a little at a time starting from the first day. If you distribute your practice, you will find it easier to learn and to remember.

When it comes time to review for the test, you will already know what to expect on the test, and

you will have learned the material by attending the lectures and reading your text. Reviewing for the test is just review; it is not original learning. It is a chance to strengthen what you have learned so that you can relax and do your best on the test. Review is one of the final steps in learning. With review, you will gain a sense of confidence and satisfaction in your studies.

If you are not prepared, you will need to cram for the test and you may not be as successful on the test as you could be. If you are not successful, you may get the mistaken idea that you cannot be successful in college. Cramming for the test produces stress, since you will need to learn a great deal of information in a short time. Stress can interfere with memory and cause you to freeze up on exams. It is also difficult to remember if you have to cram. The memory works best if you do a small amount of learning regularly over a period of time. Cramming is hard work and no fun. The worst problem with cramming is that it causes you to dislike education. It is difficult to continue to do something that you have learned to dislike.

Good preparation is the key to success in many areas of life. Whether you are taking a college course, playing a basketball game, going on vacation, planning a wedding, or building a house, good preparation will help to guarantee your success. Begin with your vision of the future and boldly take the first steps. The best preparation for the future is the good use of your time today.

> "The future starts today, not tomorrow."
>
> Pope John Paul II

Test Taking

Go to http://www.collegesuccess1.com/JournalEntries.htm for Word files of the
Journal Entries

Success over the Internet

Visit the *College Success Website* at http://www.collegesuccess1.com/

The *College Success Website* is continually updated with new topics and links to
the material presented in this chapter. Topics include:

- Tips for taking tests
- Dealing with math anxiety
- How to study for math tests
- How to take math tests
- How to guess on a test
- Test anxiety
- Multiple-choice exams
- Dealing with difficult questions

Contact your instructor if you have any problems accessing the *College Success
Website*.

Notes

1. G. A. Miller, "The Magical Number Seven, Plus or Minus Two: Some Limits on Our
    Capacity for Processing Information," *Psychological Review* 63 (March 1956): 81–97.

2. From Aguilar et al., *The Community College: A New Beginning,* 2nd ed. (Dubuque, IA:
    Kendall Hunt, 1998).

Test-Taking Checklist

Name _____ Date _____

Place checkmarks next to the test-taking skills you have now.

_____ Attend every class (or almost every class)

_____ Have a copy of the course syllabus with test dates

_____ Start test preparation early and study a little at a time

_____ Do not generally cram for exams

_____ Have a place to study (not the kitchen, TV room, or bedroom)

_____ Participate in a study group

_____ Review immediately after learning something

_____ Review previous notes and reading assignments on a regular basis

_____ Schedule a major review before the exam

_____ Know how to predict the test questions

_____ Get enough rest before a test

_____ Visualize my success on the exam

_____ Complete my math homework on a regular basis

_____ Eat a light but nutritious meal before the exam

_____ Maintain a regular exercise program

_____ Read all my textbook assignments before the exam

_____ Review my classroom notes before the exam

_____ Skim through the test and read all directions carefully before starting the test

_____ Answer the easy questions first and return later to answer the difficult questions

_____ Check over my test before handing it in

_____ Write an outline before beginning my essay answer

_____ Manage my study time to adequately prepare for the test

_____ Review my returned tests to improve future test preparation

_____ Write the test neatly and make sure my writing is legible

_____ Avoid test anxiety by being well prepared and practicing relaxation techniques

_____ Prepare adequately for tests

Analyze Your Test-Taking Skills

Name _____ Date _____

Use the test-taking checklist on the previous page to answer the following questions.

1. My strengths in test-taking skills are

2. Some areas I need to improve are

3. Write three intention statements about improving your test-taking skills.

Name _____ Date _____

Your professor may ask you to do this as a classroom exercise. Review the section in the text on how to write a short essay. Answer the following short essay question worth five points.

1. Explain how you can improve your chances of success when preparing for exams. Include the physical, mental, and emotional preparation necessary for success.

2. Rate your essay. Did you do the following?

   _____ I read the directions and the essay question thoroughly before I began.

   _____ I organized my thoughts or made a brief outline before starting.

   _____ The first sentence was a direct answer and rephrased the question.

   _____ My thesis statement or main idea was clear.

   _____ The remaining sentences in the essay supported my main idea.

   _____ Since this is a five-point essay, I made at least five key points in the essay.

   _____ My answer was written clearly and neatly. My handwriting was legible.

   _____ I spelled the words correctly and used good grammar.

   _____ I read over my essay to make sure it made sense.

3. For essay exams, I need to work on

How Well Do You Follow Directions?

Name _____   Date _____

1. Read all of the directions before you do anything.

2. Put your name at the top of this page.

3. In the bottom right-hand corner, write the name of this class.

4. In the bottom left-hand corner, write the name of your instructor.

5. Put a box around the class name.

6. Put a circle around your instructor's name.

7. Write the name of your college at the bottom of this page.

8. You have now completed the exercise, so let the class know you are finished by calling out "Done."

9. Return to the beginning and only do number one.

From Aguilar et al., *The Community College: A New Beginning*, 2nd ed. (Dubuque, IA: Kendall Hunt, 1998).

PART III

Lifelong Success

CHAPTER 8

Communication and Relationships

Learning Objectives

Read to answer these key questions:

- What is my personal communication style?

- What are some problems in communication?

- What are some techniques for being a good listener?

- What is the best way to communicate in a crisis situation?

- How does language affect behavior?

- What are some conflict management techniques?

- What are the qualities of a good friendship?

- How can I get along with my roommate?

- How can I improve my relationships?

- How is failure an opportunity for learning?

Kelly Morrissey

Hometown: Chicago, IL

Major: Social Work

Minor: Addiction Studies, Criminal Justice, and Interdisciplinary Health

Campus Involvements: Emerging Leaders, Campus Activities Board, Western Student Association Philanthropy Chair and Senator, Homecoming and Bronco Bash volunteer, Colleges Against Cancer Executive Board, Alternative Spring Break participant and site leader, Fall Into the Streets and Spring Into the Streets Site Leader, Fall Welcome Ambassador, First-Year Seminar Instructor, SALP programs, Ackley/Shilling Hall Council, Henry Hall Office Manager, and Summer Conference Worker

College is one of the greatest adventures you are going to take on your life journey. You can read all the books in the world, study for hours, and get straight As, but I believe that some of the greatest things you can learn from college is how to successfully communicate with others and build healthy long lasting relationships with faculty, staff, peers, and your professors. A majority of what you learn in college comes from the out of class experiences through getting involved, traveling, going to lectures, working, internships, conversations, debates, and finding your passions. Learning to communicate effectively will take you very far in life and allow you to achieve great success. I believe communication is the key to life. There are so many opportunities where you can meet and get to know people. You can strike up a conversation in the dining hall, the lecture hall, by joining an RSO (Registered Student Organization), or outside at the bus stop. The possibilities are endless. Through communication you can build relationships with all of the people around you. Building positive relationships brings great happiness and meaning to your life. You need to have people around to pick you up when you are down, cheer you on when you are doing great things, motivate you when you need the extra push, cry with you when things get tough, most importantly share thousands of laughs with you and make long lasting memories. It doesn't matter if you are shy or the most outgoing person in the room, this applies to all students. I have had so much fun during my time here at WMU, built so many great relationships with people all over campus, and have learned so many life lessons. The most important thing is to have fun, never stop looking for opportunities to grow, and don't sweat the small stuff. We are all in the same boat so don't ever feel that no one can relate to you! Good Luck and Go Broncos!!!

"Communication—the human connection—is the key to personal and career success."

Paul J. Meyer

"To effectively communicate, we must realize that we are all different in the way we perceive the world and use this understanding as a guide to our communication with others."

Anthony Robbins

When you look back on your college experience, what you are most likely to remember and value are the personal relationships established while in college. These relationships can be a source of great pleasure or disappointment. What makes a good relationship? The answer to this question is complex and different for each individual. Good relationships begin with an understanding of personality differences and the components of effective communication. These skills can be useful in establishing satisfying friendships, happy marriages, effective parenting skills, and good relationships in the workplace.

Understanding Your Personal Communication Style

Becoming familiar with personality types can help you better understand yourself and others. Personality has a major impact on our style of communication. While we can make some generalizations about personality types, keep in mind that each individual is unique and may be a combination of the various types. For example, some people are a combination of introvert and extravert. The following descriptions will help you begin thinking about your own communication style and understanding others who are different. Remember that each personality type has positive and negative aspects. Knowledge of these differences can help individuals accentuate the positives and keep the negatives in perspective.

Introvert and Extravert Types

Extraverts are very social types who easily start conversations with strangers as well as friends. They know a lot of people and have many friends. They like going to parties and other social events and are energized by talking to people. They like to talk on the telephone and can read while watching TV, listening to music, or carrying on a conversation with someone else. They find talking easy and sometimes dominate the conversation. They find it more difficult to listen. They tend to talk first and think later, and sometimes regret that they have put their foot in their mouths.

In personal relationships, extraverts are fun to know and get along well with others. It is easy for them to make a date and do the talking. When extraverts are in conflict situations, they just talk louder and faster. They believe that the argument can be won if they can say just one more thing or provide more explanation. If there is a problem, extraverts want to talk about it right away. If they cannot talk about it, they become very frustrated.

The introvert is the opposite of the extravert. Introverts want to rehearse what they are going to say before they say it. They need quiet for concentration and enjoy peace and quiet. They have great powers of concentration and can focus their attention on projects for a long period of time. Because they tend to be quieter than extraverts, they are perceived as great listeners. Because they need time to think before talking, they often find it difficult to add their ideas to a conversation, especially when talking with extraverts. They often wish they could participate more in conversations. Because they are reserved and reflective, people often label the introvert as shy. In American society, introverts are the minority. There are three extraverts to every introvert. For this reason, the introvert is often pressured to act like an extravert. This can cause the introvert a great deal of anxiety.

The introvert often finds it difficult to start conversations or invite someone on a date. Introverts are often attracted to extraverts because they can relax and let the extravert do the talking. In conflict situations, the introverts are at a disadvantage. They will often withdraw from conflict because they need time to think about the situation and go over in their minds what to say. Introverts become stressed if they are faced with a conflict without advance notice.

Introverts and extraverts can improve their relationship by understanding each other and respecting their differences. The extravert can improve communication with the introvert by pausing to let the introvert have time to speak. He or she has to make a conscious effort to avoid monopolizing the conversation. Introverts can improve communication by making an effort to communicate. Introverts sometimes act like extraverts in social situations. Since this takes effort, they may need quiet time to relax and recharge after social events.

Imagine that two roommates are opposite types, extravert and introvert. The extravert enjoys talking and making noises. She will have guests, take telephone calls, and play music in the background while studying. These actions will cause the introvert to withdraw and leave the room to find a quiet place to study. These two roommates need to talk about their differences and do some compromising to get along with one another.

Sensing and Intuitive Types

Sensing types collect information through the senses. Their motto could be, "Seeing is believing." They are practical and realistic. They like communication to be exact and sequential. They want details and facts. They ask specific questions and want concrete answers. About 70 percent of the population of the United States is the sensing type.

Communication Styles

- Introvert
- Extravert
- Sensing
- Intuitive
- Feeling
- Thinking
- Judging
- Perceptive

In a dating situation, the sensing type focuses on actual experience. A sensor will describe the date in terms of what his or her companion looked like, how the food tasted, how the music sounded, and the feelings involved. During the date, sensors may talk about concrete events such as people they have known, experiences they have had, and places they have visited. Sensing types are generally on time for the date and get irritated if the other person is late. In conflict situations, sensing types argue the facts. They often don't see the big issues because they are concentrating on the accuracy of the facts.

Intuitive types gather information from the senses and immediately look for possibilities, meanings, and relationships between ideas. They are often ingenious and creative. Sensing types often describe intuitives as dreamers who have their heads in the clouds. They represent about 30 percent of the population.

In social situations such as dating, the intuitive person starts to fantasize and imagine what it is going to be like before it begins. The fantasies are often more exciting than the actual date. Conversations follow many different and creative trains of thought. Intuitive types are more likely to talk about dreams, visions, beliefs, and creative ideas, skipping from one topic to another. Sensing types sometimes have difficulty following the conversation. Intuitive types are less worried about being exactly on time. They believe that time is flexible and may not be on time for the date, much to the annoyance of sensing types. In conflict situations, intuitive types like to make broad generalizations. When sensing types remind them of the facts, they may accuse them of nitpicking.

Having both sensing and intuitive types in a relationship or business environment has many advantages, as long as these types can understand and appreciate one another. Sensing types need intuitive types to bring up new possibilities, deal with changes, and understand different perspectives. Intuitive types need sensing types to deal with facts and details.

Feeling and Thinking Types

Feeling types prefer to make decisions based on what they feel to be right or wrong based on their subjective values. They prefer harmony and are often described as tenderhearted. Other people's feelings are an important consideration in any decision they make. The majority of women (60 percent) are feeling types. In a conflict situation, feeling types take things personally. They prefer to avoid disagreements and will give in to reestablish a harmonious relationship.

Thinking types are logical, detached, analytical, and objective and make decisions based on these characteristics. They like justice and clarity. The majority of men (60 percent) are thinking types. In a conflict situation, thinking types use logical arguments. They often get frustrated with feeling types and think they are too emotional.

In a dating situation, the differences between feelers and thinkers can cause much misunderstanding and conflict. Thinking types strive to understand love and intimacy. Feeling types like to experience emotions. Thinking types process and analyze their feelings. For the thinker, love is to be analyzed. For the feeling types, love just happens.

Remember that while most women are feeling types and most men are thinking types, there are still 40 percent of women who are thinking types and 40 percent of men who are feeling types. Unfortunately, because of gender stereotyping, feeling-type men are often seen as less masculine and thinking-type women are seen as less feminine.

There is much to gain from understanding and appreciating the differences between feeling and thinking types. Feeling types need thinking types to analyze, organize, follow policy, and weigh the evidence. Thinking types need feeling types to understand how others feel and establish harmony in relationships or in a business environment.

Judging and Perceptive Types

Judging types prefer their environment to be structured, scheduled, orderly, planned, and controlled. Judging types even plan and organize their recreation time. They need events to be planned and organized in order to relax. They are quick to make decisions, and once the decisions are made, they find it difficult to change them. In the social scene, judging types schedule and plan the dates. When traveling, judging types carefully pack their suitcases using a list of essential items to make sure that nothing is forgotten. In conflict situations, judging types know that they are right. They tend to see issues in terms of right and wrong, good and bad, or black and white. It is difficult to negotiate with a judging type.

Perceptive types are very much the opposite of the judging types. They prefer the environment to be flexible and spontaneous. Perceptive types find it difficult to make a decision and stick to it because it limits their flexibility. Perceptive types like to collect information and keep the options open. After all, something better might come along and they do not want to be restricted by a plan or schedule. In a social situation, these types are playful and easygoing. They provide the fun and find it easy to relax. They often feel controlled by judging types. In a conflict situation, this type sees many options to resolve the situation. They have trouble resolving conflicts because they keep finding many possible solutions.

The preference for judging or perceiving has the most potential for conflict between individuals. Judging types can drive perceptive types crazy with their need for schedules, planning, and organization. Perceptive types drive the judging types crazy with their spontaneous and easygoing nature. In spite of these differences, judging and perceptive types are often attracted to one another. Judging types need perceptive types to encourage them to relax and have fun. Perceptive types need judging types to help them be more organized and productive. These two types need understanding and appreciation of each other to have a good relationship. They also need excellent communication skills.

It is often asked whether two people should consider personality type in establishing relationships or choosing a marriage partner. There are two theories on this. One theory is that opposites attract. If two people have opposite personality types, they will have the potential for using the strengths of both types. For example, if one marriage partner is a judging type, this person can manage the finances and keep the family organized. The perceptive type can provide the fun and help the other to relax and enjoy life. A disadvantage is that opposite types have great potential for conflict. The conflict can be resolved by understanding the other type and appreciating different strengths the opposite type brings to the relationship. The relationship cannot work if one person tries to change the other. Good communication is essential in maintaining the relationship.

Another theory is that like types attract. If you have a relationship with another person of the same type, your basic preferences are similar. However, even matching types will be different depending on the strength of each preference. Communication is easier when two people have similar views of the world. One disadvantage is that the relationship can become predictable and eventually uninteresting.

Journal Entry #1

Consider how the following terms describe your communication style: extravert, introvert, sensing, intuitive, feeling, thinking, judging, perceptive. What is your personal communication style?

Communication for Success

To be an effective communicator, it is important to be a good listener and speaker. Practice the techniques of good listening and use language that helps you enhance your success and establish good relationships.

"The biggest problem in communication is the illusion that it has taken place."

George Bernard Shaw

Communication Style

Test what you have learned by selecting the correct answers to the following questions.

1. Extraverts can help introverts improve communication by

    a. clearly explaining their point of view.
    b. pausing to give the introvert time to think and respond.
    c. talking louder and faster.

2. In a dating situation, sensing types are likely to talk about

    a. concrete events such as the weather or personal experiences.
    b. dreams and visions.
    c. creative ideas.

3. In a conflict situation, feeling types

    a. use logic to analyze the situation.
    b. engage in debate based on logical arguments.
    c. take things personally.

4. Perceptive types

    a. find it difficult to make a decision and stick to it.
    b. tend to decide quickly in order to finish the project.
    c. find it easy to be on time and meet deadlines.

5. In choosing a marriage partner it is best to

    a. choose a person with the same personality.
    b. choose a person with the opposite personality.
    c. be aware of each other's personality type to appreciate each other.

How did you do on the quiz? Check your answers: 1. b, 2. a, 3. c, 4. a, 5. c

Problems in Communication

Effective communication involves a loop in which a sender sends a message and a receiver receives the message. Communications are disrupted when:

- The receiver doesn't receive the message.
- The receiver hears the wrong message.
- The receiver doesn't care about the message.
- The receiver is more interested in talking than listening.
- The receiver only hears part of the message.
- The receiver only hears what she or he wants to hear.
- The receiver feels threatened by the sender.
- The sender didn't send the message correctly.
- The sender left out part of the message.
- The sender talks so much that nobody listens.
- The sender is not someone you want to hear.
- The sender is annoying.
- The sender was upset and did not mean to send the message.
- The sender assumes that you should know the message already.

Factors That Interfere with Good Listening

- Message overload
- Worries and anxiety
- Rapid thought
- Tired, overloaded, or distracted
- Noise and hearing problems
- Faulty assumptions

There is a joke circulating on the Internet:

A man is driving up a steep, narrow mountain road. A woman is driving down the same road. As they pass each other, the woman leans out the window and yells, "Pig!" The man replies by calling the woman a name. They each continue on their way. As the man rounds the next corner, he crashes into a pig in the middle of the road. If only people would listen!

As you can see, there are many ways to disrupt communication. Just because a message was sent does not mean that it was received. The first step in communication is to be a good listener. Many factors interfere with good listening. Do you recognize some of these reasons for not listening?

- **Message overload.** There is so much communication going on today that it is difficult to keep up with it all. There are stacks of paper, multiple email messages, text messages, television, radio, and people who want to talk to you. Introverts may find this overwhelming, while extraverts may find it exciting. Both find it challenging to keep up with all these communications and to focus on the messages.

- **Worries and anxiety.** It is difficult to listen to other people when you are preoccupied with your own thoughts. You may be thinking about an upcoming test or paper that is due or worried about a personal relationship. While others are talking, you are thinking about something else of more immediate concern to yourself.

- **Rapid thought.** People think faster than they speak. We are capable of understanding speech at about 600 words per minute, but most people talk at 100 to 150 words per minute.[1] People use the spare time to become distracted. They daydream, think about what they will do next, or think about their reply.

- **Listening is hard work.** It takes effort to listen. It requires paying attention and striving to understand. People can't listen effectively if they are tired, overloaded, or distracted.

- **Noise and hearing problems.** Our world is becoming noisier. As people get older, many suffer from hearing loss. Younger persons are suffering hearing loss from listening to loud music. It is more difficult to get your message across when people can't hear everything you are saying.

- **Faulty assumptions.** People often make faulty assumptions. They may assume that other people also know the information, and therefore they do not communicate well. People listening may assume that they know the information already or that the information is easy, so it is not necessary for them to pay attention. Or they may assume the material is too difficult to understand and block it out.

- **Talking too much.** Since listening involves effort, people consider what they have to gain before they invest the effort in listening. They might think that there is more to gain in speaking than in listening. The speaker often feels that he or she has control. You might feel that in speaking you gain the attention or admiration of others. If you are speaking or telling a joke and everyone is listening, you feel important. Also, through speaking people release their frustration and think about their problems. They need to stop speaking in order to listen.

How to Be a Good Listener

Being a good listener takes practice and effort. Here are some tips on becoming a good listener:

- **Talk less.** It does no good to talk if no one is listening, if no one understands your message, or if your message is irrelevant to the situation. To have a better chance of communicating your message, it is important first to listen to gain an understanding of the other person and then to speak. In marriage counseling, a common technique is to have one person talk and express his or her point of view. Before the other person

To Be a Good Listener

- Talk less
- Minimize distractions
- Don't judge too soon
- Look for main point
- Ask questions
- Feed back meaning
- Be careful with advice

"We have two ears and one mouth, so we should listen twice as much as we speak."

Epictetus

"Life is an echo: what you send out comes back."

Chinese Proverb

can talk, he or she has to accurately summarize what the previous person said. Too often people do not really listen; instead they are composing their own messages in their heads. It is a Native American custom that when members of the group assemble to talk about an important issue, a talking stick is used. Persons can only talk when they have the talking stick. When the person holding the talking stick is finished, it is passed to the next person who wants to talk. In this way, only one person can talk at a time, and the others listen.

- **Minimize distractions.** For important conversations, turn off the TV or the music. Find quiet time to focus on the communication. Manage your internal distractions as well. Focus your attention on listening first and then speaking.

- **Don't judge too soon.** Try to understand first and then evaluate. If you judge too soon, you may not have the correct information and might make a mistake. People are especially vulnerable to this problem when their ideas do not agree with those of the speaker. They focus on defending their position without really listening to the other point of view.

- **Look for the main point.** You may become distracted or impatient with people who talk too much. Try to be patient and look for the main points. In a lecture, write these points down.

- **Ask questions.** You will need to ask questions to make sure that you understand. Each person looks at the world in a different way. The picture in my mind will not match the picture in your mind. We will have a better idea of each other's pictures if we ask for more information.

- **Feed back meaning.** This communication technique involves restating the speaker's ideas in your own words to check the meaning. This is important because speakers often:

  - say one thing and mean something else.
  - say something but don't mean it, especially if emotions are involved.
  - speak in a way that causes confusion.

Feeding back meaning has two important benefits. It helps speakers to clarify their thoughts and it helps listeners make sure that they have received the correct message. Here are several ways to feed back meaning:

1. **Restate what has been said.** Sometimes this is called parroting. It is useful for clarifying information, but sometimes it annoys people if you use it too much.
   Statement: Turn right at the light.
   Feedback: Okay. So you want me to turn right at the light?

2. **Ask for clarification.**
   Statement: Take the next exit on the freeway.
   Feedback: Do you mean this exit coming up now or the next one?
   Statement: Pig! (referring to the joke about the man and woman on the mountain road)
   Feedback: What do you mean by "pig"?
   Statement: Be careful. There is a pig in the road ahead.

3. **Reword the message to check your understanding.** First, restate what you have heard and then ask for clarification. This is called active listening.
   Statement: Turn in the draft of your paper next week.
   Feedback: You want the draft next week. Does that include the outline, the draft of the entire paper, and the bibliography? Should it be typed, or is handwritten okay?

Statement: Don't worry about your grade on this quiz.

Feedback: You said not to worry about my grade on this quiz. Does that mean that the grade won't count or that I can make up the quiz?

Statement: I need this project completed by Friday.

Feedback: So this project needs to be done by Friday. What parts do you want included and how would you like me to do it?

4. **Listen for feelings.** Feelings get in the way of clear thinking. A person may say one thing and mean something else.

    Statement: Just forget about it!

    Feedback: I'm confused. You ask me to forget about it, but you sound angry.

5. **Use your own words to restate what the speaker has said.** In this way, you help the speaker to clarify his or her thoughts and hopefully to come up with some solutions.

    Statement: I wish I didn't have to work so much. I'm getting behind in school, but I have bills to pay. I have to work.

    Feedback: You seem to be caught in a bind between school and work.

    Statement: That's right. I just can't keep working so much. Maybe I should go check out financial aid and scholarships.

- **Be careful about giving advice.** Whenever possible, listen closely and be an active listener. This helps the person speaking to you to clarify his or her thoughts and think about alternatives. When you listen, it is tempting to offer advice because you may have had similar experiences. You can share your experiences and offer suggestions, but beware of giving advice for these reasons:

    - If you give advice and it turns out badly, you may be blamed.

    - If you give advice and it turns out right, the person may become dependent on you.

    - People are unique individuals with unique life situations. Something that works for one person may not work for another person at all.

Journal Entry #2

Review the section on "Communication for Success." What are three ways to improve your communication and listening skills?

I can improve my communication and listening skills by . . . .

Helpful Communication in a Crisis Situation

Most people have been in a situation where their friends or family are in distress and need immediate help. If you become aware of a dangerous or critical situation, seek professional help. Go to your college counseling center, a community service organization, your doctor, or a religious leader for help. Here are some general ideas for being a helpful listener:

- Let the person talk. Talking helps to clarify thinking.
- Paraphrase or feed back meaning.
- Avoid being critical. Comments such as "You asked for it" or "I told you so" do not help. They just make the person angry.

- Help the person analyze the situation and come up with alternatives for solving the problem.
- Share your experiences but resist giving advice.
- Ask questions to clarify the situation.
- Offer to be supportive. Say, "I'm here if you need me" or "I care about you."
- Let people express their feelings. It is not helpful to say, "Don't feel sad," for example. A person may need to feel sad and deal with the situation. The emotion can be a motivation for change.
- Don't minimize the situation. Saying, "It's only a grade (job, promotion)," minimizes the situation. It might not be important to the listener, but it is causing pain for the speaker. Give him or her time to gain perspective on the problem.
- Replace pity with understanding. It is not helpful to say, "You poor thing."

The following anonymous poem summarizes some ideas on how to be a helpful listener.

When I ask you to listen to me
    and you give me advice
    you have not done what I asked.

When I ask you to listen to me
    and you begin to tell me why I shouldn't feel that way,
    you are trampling on my feelings.

When I ask you to listen to me
    and you feel you have to do something to solve my problem,
    you have failed me, strange as that may seem.

Listen! All I asked was that you listen.
    Not talk or do—just hear me.

Advice is cheap: 50 cents will get you both Dear Abby and
    Billy Graham in the same newspaper.

And I can do for myself; I'm not helpless.
    Maybe discouraged and faltering, but not helpless.

When you do something for me that I can and need to do
    for myself, you contribute to my fear and weakness.

But, when you accept as a simple fact that I do feel what I feel,
    no matter how irrational, then I can quit trying to convince
    you and can get about the business of understanding what's
    behind this irrational feeling.
    And when that's clear, the answers are obvious and I
    don't need advice.

Irrational feelings make sense when we understand what's
    behind them.

Perhaps that's why prayer works, sometimes, for some people
    because God is sometimes mute and doesn't give advice or
    try to fix things. He often listens and lets you
    work it out for yourself.

So please listen and hear me. And, if you want to
    talk, wait a minute for your turn; and I'll listen to you.[2]

Communication for Success, Part I

Test what you have learned by selecting the correct answers to the following questions.

1. One of the biggest problems with communication is that the message sent is not always the message that is

   a. appreciated.
   b. intended.
   c. received.

2. To be a good listener, it is important to remember that

   a. it is important to listen first, so that you can understand before speaking.
   b. it is important to talk first to make sure the other has heard your point of view.
   c. it is important to assume that the other knows what you are talking about.

3. Feeding back meaning is

   a. responding to questions.
   b. restating what has been said to check understanding.
   c. unnecessary because some people find it irritating.

4. Giving advice is

   a. generally not a good idea.
   b. only a good idea if you know what is best.
   c. a good idea if the other person does not know what to do.

5. In a crisis situation, it is best to

   a. tell the person not to feel sad.
   b. show your pity for the person.
   c. let the person talk in order to clarify thinking.

How did you do on the quiz? Check your answers: 1. c, 2. a, 3. b, 4. a, 5. c

The Language of Responsibility

The way we use language reflects our willingness to take responsibility for ourselves and affects our relationships with others. Knowing about "I" and "you" messages, as well as how we choose certain words, can help us to improve communications. We can become aware of how our thoughts influence our behavior and communication. We can choose to use cooperation in dealing with conflicts.

"I" and "You" Statements

When communicating, watch how you use the pronouns "I" and "you." For example, if you walk in and find your apartment a mess, you might say to your roommate, "Just look at this mess! You are a slob!" Your roommate will probably be angry and reply by calling you an equally offensive name. You have accomplished nothing except becoming angry and irritating your roommate. Using the pronoun "you" and calling a person a name implies that you are qualified to make a judgment about another person. Even if this is true, you will not make any friends or communicate effectively.

"You" statements label and blame. They demand a rebuttal. They cause negative emotions and escalate the situation. How would you react to these statements?

You must be crazy.
You are really a jerk!

You would probably get angry and think of a nasty reply in return. When you use an "I" message, you accept responsibility for yourself. You might say something like this:

I don't understand.
I feel angry.

There are many ways to make "I" statements. Instead of calling your roommate a slob, you could:

1. **Make an observation.** Describe the behavior.
   Your things are all over the floor.

2. **State your feelings.** Tell how you feel about the behavior.
   I get angry when I have to step over your things on the floor.

3. **Share your thoughts.** Say what you think about the situation, but beware of disguised "you" messages such as,
   "I think you are a slob."
   I think it is time to clean up.

4. **State what you want.**
   Please pick up your things.

5. **State your intentions.** Say what you are going to do.
   If you do not pick up your things, I will put them in your room.

Here are some examples of "I" statements that can be used to express various feelings:

To express anger	To express sadness
I don't like	I feel disappointed
I feel frustrated	I am sad that
I am angry that	I feel hurt
I feel annoyed	I wanted
I want	I want
To express fear	To say you are sorry
I feel worried	I feel embarrassed
I am afraid	I am sorry
I feel scared	I feel ashamed
I do not want	I didn't want
I need, I want	I want

A complete "I" message describes the other person's behavior, states your feelings, and describes the effect of the other's behavior on you. For example, "When your things are all over the floor (behavior), I feel angry (feeling) because I have to pick up after you (how it affects me)." A variation on the "I" message is the "we" message. The "we" statement assumes that both persons need to work on the problem. For example, "We need to work on this problem so that we don't have to argue."

Words Are Powerful

The words that we choose have a powerful influence on behavior. One of the least powerful words is the word "should." This word is heard frequently on college campuses:

I should do my homework.
I should go to class.
I should get started on my term paper.

The problem with "should" is that it usually does not lead to action and may cause people to feel guilty. If you say, "I should get started on my term paper," the chances are that you will not start on it.

If you say, "I might get started on my term paper," at least you are starting to think about possibilities. You might actually get started on your term paper. If you say, "I want to get started on my term paper," the chances are getting better that you will get started. You are making a choice. If you say, "I intend to start on my term paper," you have at least expressed good intentions. The best way to get started is to make a promise to yourself that you will start. The words "should," "might," "want," "intend," and "promise" represent a ladder of powerful communication. As you move up the ladder, you are more likely to accomplish what you say you will do. This ladder moves from obligation to promise, or a personal choice to act:

Figure 8.1 The Ladder of Powerful Speaking.

"I promise" or "I will"

"I intend to"

"I want to"

"I might"

"I should"

Next time you hear yourself saying that you "should" do something, move one more step up the ladder. Move from obligation to making a personal decision to do what is important to you. For example, if a friend wants to borrow money from you, which response is the most powerful?

- I really should pay the money back.
- Well, I might pay the money back.
- I really want to pay the money back.
- I intend to pay the money back.
- I promise to pay the money back.

Negative Self-Talk

Self-talk is what you say to yourself. It is the stream of consciousness or the little voice in your head. This self-talk affects how you communicate with others. If your self-talk is negative, you will have lower self-esteem and find it more difficult to communicate with others. There are some common irrational beliefs that lead to negative self-talk. Becoming aware of these beliefs can help you to avoid them.

- **I have to be perfect.** If you believe this, you will think that you have to be a perfect communicator and deliver flawless speeches. Since this goal is unattainable, it causes stress and anxiety. If you believe in this idea, you may try to pretend or act as if you

eliefs that Lead to egative Self-Talk

have to be perfect.

need everyone's approval.

That's always the way it is.

You made me feel that way.

I'm helpless.

If something bad can happen, it will.

were perfect. This takes up a lot of energy and keeps others from liking you. Everyone makes mistakes. When people stop trying to be perfect and accept themselves as they are, they can begin to relax and work on the areas needing improvement. They can write papers and make speeches knowing that they will probably make mistakes, just like the rest of the human population.

- **I need the approval of everyone.** A person who believes this finds it necessary to have the approval of almost everyone. Much energy is spent in gaining approval from others. If approval is not obtained, the person may feel nervous, embarrassed, or apologetic. It is not possible to win the approval of everyone because each individual is unique. Those who constantly seek approval will sacrifice their own values and what they think is right just to please others.

- **That's always the way it is.** People who believe this statement are making a generalization. They take a few events and use them to predict the future or exaggerate their shortcomings. Here are some examples:

  - I'm not a technical person. I can't install my computer.
  - I'm not good at numbers. I'll never to able to pass algebra.
  - Some husband (wife) I am! I forgot our anniversary.
  - You never listen to me.

Notice the absolute nature of these statements. Absolute statements are almost always false and lead to anger and negative thinking. Remember that with a positive attitude, things can change in the future. Just because it was one way in the past does not mean it has to be the same in the future. Beware of "always" and "never" statements.

- **You made me feel that way.** Your own self-talk, rather than the actions of others, is what causes emotions. No one can make you feel sad or happy. You feel sad or happy based what you say to yourself about an event. If someone makes a negative comment about you, you can say to yourself that it is only the other person's opinion and choose how you react. Your reactions and emotions depend on how much importance you decide to attach to the event. People tend to react strongly to a comment if it is from someone they care about.

  People also do not cause the emotions of others. Some people do not communicate honestly because they are afraid of causing negative emotions in the other person. They may hesitate to tell someone how they really feel. This lack of honesty leads to increasing hostility over time and difficulties in communication.

- **I'm helpless.** If you believe that what happens to you is beyond your control, you will be unlikely to do something to make the situation better. Here are some examples of helpless self-talk:

  - I'm a shy person. It is hard for me to talk to people.
  - I won't consider that career. Women are always discriminated against in that field.
  - It's difficult for me to meet people.

  Believing such statements, shy people don't attempt to talk to others, women limit their career options, and people give up trying to make friends. Believe that there is a way to change, and you can make your life better.

- **If something bad can happen, it will happen.** If you expect the worst, you may take actions that make it happen. If you expect that your speech will be a disaster, you may not prepare or you may forget your notes or props. If you believe that you will not pass the interview and will never get hired, you may not even apply for the job or attempt the interview. If you believe that your personal relationships will not get better, you will not invest the effort to make things better. There will be times when you make a poor speech, get turned down for a job, or have a relationship fail. Learn from these mistakes and do better the next time.

Barriers to Effective Communication

We all want to communicate effectively and get along with people whom we care about. We want to get along with our families, be a good parent, have friends at school, and get along with the boss and our coworkers on the job. Life is just more enjoyable when we have good communication with others. Watch for these barriers to effective communication:

- **Criticizing.** Making negative evaluations of others by saying, "It's your fault" or "I told you so" causes anger, which gets in the way of communication.
- **Name-calling and labeling.** If you call someone a name or put a label on them, they will attack you rather than communicate with you in any meaningful way.
- **Giving advice.** Giving advice may be viewed as talking down to a person. The person may resent your advice and you as well.
- **Ordering or commanding.** If you order someone to do something, they are likely to sabotage your request.
- **Threatening.** Trying to control someone by making threats causes resentment.
- **Moralizing.** Preaching about what a person should or should not do doesn't work because it causes resentment.
- **Diverting.** Changing the subject to talk about your own problems tells the person that you do not care about them.
- **Logical arguing.** Trying to use facts to convince without taking feelings into account is a barrier to communication. Present your facts and state your point of view, but respect the other person's feelings and different point of view.[3]

QUIZ

Communication for Success, Part II

Test what you have learned by selecting the correct answers to the following questions.

1. The following is a good example of an "I" statement.

    a. I think you need to explain.
    b. I do not understand.
    c. I think you are crazy.

2. "You" statements

    a. put the blame where it needs to be.
    b. results in anger and rebuttal.
    c. are effective communication tools.

3. Which statement is the most powerful?

    a. I should get started on my paper.
    b. I want to get started on my paper.
    c. I will get started on my paper.

4. The following statement is an irrational belief.

    a. I have to be perfect.
    b. I don't need the approval of everyone.
    c. I make mistakes sometimes.

5. This technique is used in effective communication:

    a. moralizing.
    b. logical arguing.
    c. listen and then respond.

How did you do on the quiz? Check your answers: 1. b, 2. b, 3. c, 4. a, 5. c

Dealing with Conflict

There are several ways to approach a conflict. In every conflict, there is the potential to be a winner or a loser.

- **Win-lose.** With this approach to conflict management, one person wins and the other loses, just as in a game or sport. Competition is part of the win-lose approach. In competition, power is important. In sports, the best and most powerful team wins.

  There are many kinds of power, however. Power may be based on authority. Examples might include your boss at work, your teacher, or even your parents. Another kind of power is based on mental ability or cleverness. Sometimes battles are not won by the strongest, but by the cleverest person. Another kind of power is majority rule. In many settings in a democratic society, the person with the most votes wins.

  In many situations, we cannot avoid the win-lose approach. Only one team can win, only one person can get the job, and only one person can marry another. In some circumstances the person you are communicating with does not want to cooperate but to compete.

  The problem with this approach is that there is only one winner. What happens to the loser? The loser can feel bad, resent the winner, give up, or try again for victory. These are not always the best alternatives.

- **Lose-lose.** Lose-lose is another option for resolving conflicts. Both parties lose. Both parties strive to be winners, but the struggle causes damage to both sides. Wars are often lose-lose situations. In World War II, dropping an atomic bomb caused the surrender of Japan, but it contaminated the environment with radioactive material and set a dangerous precedent for nuclear war. Russia was able to stop a civil war by destroying Grozny, the capital of Chechnya. The city became nearly uninhabitable. Everyone lost. On an interpersonal level, divorce can be a lose-lose situation if the struggle becomes destructive to both parties.

- **Compromise.** Another approach to solving conflict is compromise, where both parties to the conflict have some of their needs met. Both make some sacrifice in order to resolve the situation. For example, the buyer and seller of a used car may agree on a price somewhere between what the seller wants to get and the buyer wants to pay. As long as both parties are satisfied with the outcome, the results are satisfactory. Difficulties arise when people are asked to compromise their values. If they must compromise on something that is truly important, they may be dissatisfied with the outcome.

- **Win-win.** In a win-win approach, both parties work together to find a solution that meets everyone's needs. There is no loser. To reach a win-win solution, set aside competition and replace it with cooperation. This is often difficult to do because emotions are involved. Put aside emotions to discuss the issue. This may mean waiting until both parties have had the opportunity to calm down. This approach can be impossible, however, when one person wants to cooperate and the other person wants to win.

These are the steps in a win-win approach:

1. **Identify the problem.** Identify the problem as your own. If your roommate is having a party and you cannot study, it is your problem. You need to find a quiet place to study.

2. **Set a good time to discuss the issue.** When you are feeling angry is usually not a good time to discuss issues. Set a time when both parties can focus on the problem. A good rule is to wait 24 hours to let the emotions cool down and gain some perspective.

3. **Describe your problem and needs.** Use "I" messages. Resist the temptation to label and call names. Goodwill is important.

> **Approaches to Conflict**
>
> - Win-Lose
> - Lose-Lose
> - Compromise
> - Win-Win

4. **Look at the other point of view.** Understand the other person's needs, and make sure the other person understands your needs.

5. **Look for alternatives that work for both parties.**

6. **Decide on the best alternative.**

7. **Take action to implement the solution.**

The win-win approach is a good tool for effective communication and maintaining good relationships.

Journal Entry #4

Review the section on "Barriers to Effective Communication" and "Dealing with Conflict." What are some common mistakes that people make when trying to resolve problems and communicate effectively?

Friendships

College provides the opportunity to make new friends. These friends can broaden your perspective and make your life richer and more enjoyable. What do you value in a friendship? How can you establish and maintain good friendships?

ACTIVITY

Friendship

Friendship is a relationship that involves trust and support. Beyond this basic definition, we all have different ideas about what is important in a friendship. Here is a list of common qualities of friends. Place a checkmark next to those qualities that are important to you in establishing your personal friendships. A friend is a person who:

_____ can keep information confidential.	_____ spends time with me.
_____ is loyal.	_____ has a sense of humor.
_____ can be trusted.	_____ is independent.
_____ is warm and affectionate.	_____ has good communication skills.
_____ is supportive of who I am.	_____ is an educated person.
_____ is honest.	_____ is an intelligent person.
_____ is a creative person.	_____ knows how to have fun.
_____ encourages me to do my best.	_____ cares about me.

What are the top three qualities you would look for in a friend? List them below.

1. _____

2. _____

3. _____

The friends that you choose can have a big influence on your life, so it is important to choose them wisely. In college and in the workplace, you will have the opportunity to make new friends who can add a new dimension and perspective to your life. For example, if your friends have goals for the future and believe that completing college is important, you will be more likely to finish your own education. If your friends distract you with too many activities outside of school, your college performance may suffer.

Some students naturally make friends easily; others find making new friends more difficult. Here are some ideas for making new friends:

- **Be a good listener.** Spend equal time listening and talking. If you are doing all the talking, the other person is likely to feel left out of the conversation. Show interest in the other person's interests and ideas.

- **Talk about yourself.** Let others get to know you by sharing your interests, where you come from, and what is important to you. In this way, you can find mutual interests to enjoy.

- **Be supportive and caring.** We all have good days and bad ones. Help your friends to celebrate the good days and be supportive through life's challenges. Showing that you care is the basis of developing trust and friendship.

- **Be a friend.** Treat your friends the way you would like to be treated.

- **Spend time with your friends.** It is difficult to maintain relationships if you do not spend time sharing activities. Make spending time with friends a high priority.

- **Accept your friends for who they are.** Everyone has good and bad qualities. Accept the idea that you are not going to be able to change people to match your expectations.

- **Show appreciation.** Say thank you and make honest compliments. Think of something positive to say.

- **Be assertive.** This means that you ask for what you want and that you don't give in to doing something that you don't want to do. Being assertive means that you have the right to your feelings and opinions. There is a fine line, though, between being assertive and being aggressive. Aggressive behavior is domineering, rude, and intimidating. Aggressive individuals act without consideration of other people's rights and feelings.

- **Be selective.** Not everyone makes a good friend. Make friends with people you respect and admire. Stay away from people who are critical or make you feel unhappy. Avoid those who cause you to do things that you do not want to do. Choose friends that make you happy and encourage you to do your best.

"Lots of people want to ride with you in the limo, but what you want is someone who will take the bus with you when the limo breaks down."

Oprah Winfrey

Communication and Relationships   Chapter 8   267

Roommates

Getting along with a roommate can be a challenge. It can be your best or worst college experience or somewhere in between. The key to getting along with a roommate is to understand differences and to work on compromise or win-win solutions. Making a wise choice of a roommate can make the situation much easier. Below are some areas of possible disagreement for roommates:

- **Neatness.** Some students like to keep their rooms neat and others can tolerate messiness.
- **Smoking.** Some students like to smoke and others are offended by smoking.
- **Noise.** Some students need quiet for study, while others like to study with music and friends.
- **Guests.** Some students like to have guests in the room, and others do not want guests.
- **Temperature.** Some like it warm and some like it cold.
- **Studying.** Is the room a place to study or to have fun?
- **Borrowing.** Some think that borrowing is okay and some do not.
- **Sleeping.** Some go to bed early and some go to bed late. Some need quiet for sleeping.

If you have a choice of roommates, it is a good idea to discuss the above issues in advance. Even best friends can part company over some of these issues. If you are assigned a roommate, discuss the above issues to avoid conflict later on. Aim for a win-win solution or at least a compromise. If there is some conflict, following these guidelines may help.

1. Discuss problems as they arise. If you do not discuss problems, it is likely that anger and resentment will increase, causing a more serious problem at a later date.

2. Ask for what you want. Subtle hints often do not work.

3. Be nice to your roommate and treat him or her as you would want to be treated.

4. Be reasonable and overlook small problems. No one is perfect.

Relationships

A relationship starts as a friendship and then moves a step further. A relationship involves emotional attachment and interdependence. We often get our ideas about good relationships through practice and trial and error. When we make errors, the results are often painful. Although we all have different ideas about what constitutes a good relationship, at a minimum it includes these components:

- Love and caring
- Honesty
- Trust
- Loyalty
- Mutual support
- Acceptance of differences

Relationships between Men and Women

According to John Gray, popular author of *Men Are from Mars, Women Are from Venus,* men and women have such different values and needs in a relationship, it is as if they came from different planets.[4] He states that men generally value power, competency, efficiency, and achievement. He says, "A man's sense of self is defined through his ability to achieve results." While women are fantasizing about romance, a man is fantasizing about "powerful cars, faster computers, gadgets, gizmos, and new and more powerful technology."[5] The worst thing that women can do to men, according to Gray, is to offer unsolicited advice or to try to change them. These actions conflict with men's needs for power and competence and imply that they don't know what to do or can't do it on their own. We can communicate our honest feelings about our partner's behavior and ask for what we want and need. However, we should not use our feelings and requests to manipulate another person to change. Gray identifies the most important needs for men as trust, acceptance, appreciation, admiration, approval, and encouragement.

Gray says that women generally value love, communication, beauty, and relationships. Their sense of self-worth is defined through their feelings and the quality of their relationships. The worst thing that men can do to women is to offer solutions too quickly when women are talking about their feelings, rather than listening and understanding those feelings. When this happens, women get frustrated and feel a lack of intimacy. It is possible to listen carefully and understand these feelings without necessarily agreeing with them. The most important needs for women are caring, understanding, respect, devotion, validation, and reassurance.

Gray's ideas about men and women parallel the thinking and feeling dimensions of personality presented earlier. Men are 60 percent thinking types and women are 60 percent feeling types. His ideas are interesting for discussion and apply in many relationships, but it is important to be aware of gender stereotypes. Remember that 40 percent of women are thinking types and 40 percent of men are feeling types, so not all individuals will fit into the same categories that Gray describes.

Although Gray proposes that men and women generally differ in what they consider most important, he lists the following 12 components of love.[6] Men and women can improve their relationships when they demonstrate the following:

1. **Caring.** Show that you are interested and concerned about each other.

2. **Trust.** Have a positive belief in the intentions and abilities of each other.

3. **Understanding.** Listen without judgment and without presuming that you understand the feelings of the other person. In this way, both men and women can feel free to discuss what is important to them.

4. **Acceptance.** It is probably not a good idea to marry a person if you think you can change him or her into the ideal person you have in mind. Love your partner without trying to change him or her. No one is perfect; we are each a work in progress. The key is to trust the people we love to make their own improvements.

5. **Respect.** Have consideration for the thoughts and feelings of each other.

6. **Appreciation.** Acknowledge the behavior and efforts of your partner. Appreciation can be in the form of a simple "Thank you" or sending cards or flowers.

7. **Devotion.** Give priority to the relationship so that the other person feels important.

8. **Admiration.** Show approval for the unique gifts and talents of your partner.

9. **Validation.** Do not argue with feelings. Each person has a right to his or her own feelings. We can acknowledge, try to understand, and respect the feelings of another without necessarily agreeing with them.

10. **Approval.** Show approval by acknowledging the goodness and satisfaction you have with each other.

11. **Reassurance.** Show reassurance by repeatedly showing that you care, understand, and respect each other.

12. **Encouragement.** Notice the good characteristics of each other and provide encouragement and support.

How to Survive the Loss of a Relationship

Relationships require work and good communication to keep them going strong. Relationships also change over time as people grow and change. As we search for our soul mates, we may need to end some relationships and start new ones. This process can be very painful. Following the breakup of a relationship, people generally go through three predictable stages:

1. Shock or denial

2. Anger or depression

3. Understanding or acceptance[7]

Dealing with pain is a necessary part of life. Whether the pain is a result of the loss of a relationship or the death of someone important to you, there are some positive steps you can take along the road to acceptance and understanding.

- Recognize that a loss has taken place and give yourself time to adjust to this situation. The greater the loss, the more time it will take to feel better. In the meantime, try to keep up with daily routines. It is possible to feel sad and to go to work and to school. Daily routines may even take your mind off your troubles for a while.

- It is healthy to feel sad and cry. You will need to experience the pain to get over it. It is not helpful to deny pain, cover it up, or run away from it, because it will take longer to feel better.

- Talk to a friend or a counselor. Talking about how you feel will help you to understand and accept the loss.

- Don't punish yourself with thoughts that begin "If only I had . . ."
- Realize that there is a beginning and an end to pain.
- Get plenty of rest and eat well.
- Accept understanding and support from friends and family.
- Ask for help if you need it.
- Don't try to get the old relationship going again. It will just prolong the pain.
- Anticipate a positive outcome. You will feel better in the future.
- Beware of the rebound. It is not a good idea to jump into a new relationship right away.
- Beware of addictive activities such as alcohol, drugs, smoking, or overeating.
- Take time to relax and be kind to yourself.
- Use exercise as a way to deal with stress and feel better.
- Keep a journal to help deal with your emotions and learn from the situation.[8]

KEYS TO SUCCESS

Failure Is an Opportunity for Learning

Everyone makes mistakes and experiences failure. This is the human condition. There is also a saying that falling down is not failure, but not getting up is. If you can view failure as an opportunity for learning, you can put it into perspective and continue making progress toward your goals. It has been said that the famous inventor Thomas Edison tried 9,999 times to invent the light bulb. When asked if he was going to fail 10,000 times, he answered, "I didn't fail. I just discovered another way not to invent the light bulb." Failure allows you to collect feedback about how you are doing.

Imagine that your life is like a ship heading toward a destination. Sometimes the sailing is smooth, and sometimes the water is choppy and dangerous and knocks you off course. Failure acts like the rudder of the ship. It helps you to make adjustments so that you stay on course. Too often we do not learn from failure because shame and blame get in the way. Gerard Nierenberg, author of *Do It Right the First Time*, advocates the "no shame, no blame" approach to dealing with errors, mistakes, or failure.[9] The first step is to identify the mistake that has been made. What went wrong? Then you look at how much damage has been done. The next step is to take an honest look at what caused the problem. The last step is to figure out a way to fix the problem and see that it does not happen again. There is no shame or blame in the process. Following this approach results in fewer errors and failures.

Harold Kushner has another view about failure:

Life is not a spelling bee, where no matter how many words you have gotten right, if you make one mistake you are disqualified. Life is more like a baseball season, where even the best team loses one-third of its games and even the worst team has its days of brilliance. Our goal is not to go all year without ever losing a game. Our goal is to win more than we lose, and if we can do that consistently enough, then when the end comes, we will have won it all.[10]

Like a baseball player, if you lose a game, analyze what went wrong and keep on practicing. Remember that you will eventually be a winner. Everyone remembers that Babe Ruth was a great baseball player and that he had 714 home runs. People do not remember that he also struck out 1,330 times. If you can look honestly at your mistakes and learn from them, you can have many winning seasons.

Journal Entry #5

Describe a situation in which you have been disappointed, such as a poor grade or the loss of a job or a relationship. Was there an opportunity to learn from the situation?

"Work as hard as you ask others to. Strive for what you believe is right, no matter the odds. Learn that mistakes can be the best teacher."

George Steinbrenner

JOURNAL ENTRIES

Communication and Relationships

Go to http://www.collegesuccess1.com/JournalEntries.htm for Word files of the Journal Entries

Success over the Internet

Visit the *College Success Website* at http://www.collegesuccess1.com/

The *College Success Website* is continually updated with new topics and links to the material presented in this chapter. Topics include:

- Expectations in relationships
- Common mistakes in relationships
- Beginning, enhancing, and ending relationships
- Dealing with anger
- Personality and relationships

Contact your instructor if you have any problems accessing the *College Success Website*.

Notes

1. A. Wolvin and C. G. Coakley, *Listening*, 3rd ed. (Dubuque, IA: W. C. Brown, 1988), 208.
2. *Care of the Mentally Ill* (F.A. Davis, 1977).
3. T. Gordon, *Parent Effectiveness Training* (New York: McGraw-Hill, 1970).
4. John Gray, *Men Are from Mars, Women Are from Venus* (New York: HarperCollins, 1992).
5. Ibid., 16.

6. Ibid., 133–37.

7. Melba Colgrove, Harold Bloomfield, and Peter McWilliams, *How to Survive the Loss of a Love* (New York: Bantam Books, 1988).

8. Adapted from Colgrove, Bloomfield, and McWilliams, *How to Survive the Loss of a Love.*

9. Gerard Nierenberg, *Doing It Right the First Time* (New York: John Wiley and Sons, 1996).

10. Harold Kushner, *Becoming Aware* (Dubuque, IA: Kendall Hunt).

Communication Scenarios

Name _____ Date _____

In the following scenarios, think about how personality type influences communication style. Knowing about your personality type and understanding opposite types can help to improve your communication. Your instructor may want to do this as a group activity in the classroom.

1. An introvert and an extravert are having an argument.

   How is the introvert likely to act?

   How is the extravert likely to act?

   How can the extravert improve communication?

   How can the introvert improve communication?

2. A sensing and an intuitive type are on a date.

   What is the sensing person likely to talk about?

   What is the intuitive type likely to talk about?

3. A thinking type and a feeling type are dating.

   When there are problems in the relationship, how is the thinking type likely to approach the problem?

   How will the feeling type approach the problem?

How can the thinking type improve communication?

How can the feeling type improve communication?

4. A judging type and a perceptive type are married. The judging type likes to keep the house neat and orderly. The perceptive type likes creative disorder. How can they resolve this conflict?

"I" and "You" Messages

Name _____ Date _____

Part 1. "You" messages label, judge, and blame; they demand counterattack.

"I" messages describe yourself and help improve understanding.

Examples:

You are rude.	I feel upset.
You make me mad.	I feel angry.
You must be crazy.	I don't understand.

Change the following statements from a "you" message to an "I" or "we" message.

1. Your class is boring.

2. That was a stupid joke.

3. You gave me an F.

4. You don't understand.

Part 2. For each situation below, state the behavior, the consequences, and your feelings in any order.

Example: When you play your stereo this loud after midnight (behavior),
I can't sleep (consequence) and I get really irritable (feelings).

1. Your date, who is supposed to arrive at 6:00, arrives at 7:00. The dinner you have fixed is ruined and you won't have time to catch that late movie after dinner. What do you say?

_____

_____

2. A student who sits next to you in class constantly asks you questions and tries to talk to you during the lecture. You find it difficult to concentrate and take notes. What do you say?

_____

_____

_____

Name _____ Date _____

Rewrite the script in the following scenario using "I" messages to try to improve the situation and come up with a win-win solution.

Eric and Jason are roommates who have known each other since childhood. Because they are good friends, they decide to be roommates in college. They rent an apartment together and sign a one-year lease.

Eric: Look at this place. It's trashed! You're really a pig! There are pieces of leftover pizza and empty beer bottles everywhere from that party you had. Your stupid friends spilled soda on the floor and broke the lamp. Are you going to pay for that?

Jason: Why do you always have to be so hostile? We were just having some fun. I was going to clean it up in the morning but I accidentally slept in. Then I had to go to class. Do you want me to miss class and fail? I'm still going to clean it up. Chill out!

Eric: Maybe I wouldn't be so irritated if you guys didn't keep me up all night. I had a test this morning at 8:00. You don't think of anyone but yourself. How can you be so irresponsible?

Jason: Whatever, dude.

Name _____ Date _____

List 10 ideas from this chapter that will help you to improve communication with others who are important to you.

1.

2.

3.

4.

5.

6.

7.

8.

9.

10.

Planning Your Career and Education

Learning Objectives

Read to answer these key questions:

- What are some employment trends for the future?

- What are work skills necessary for success in the twenty-first century?

- How do I research a career?

- How do I plan my education?

- How can I make good decisions about my future?

- How can I obtain my ideal job?

- What is a dangerous opportunity?

Name: Diamond Nicole Hall

Major: Social Work   **Minor:** Gerontology

Career aspirations: To attend graduate school for social work and eventually open my own clinical practice as a family and marriage counselor.

Hometown: Detroit, MI

Campus Involvement: While at WMU I've been involved in multiple student organizations and with great leadership roles. I've been a Bronco Buddy coordinator, Alpha program peer mentor, a First-Year Seminar Instructor and Fall Welcome Ambassador.

Hobbies and interests: Enjoying the sunshine, reading, meeting new people, and exploring new things.

Favorite quote on success: "It always seems impossible until it's done."— Nelson Mandela

By coming to WMU you are improving yourself as an individual. Western Michigan University gives you a chance to broaden your experience by opening you up to your new environment and helping you to make friendships while obtaining an education. Educating yourself will improve your overall quality of life and attending WMU will make learning enjoyable! You have already made one of the many great decisions of your life by attending WMU! Western Michigan University has some of the most energetic and welcoming students and faculty members. Another reason why WMU is so cool is the connections you can make that will help you to advance in your future career. The WMU career center (Career and Student Employment Services) can direct you to options that are available for you. WMU has a number of resources for students to be successful and the professors take time to know you as a person! You're not just another incoming student; they connect names, with faces to build a relationship with their students. Building a healthy relationship with your professors and peers will enhance the overall college experience for you. It is most important to build relationships with your peers around campus. One way to do this is by joining some of the many RSOs (Registered Student Organizations) WMU has to offer. Introducing yourself to your professors and peers on the first day of class helps to make those connections you will need and I highly recommend this practice. Many programs and jobs require letters of recommendation and your professors are the best people to write them. Lastly, communicating with your professors through email and attending their office hours can benefit you, especially, if you find that you are struggling in their class. Some professors may take your early interest in your performance into account and give you extra credit for your efforts.

> "What is the recipe for successful achievement? To my mind there are just four essential ingredients: Choose a career you love, give it the best there is in you, seize your opportunities, and be a member of the team."
>
> Benjamin Fairless

It is always easier to get where you are going if you have a road map or a plan. To start the journey, it is helpful to know about yourself, including your personality, interests, talents, and values. Once you have this picture, you will need to know about the world of work and job trends that will affect your future employment opportunities. Next, you will need to make decisions about which road to follow. Then, you will need to plan your education to reach your destination. Finally, you will need some job-seeking skills such as writing a resume and preparing for a successful interview.

Employment Trends

The world is changing quickly, and these changes will affect your future career. To assure your future career success, you will need to become aware of career trends and observe how they change over time so that you can adjust your career plans accordingly. For example, recently a school was established for training bank tellers. The school quickly went out of business and the students demanded their money back because they were not able to get jobs. A careful observer of career trends would have noticed that bank tellers are being replaced by automatic teller machines (ATMs) and would not have started a school for training bank tellers. Students observant of career trends would not have paid money for the training. It is probably a good idea for bank tellers to look ahead and plan a new career direction.

How can you find out about career trends that may affect you in the future? Become a careful observer by reading about current events. Good sources of information include:

- Your local newspaper, especially the business section
- News programs
- Current magazines
- Government statistics and publications
- The Internet

When thinking about future trends, use your critical thinking skills. Sometimes trends change quickly or interact in different ways. For example, since we are using email to a great extent today, it might seem that mail carriers would not be as much in demand in the future. However, since people are buying more goods over the Internet, there has been an increased demand for mail carriers and other delivery services. Develop the habit of looking at what is happening to see if you can identify trends that may affect your future.

Usually trends get started as a way to meet the following needs:[1]

- To save money
- To reduce cost
- To do things faster
- To make things easier to use
- To improve safety and reliability
- To lessen the impact on the environment

The following are some trends to watch that may affect your future career. As you read about each trend, think about how it could affect you.

Baby Boomers, Generation X, and the Millennial Generation

About every 20 years, sociologists begin to describe a new generation with similar characteristics based on shared historical experiences. Each generation has different opportunities and challenges in the workplace.

The Baby Boomers were born following World War II between 1946 and 1964. Four out of every 10 adults today are in this Baby Boom Generation.[2] Because there are so many aging Baby Boomers, the average age of Americans is increasing. Life expectancy is also increasing. By 2015 the projected life expectancy will be 76.4 for men and 81.4 for women.[3] In the new millennium, many more people will live to be 100 years old or more! Think about the implications of an older population. Older people need such things as health care, recreation, travel, and financial planning. Occupations related to these needs are likely to be in demand now and in the future.

Those born between 1965 and 1977 are often referred to as Generation X. They are sometimes called the "baby bust" generation because fewer babies were born during this period than in the previous generations. There is much in the media about this generation having to pay higher taxes and Social Security payments to support the large number of aging Baby Boomers. Some say that this generation will not enjoy the prosperity of the Baby Boomers. Those who left college in the early nineties faced a recession and the worst job market since World War II.[4] Many left college in debt and returned home to live with their parents. Because of a lack of employment opportunities, many in this generation became entrepreneurs, starting new companies at a faster rate than previous generations.

Jane Bryant Quinn notes that in spite of economic challenges, Generation Xers have a lot going for them:[5]

- They have record-high levels of education, which correlate with higher income and lower unemployment.
- There is a demand for more skilled workers, so employers are more willing to train employees. Anthony Carnevale, chairman of the National Commission for Employment Policy, "sees a big demand for 'high-school plus'—a high school diploma plus technical school or junior college."
- Generation Xers are computer literate, and those who use computers on the job earn 10 to 15 percent more than those who don't.
- This group often has a good work ethic valued by employers. However, they value a balanced lifestyle with time for outside interests and family.
- As Baby Boomers retire, more job opportunities are created for this group.
- Unlike the Baby Boomers, this generation was born into a more integrated and more diverse society. They are better able than previous generations to adapt to diversity in society and the workplace.

Many of today's college students are part of the Millennial Generation, born between 1977 and 1995. This generation is sometimes called Generation Y or the Echo Boomers, since they are the children of the Baby Boomers.[6] This new generation of approximately 60 million is three times larger than Generation X and will eventually exceed the number of Baby Boomers. In this decade, they will become the largest teen population in U.S. history. As the Millennials reach college age, they will attend college in increasing numbers. In the next 10 years, college enrollments will increase by approximately 300,000 students per year. Colleges will find it difficult to accommodate rapidly increasing numbers of students, and as a result, the Millennial Generation will face increasingly competitive college admissions criteria.

Millennials are more ethnically diverse than previous generations with 34 percent ethnic minorities. One in four lives with a single parent; three in four have working mothers. Most of them started using computers before they were five years old. Marketing researchers describe this new generation as "technologically adept, info-savvy, a cyber-generation, the clickeratti."[7] They are the connected generation, accustomed to cell phones, chatting on the Internet, and listening to downloaded music.

Young people in the Millennial Generation share a different historical perspective from the Baby Boom Generation. Baby Boomers remember the Vietnam War and the assassinations of President John F. Kennedy and Martin Luther King. For Millennials, school shootings such as Columbine and acts of terrorism such as the Oklahoma City bombing and the 9–11 attack on New York City stand out as important events. The Millennial Generation will see their main problems as dealing with violence, easy access to weapons, and the threat of terrorism.

Neil Howe and William Strauss paint a very positive picture of this new generation in their book *Millennials Rising: The Next Great Generation*:

- Millennials will rebel by tearing down old institutions that do not work and building new and better institutions. The authors predict that this will be the can-do generation filled with technology planners, community shapers, institution builders, and world leaders.
- Surveys show that this generation describes themselves as happy, confident, and positive.
- They are cooperative team players.
- They generally accept authority and respect their parents' values.

- They follow rules. The rates of homicides, violent crime, abortion, and teen pregnancy are decreasing rapidly.
- The use of alcohol, drugs, and tobacco is decreasing.
- Millennials have a fascination with and mastery of new technology.
- Their most important values are individuality and uniqueness.[8]

It is predicted that the world of work for the Millennials will be dramatically different. Previous generations anticipated having a lifetime career. By the year 2020, many jobs will probably be short-term contracts. This arrangement will provide cost savings and efficiency for employers and flexibility for employees to start or stop work to take vacations, train for new jobs, or meet family responsibilities. One in five people will be self-employed. Retirement will be postponed as people look forward to living longer and healthier lives.[9]

Journal Entry #1

> Describe your generation (Baby Boomer, Generation X, or New Millennial). What are your best qualities and challenges?

Moving from Goods to Services and Technology

Human society has moved through several stages. The first stage, about 20,000 years ago, was the hunting and gathering stage. During this time, society depended on the natural environment for food and other resources. When natural resources were depleted, the community moved to another area. The second stage, some 10,000 years ago, was the agricultural stage. Human beings learned to domesticate animals and cultivate crops. This allowed people to stay in one place and develop more permanent villages. About 200 years ago, industrial societies came into being by harnessing power sources to produce goods on a large scale.

Today in the United States, we are evolving into a service, technology, and information society. Fewer people are working in agriculture and manufacturing. Futurists John Naisbitt et al. note that we are moving toward a service economy based on high technology, rapid communications, biotechnology for use in agriculture and medicine, health care, and sales of merchandise.[10] Service areas with increasing numbers of jobs include health care and social assistance; professional, scientific, and technical services; educational services; administrative and support services; waste management and remediation services; accommodation and food services; government; retail trade; transportation and warehousing, finance and insurance; arts, entertainment, and recreation; wholesale trade; real estate, rental, and leasing; and information and management.

Increased Opportunities in Health Care

If you are interested in science and technology along with helping other people, there are many career opportunities in health care. It is estimated that by 2018, there will be an increase of four million new jobs in health care, which will account for 26 percent of all new jobs.[11] This trend is being driven by an aging population, increased longevity, health care reform, and new developments in the pharmaceutical and medical fields. Because of increased health care costs, many of the jobs done by doctors, nurses, dentists, or physical therapists are now being done by physician's assistants, medical assistants, dental assistants, physical therapy aides, and home health aides. Health care workers will increasingly use technology to do their work. For example, a new occupation is nursing informatics, which combines traditional nursing skills with computer and information science.

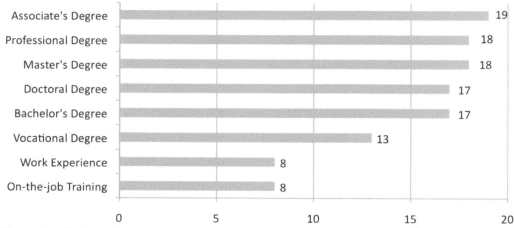

Figure 9.1 Projected percent increase in employment, 2008 through 2018.[13]

Increased Need for Education

In the past, the life pattern for many people was to graduate from school, go to work, and eventually retire. Because of the rapid changes in technology and society today, workers will need additional training and education over a lifetime. Education will take place in a variety of forms: community college courses, training on the job, private training sessions, and learning on your own. Those who do not keep up with the new technology will find that their skills quickly become obsolete. Those who do keep up will find their skills in demand.

As we transition from manufacturing to service and technical careers, education beyond high school will become increasingly important. According to the Bureau of Labor Statistics, occupations that require a postsecondary degree will account for nearly half of all new jobs from 2008 to 2018, with the fastest growth in jobs requiring an associate's degree or higher. In addition, higher education will result in higher earnings and lower unemployment.[12]

Young people who do not continue their education are likely to be stuck in lower-paying jobs, while those who continue their education will have higher-paying jobs. Author Joyce Lain Kennedy believes that the middle class is becoming an endangered species.[15] She states that many jobs traditionally held by the middle class have been "dumbed down," making them so simple that anyone can do them. These jobs pay very little and offer no benefits, no employment stability, and little opportunity for advancement. Young people often hold these jobs in their teens and twenties.

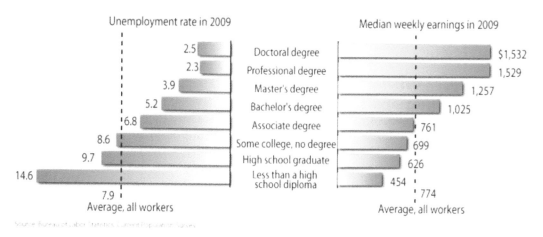

Figure 9.2 Education pays, unemployment rate and median weekly earnings, 2009.[14]

At the other end of the job continuum are jobs requiring a college education or training beyond high school. These high-end jobs often require technical or computer skills. These are the jobs that pay better and offer benefits. It seems that we are becoming a nation of haves and have-nots who are separated by their education and technical skills.

Going Green!

Have you purchased organic products or an energy-efficient light bulb, appliance, or car? If so, you are part of a new environmental movement that is gaining impetus in the U.S., the rise of social responsibility and the citizen consumer. Businesses that are seen as green attract consumers who are concerned about using energy efficiently, new sources of energy, and preserving the environment. In addition to profit, businesses are now concerned about the planet and working conditions for people.

As fossil fuels are depleted, the world is facing a major transformation in how energy is generated and used. Sustainability, wind turbines, solar panels, farmer's markets, biofuels, and wind energy are just some of the ways to transition to a post-fossil-fuel world. Jobs in this field will include engineers who design new technology, consultants to audit energy needs, and installers who install and maintain systems. Here are some titles of green jobs: environmental lawyer, environmental technician, sustainability consultant, sustainability project director, green architect, green building project manager, marine biologist, environmental technician, energy efficiency specialist, organic farmer, compliance manager, product engineer, wind energy engineer, and solar engineer.

A Diverse Workforce

The workforce in the United States is becoming increasingly more diverse. Diversity includes many demographic variables such as ethnicity, religion, gender, national origin, disability, sexual orientation, age, education, geographic origin, and skill characteristics. Having an appreciation for diversity is important in maintaining a work environment that is open and allows for individual differences. Increasing diversity provides opportunities for many different kinds of individuals and makes it important to be able to have good working relationships with all kinds of people.

The U.S. Bureau of Labor Statistics has described some trends that will affect the workplace by 2018.[16]

- Whites are expected to make up a decreasing share of the labor force, while Blacks, Asians, and all other groups will increase their share. Persons of Hispanic origin will increase their share of the labor force from 14.3 to 17.6 percent, reflecting a 33.1 percent growth.
- The number of women in the labor force will grow at a slightly faster rate than the number of men. The male labor force is projected to grow by 7.5 percent, as compared with 9.0 percent for the female labor force.
- The number of workers in younger age groups will decline, while workers in the 55 years and older group will increase, reflecting the increase of aging Baby Boomers.
- Total employment is expected to increase by 10 percent from 2008 to 2018. Changes in consumer demand and advances in technology will continue to change the structure of the economy, with decreasing jobs in manufacturing and increasing numbers of jobs in service and technology.

E-Commerce Is Changing the Way We Do Business

E-commerce, the purchasing of goods, services, and information over the Internet, is a new technology that has revolutionized the way business is done in the 21st century. More people are using e-commerce because of convenience, selection, and the ease of shopping for goods at the best price. Online sales are a growing part of the market, increasing 10 to 20 percent a year for the last several years. In 2010, online shopping accounted for 7 percent of all sales, and 42 percent of retail sales were influenced by online marketing.[17] This growth in e-commerce will have implications for education and business. More colleges are offering courses in e-commerce and incorporating e-commerce topics into traditional business offerings. There are more career opportunities in e-commerce and related fields such as computer graphics, web design, online marketing, and package delivery services.

The Microprocessor

The microprocessor is a silicon chip containing transistors that determine the capability of a computer. In the past 20 years, the power of the microprocessor has increased more than one million times. In the next 20 years, the power will increase a million times again.[18] Because of the increased power of the microprocessor, it will be used in new ways and with new devices. Consider the "smart home" of the future:

> As you reach the front door, you are welcomed by a flat screen, rather than a doorbell. You can use this screen to ring the doorbell, talk to the person inside the home or leave a message, which can be accessed by telephone or e-mail.

> If you're the homeowner, walk through the door and the curtains go up, letting light in, and the entire house is soon subtly illuminated. The hi-fi will access its database to play your favorite music, and the air-conditioning will be preset to the temperature you prefer.

> As you move to the kitchen, you take the ingredients for your lunch—say, flour, a piece of fish and a few stalks of broccoli—to a networked table. This will activate a system that will immediately offer you a range of appropriate recipes. Your smart microwave will fix the dish for you, consulting the recipe you prefer, via the Internet.[19]

The microprocessor is increasingly available to all and for less cost. The personal computer would have occupied an entire building 35 years ago. Today we have access to powerful computers and mobile devices that will play an ever greater role in our daily lives.

> It's remarkable how we now take all that power for granted. Using a basic home PC costing less than $1,000, you can balance your household budget, do your taxes, write letters to friends and fax or e-mail them over the Internet, listen to CDs or the radio, watch the news, consult a doctor, play games, book a vacation, view a house, buy a book or a car. The list is endless.[20]

New Advances in Technology and Communication

There has been a recent rapid increase in the development of cell phones and other mobile devices, as well as the use of social media, which will continue to have a major impact on career opportunities. Those who can keep up with the current technology will find increasing career and business opportunities. Graduates will become more marketable if they combine traditional career areas with technology such as social media. For example, students in a marketing degree program will be more in demand if they can use Facebook, LinkedIn, or Twitter to market products.

The Bureau of Labor Statistics reports that two million technology-related jobs will be created by 2018. Jobs in computer systems design and related services are expected to increase by 34 percent by 2018. Jobs that will grow faster than the average include computer-network administrators, data-communications analysts, and Web developers. Some new fields include data-loss prevention, online security, and risk management. Computer science degrees are especially marketable when combined with traditional majors such as finance, accounting, or marketing.[21]

Because we are living in the Information Age, information and technology workers are now the largest group of workers in the United States. Careers in information technology include the design, development, and support of computer software, hardware, and networks. Some newer jobs in this area include animation for video games, films, and videos as well as setting up websites and Internet security. There are also good opportunities for network programmers who can program a group of computers to work together. Because computer use has increased greatly, it is expected that computer-related jobs will expand by 40 percent or more in the next decade.[22]

In the future, computers will continue to become more powerful, mobile, and connected. It is predicted that by 2018, microprocessors will be replaced by optical computers that function at the speed of light. Technology will be embedded in products used for entertainment as well as for home and business use. It is predicted that in the future, the desktop computer as we know it will cease to exist. Instead of a home computer, we will have computerized homes with sensors that monitor energy use and smart appliances with computer chips. Gestures, touch, and voice communication will rapidly replace computer keyboards. The Nintendo Wii™ and the iPhone are current examples. Computers will move from homes and offices into human bodies. Microchips may be embedded in human bodies to monitor health conditions and to deliver medical care. Some futurists forecast a time when computer chips will be embedded in the brain and connected to the Internet. Of course, computer security will become increasingly important with these new advances.[23]

Radiation and laser technologies will provide new technical careers in the future. It has been said that lasers will be as important to the 21st century as electricity was for the 20th century. New uses for lasers are being found in medicine, energy, industry, computers, communications, entertainment, and outer space. The use of lasers is creating new jobs and causing others to become obsolete. For example, many welders are being replaced by laser technicians, who have significantly higher earnings. New jobs will open for people who purchase, install, and maintain lasers.

Careers in fiber optics and telecommunications are among the top new emerging fields in the 21st century. Fiber optics are thin glass fibers that transmit light. This new technology may soon make copper wire obsolete. One of the most important uses of fiber optics is to speed up delivery of data over the Internet and to improve telecommunications. It is also widely used in medical instruments, including laser surgery.

Another interesting development to watch is artificial intelligence software, which enables computers to recognize patterns, improve from experience, make inferences, and approximate human thought. Scientists at the MIT Artificial Intelligence Lab have developed a robot named Cog. Here is a description of Cog and its capabilities:

We have given it a multitude of sensors to "feel" and learn what it is like to be touched and spoken to. Cog's ability to make eye contact and reach out to moving objects is also meant to motivate people to interact with it. These features have taught Cog, among other things, to distinguish a human face from inanimate objects (this puts its development at about a 3-month-old's). It can also listen to music and keep rhythm by tapping on a drum (something a 5-year-old can do). One of the most startling moments in Cog's development came when it was learning to touch things. At one point, Cog began to touch and discover its own body. It looked so eerie and human, I was stunned.[24]

Beware of Outsourcing

To reduce costs and improve profits, many jobs in technology, manufacturing, and service are being outsourced to countries such as India, China, and Taiwan, where well-educated, English-speaking workers are being used to do these jobs. For example, programmers in India can produce software at only 10 percent of the cost of these services in the United States. Jobs that are currently being outsourced include accounting, payroll clerks, customer service, data entry, assembly line workers, industrial and production engineers, machine operators, computer-assisted design (CAD) technicians, purchasing managers, textile workers, software developers, and technical support. It is a good idea to consider this trend in choosing your future career and major. Jobs that are most likely to be outsourced are: [25]

- Repetitive jobs, such as accounting,
- Well-defined jobs, such as customer service,
- Small manageable projects, such as software development,
- Jobs in which proximity to the customer is not important, such as technical support.

Jobs that are least likely to be outsourced include:

- Jobs with ambiguity, such as top management jobs,
- Unpredictable jobs, such as troubleshooters,
- Jobs that require understanding of the culture, such as marketing,
- Jobs that require close proximity to the customer, such as auto repair,
- Jobs requiring a high degree of innovation and creativity, such as product design,
- Jobs in entertainment, music, art, and design.

To protect yourself from outsourcing:

- Strive to be the best in the field.
- Be creative and innovative.
- Avoid repetitive jobs that do not require proximity to the customer.
- Choose a career where the demand is so high that it won't matter if some are outsourced.
- Consider a job in the skilled trades; carpenters, plumbers, electricians, hair stylists, construction workers, auto mechanics, and dental hygienists will always be in demand.

New Advances in Biology

Future historians may describe the 21st century as the biology century because of all the developments in this area. If you are interested in biology, it can lead to good careers in the future. One of the most important developments is the Human Genome Project, which has identified the genes in human DNA, the carrier of genetic material. The research done on the human genome has been an impetus for development in some new careers in biotechnology and biomedical technology. Watch the news for future developments that will affect how we all live and work.

Biotechnology will become increasingly important as a way to combat disease, develop new surgical procedures and devices, increase food production, reduce pollution, improve recycling, and provide new tools for law enforcement. Biotechnology includes genomic profiling, biomedical engineering, new pharmaceuticals, genetic engineering, and DNA identification. One of the most promising outcomes of biotechnology will be the production of new pharmaceuticals. About 90 percent of all drugs ever invented have been developed since 1975, and about 6,000 new drugs are waiting for regulatory approval.[26] In the future, biotechnology may be used to find cures for diabetes, arthritis, Alzheimer's disease, and heart disease.

The field of biomedical engineering, which involves developing and testing health care innovations, is expected to grow by 72 percent by 2018.[27] Biomedical technology is the field in which bionic implants are being developed for the human body. Scientists are working on the development of artificial limbs and organs including eyes, ears, hearts, and kidneys. A promising new development in this field is brain and computer interfaces. Scientists recently implanted a computer chip into the brain of a quadriplegic, enabling him to control a computer and television with his mind.[28] Biotechnology also develops new diagnostic test equipment and surgical tools.

Increase in Entrepreneurship

An important trend for the new millennium is the increase in entrepreneurship, which means starting your own business. For the Baby Boom Generation, it was expected that one would have a job for life. Because of rapid changes in society and the world of work, Millennials can expect to have as many as 10 different jobs over a lifetime.[29] A growing number of entrepreneurs operate their small businesses from home, taking advantage of telecommuting and the Internet to communicate with customers. While being an entrepreneur has some risks involved, there are many benefits, such as flexible scheduling, being your own boss, taking charge of your own destiny, and greater potential for future income if your company is successful. You won't have to worry about being outsourced, either.

The Effect of Terrorism and Need for Security

Fear of terrorism has changed attitudes that will affect career trends for years to come. Terrorist attacks have created an atmosphere of uncertainty that has had a negative effect on the economy and has increased unemployment. For example, the airline industry is struggling financially as people hesitate to fly to their vacation destinations. People are choosing to stay in the safety of their homes, offices, cars, and gated communities. Since people are spending more time at home, they spend more money making their homes comfortable. Faith Popcorn, who is famous for predicting future trends, has called this phenomenon "cocooning," which is "our desire to build ourselves strong and cozy nests where we can retreat from the world, enjoying ourselves in safety and comfort."[30] As a result, construction, home remodeling, and sales of entertainment systems are increasing.

Another result of terrorism is the shift toward occupations that provide value to society and in which people can search for personal satisfaction.[31] More people volunteer their time to help others, and are considering careers in education, social work, and medical occupations. When people are forced to relocate because of unemployment, they are considering moving to smaller towns that have a sense of community and a feeling of safety.

As the world population continues to grow, there is continued conflict over resources and ideologies and an increased need for security and safety. Law enforcement, intelligence, forensics, international relations, foreign affairs, and security administration careers will be in demand.

Nontraditional Workers

Unlike traditional workers, nontraditional workers do not have full-time, year-round jobs with health and retirement benefits. Employers are moving toward using nontraditional workers, including multiple job holders, contingent and part-time workers, independent contractors, and temporary workers. Nearly four out of five employers use nontraditional workers to help them become more efficient, prevent layoffs, and access workers with special skills. There are advantages and disadvantages to this arrangement. Nontraditional workers have no benefits and risk unemployment. However, this arrangement can provide workers with a flexible work schedule in which they work during some periods and pursue other interests or gain new skills when not working.

Journal Entry #2

Do a quick review of the career trends presented in this chapter:

- Moving from the production of goods to service and technology
- Increased opportunities in health care occupations
- Increased need for education
- New green careers
- Increasing diversity in the workplace
- Increased e-commerce and entrepreneurship
- New developments in technology, communication, and biology
- The effect of terrorism and the need for security
- Nontraditional workers

Write one paragraph about how any of these trends might affect your future.

Top Jobs for the Future[32]

Based on current career trends, here are some jobs that should be in high demand for the next 10 years.

Field of Employment	Job Titles
Business	Marketing Manager, Security and Financial Service, Internet Marketing Specialist, Advertising Executive, Buyer, Sales Person, Real Estate Agent, Business Development Manager, Marketing Researcher, Recruiter
Education	Teacher, Teacher's Aide, Adult Education Instructor, Math and Science Teacher
Entertainment	Dancer, Producer, Director, Actor, Content Creator, Musician, Artist, Commercial Artist, Writer, Technical Writer, Newspaper Reporter, News Anchor Person
Health	Emergency Medical Technician, Surgeon, Chiropractor, Dental Hygienist, Registered Nurse, Medical Assistant, Therapist, Respiratory Therapist, Home Health Aide, Primary Care Physician, Medical Lab Technician, Radiology Technician, Physical Therapist, Dental Assistant, Nurse's Aide
Information Technology	Computer Systems Analyst, Computer Engineer, Web Specialist, Network Support Technician, Java Programmer, Information Technology Manager, Web Developer, Database Administrator, Network Engineer
Law/Law Enforcement	Correction Officer, Law Officer, Anti-Terrorist Specialist, Security Guard, Tax/Estate Attorney, Intellectual Property Attorney
Services	Veterinarian, Social Worker, Hair Stylist, Telephone Repair Technician, Aircraft Mechanic, Guidance Counselor, Occupational Therapist, Child Care Assistant, Baker, Landscape Architect, Pest Controller, Chef, Caterer, Food Server
Sports	Athlete, Coach, Umpire, Physical Trainer
Technology	Electrical Engineer, Biological Scientist, Electronic Technician, CAD Operator, Product Designer, Sales Engineer, Applications Engineer, Product Marketing Engineer, Technical Support Manager, Product Development Manager
Trades	Carpenter, Plumber, Electrician
Travel/Transportation	Package Delivery Person, Flight Attendant, Hotel/Restaurant Manager, Taxi Driver, Chauffeur, Driver

Work Skills for the 21st Century

Because of rapid changes in technology, college students of today may be preparing for jobs that do not exist right now. After graduation, many college students find employment that is not even related to their college majors. One researcher found that 48 percent of college graduates find employment in fields not related to their college majors.[33] More important than one's college major are the general skills learned in college that prepare students for the future.

To define skills needed in the future workplace, the U.S. Secretary of Labor created the Secretary's Commission on Achieving Necessary Skills (SCANS). Based on interviews with employers and educators, the members of the commission outlined foundation skills and workplace competencies needed to succeed in the workplace in the 21st century.[34] The following skills apply to all occupations in all fields and will help you to become a successful employee, regardless of your major. As you read through these skills, think about your competency in these areas.

Foundation Skills
Basic Skills

- Reading
- Writing
- Basic arithmetic
- Higher-level mathematics
- Listening
- Speaking

Thinking Skills

- Creative thinking
- Decision making
- Problem solving
- Mental visualization
- Knowing how to learn
- Reasoning

Personal Qualities

- Responsibility
- Self-esteem
- Sociability
- Self-management
- Integrity/honesty

Workplace Competencies

Resources

- **Time.** Selects relevant goals, sets priorities, and follows schedules.
- **Money.** Uses budgets, keeps records, and makes adjustments.
- **Materials and facilities.** Acquires, stores, and distributes materials, supplies, parts, equipment, space, or final products.
- **Human resources.** Assesses knowledge and skills, distributes work, evaluates performance, and provides feedback.

Interpersonal

- **Participates as a member of a team.** Works cooperatively with others and contributes to group efforts.
- **Teaches others.** Helps others learn needed skills.
- **Serves clients/customers.** Works and communicates with clients and customers to satisfy their expectations.
- **Exercises leadership.** Communicates, encourages, persuades, and convinces others; responsibly challenges procedures, policies, or authority.
- **Negotiates to arrive at a decision.** Works toward an agreement involving resources or diverging interests.
- **Works with cultural diversity.** Works well with men and women and with people from a variety of ethnic, social, or educational backgrounds.

Information

- **Acquires and evaluates information.** Identifies the need for information, obtains information, and evaluates it.
- **Organizes and maintains information.** Organizes, processes, and maintains written or computerized records.
- **Uses computers to process information.** Employs computers to acquire, organize, analyze, and communicate information.

Systems

- **Understands systems.** Knows how social, organizational, and technological systems work and operates efficiently within them.
- **Monitors and corrects performance.** Distinguishes trends, predicts impacts of actions on systems operations, and takes action to correct performance.
- **Improves and designs systems.** Develops new systems to improve products or services.

Technology

- **Selects technology.** Judges which procedures, tools, or machines, including computers, will produce the desired results.
- **Applies technology to tasks.** Understands the proper procedures for using machines and computers.
- **Maintains and troubleshoots technology.** Prevents, identifies, or solves problems with machines, computers, and other technologies.

Because the workplace is changing, these skills may be more important than the background acquired through a college major. Work to develop these skills and you will be prepared for whatever lies ahead.

How to Research Your Career

After you have assessed your personality, interests, values, and talents, the next step is to learn about the world of work. If you can match your interests to the world of work, you can find work that is interesting and you can excel in it. To learn about the world of work, you will need to research possible careers. This includes reading career descriptions and investigating career outlooks, salaries, and educational requirements.

Career Descriptions

The career description tells you about the nature of the work, working conditions, employment, training, qualifications, advancement, job outlook, earnings, and related occupations. The two best sources of job descriptions are the *Occupational Outlook Handbook* and *Occupational Outlook Quarterly*. The *Handbook*, published by the Bureau of Labor Statistics, is like an encyclopedia of careers. You can search alphabetically by career or by career cluster.

The *Occupational Outlook Quarterly* is a periodical with up-to-date articles on new and emerging occupations, training opportunities, salary trends, and new studies from the Bureau of Labor Statistics. You can find these resources in a public or school library, at a college career center, or on the *College Success Website* at http://www.collegesuccess1.com/Links9Career.htm.

Career Outlook

It is especially important to know about the career outlook of an occupation you are considering. Career outlook includes salary and availability of employment. How much does the occupation pay? Will the occupation exist in the future, and will there be employment opportunities? Of course, you will want to prepare yourself for careers that pay well and have future employment opportunities.

You can find information about career outlooks in the sources listed above, current periodicals, and materials from the Bureau of Labor Statistics. The following table, for example, lists the fastest-growing occupations, occupations with the highest salaries, and occupations with the largest job growth. Information from the Bureau of Labor Statistics is also available online.

Employment Projections 2008–2018[35]

10 Fastest-Growing Occupations	10 Industries with the Largest Wage and Salary Employment Growth	10 Occupations with the Largest Numerical Job Growth
Biomedical engineers	Management, scientific, technical	Registered nurses
Network systems and data communications analysts	Physicians	Home health aides
Home health aides	Computer systems design and related	Customer service representatives
Personal and home care aides	General merchandise stores	Food preparation workers
Financial examiners	Employment services	Personal and home care aides
Medical scientists	Local government	Retail salespersons
Physician assistants	Home health care services	Office clerks
Skin care specialists	Services for elderly and disabled	Accountants and auditors
Biochemists and biophysicists	Nursing care facilities	Nursing aides, orderlies
Athletic trainers	Full-service restaurants	Postsecondary teachers

Planning Your Education

Once you have assessed your personal characteristics and researched your career options, it is important to plan your education. If you have a plan, you will be able to finish your education more quickly and avoid taking unnecessary classes. You can begin work on your educational plan by following the steps below. After you have done some work on your plan, visit your college counselor or advisor to make sure that your plan is appropriate.

"Think not of yourself as the architect of your career but as the sculptor. Expect to have a lot of hard hammering, chiseling, scraping and polishing."

B.C. Forbes

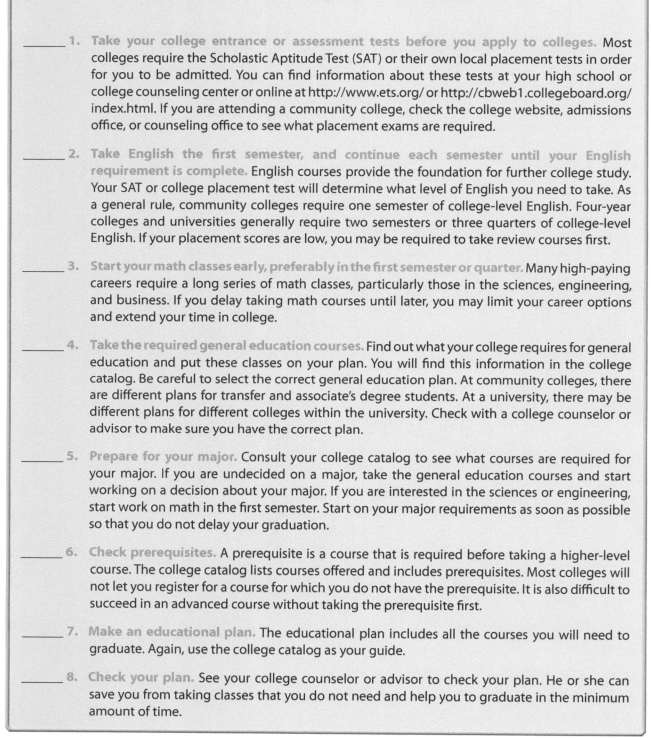

ACTIVITY

Steps in Planning Your Education

_____ 1. **Take your college entrance or assessment tests before you apply to colleges.** Most colleges require the Scholastic Aptitude Test (SAT) or their own local placement tests in order for you to be admitted. You can find information about these tests at your high school or college counseling center or online at http://www.ets.org/ or http://cbweb1.collegeboard.org/index.html. If you are attending a community college, check the college website, admissions office, or counseling office to see what placement exams are required.

_____ 2. **Take English the first semester, and continue each semester until your English requirement is complete.** English courses provide the foundation for further college study. Your SAT or college placement test will determine what level of English you need to take. As a general rule, community colleges require one semester of college-level English. Four-year colleges and universities generally require two semesters or three quarters of college-level English. If your placement scores are low, you may be required to take review courses first.

_____ 3. **Start your math classes early, preferably in the first semester or quarter.** Many high-paying careers require a long series of math classes, particularly those in the sciences, engineering, and business. If you delay taking math courses until later, you may limit your career options and extend your time in college.

_____ 4. **Take the required general education courses.** Find out what your college requires for general education and put these classes on your plan. You will find this information in the college catalog. Be careful to select the correct general education plan. At community colleges, there are different plans for transfer and associate's degree students. At a university, there may be different plans for different colleges within the university. Check with a college counselor or advisor to make sure you have the correct plan.

_____ 5. **Prepare for your major.** Consult your college catalog to see what courses are required for your major. If you are undecided on a major, take the general education courses and start working on a decision about your major. If you are interested in the sciences or engineering, start work on math in the first semester. Start on your major requirements as soon as possible so that you do not delay your graduation.

_____ 6. **Check prerequisites.** A prerequisite is a course that is required before taking a higher-level course. The college catalog lists courses offered and includes prerequisites. Most colleges will not let you register for a course for which you do not have the prerequisite. It is also difficult to succeed in an advanced course without taking the prerequisite first.

_____ 7. **Make an educational plan.** The educational plan includes all the courses you will need to graduate. Again, use the college catalog as your guide.

_____ 8. **Check your plan.** See your college counselor or advisor to check your plan. He or she can save you from taking classes that you do not need and help you to graduate in the minimum amount of time.

Making Good Decisions

Knowing how to make a good decision about your career and important life events is very important to your future, as this short poem by J. Wooden sums up:

> There is a choice you have to make,
> In everything you do.
> And you must always keep in mind,
> The choice you make, makes you.[36]

Sometimes people end up in a career because they simply seized an opportunity for employment. A good job becomes available and they happen to be in the right place at the right time. Sometimes people end up in a career because it is familiar to them, because it is a job held by a member of the family or a friend in the community. Sometimes people end up in a career because of economic necessity. The job pays well and they need the money. These careers are the result of chance circumstances. Sometimes they turn out well, and sometimes they turn out miserably.

Whether you are male or female, married or single, you will spend a great deal of your life working. By doing some careful thinking and planning about your career, you can improve your chances of success and happiness. Use the following steps to do some careful decision making about your career. Although you are the person who needs to make the decision about a career, you can get help from your college career center or your college counselor or advisor.

Steps in Making a Career Decision

1. **Begin with self-assessment.**
   - What is your personality type?
   - What are your interests?
   - What are your talents, gifts, and strengths?
   - What is your learning style?
   - What are your values?
   - What lifestyle do you prefer?

2. **Explore your options.**
   - What careers match your personal characteristics?

3. **Research your career options.**
   - Read the job description.
   - Investigate the career outlook.

- What is the salary?

- What training and education is required?

- Speak with an advisor, counselor, or person involved in the career that interests you.

- Choose a career or general career area that matches your personal characteristics.

4. **Plan your education to match your career goal.**

   - Try out courses in your area of interest.

   - Start your general education if you need more time to decide on a major.

   - Try an internship or part-time job in your area of interest.

5. **Make a commitment to take action and follow through with your plan.**

6. **Evaluate.**

   - Do you like the courses you are taking?

   - Are you doing well in the courses?

   - Continue research if necessary.

7. **Refine your plan.**

   - Make your plan more specific to aim for a particular career.

   - Select the college major that is best for you.

8. **Change your plan if it is not working.**

   - Go back to the self-assessment step.

> "Find a job you like and add five days to every week."
>
> H. Jackson Browne

The Decision-Making Process

- **Dependent decisions.** Different kinds of decisions are appropriate in different situations. When you make a dependent decision, you depend on someone else to make the decision for you. The dependent decision was probably the first kind of decision that you ever made. When your parents told you what to do as a child, you were making a dependent decision. As an adult, you make a dependent decision when your doctor tells you what medication to take for an illness or when your stockbroker tells you what stock you should purchase. Dependent decisions are easy to make and require little thought. Making a dependent decision saves time and energy.

  The dependent decision, however, has some disadvantages. You may not like the outcome of the decision. The medication that your doctor prescribes may have unpleasant side effects. The stock that you purchased may go down in value. When students ask a counselor to recommend a major or a career, they are making a dependent decision. When the decision does not work, they blame the counselor. Even if the dependent decision does have good results, you may become dependent on others to continue making decisions for you. Dependent decisions do work in certain situations, but they do not give you as much control over your own life.

- **Intuitive decisions.** Intuitive decisions are based on intuition or a gut feeling about what is the best course of action. Intuitive decisions can be made quickly and are useful in dealing with emergencies. If I see a car heading on a collision path toward me, I have to swerve quickly to the right or left. I do not have time to ask someone else what to do or think much about the alternatives. Another example of an intuitive decision is in gambling. If I am trying to decide whether to bet a dollar on red or black, I rely on my gut feeling to make a choice. Intuitive decisions may work out or they may not. You could make a mistake and swerve the wrong way as the car approaches or you could lose your money in gambling.

- **Planful decisions.** For important decisions, it is advantageous to use what is called a planful decision. The planful decision is made after carefully weighing the consequences and the pros and cons of the different alternatives. The planful decision-making strategy is particularly useful for such decisions as:
  - What will be my major?
  - What career should I choose?
  - Whom should I marry?

Types of Decisions
- Dependent
- Intuitive
- Planful

The steps in a planful decision-making process:

1. **State the problem.** When we become aware of a problem, the first step is to state the problem in the simplest way possible. Just stating the problem will help you to clarify the issues.

2. **Consider your values.** What is important to you? What are your hopes and dreams? By keeping your values in mind, you are more likely to make a decision that will make you happy.

3. **What are your talents?** What special skills do you have? How can you make a decision that utilizes these skills?

4. **Gather information.** What information can you find that would be helpful in solving the problem? Look for ideas. Ask other people. Do some research. Gathering information can give you insight into alternatives or possible solutions to the problem.

5. **Generate alternatives.** Based on the information you have gathered, identify some possible solutions to the problem.

6. **Evaluate the pros and cons of each alternative.** List the alternatives and think about the pros and cons of each one. In thinking about the pros and cons, consider your values and talents as well as your future goals.

7. **Select the best alternative.** Choose the alternative that is the best match for your values and helps you to achieve your goals.

8. **Take action.** You put your decision into practice when you take some action on it. Get started!

The Resume and Job Interview

After investing your time in achieving a college education, you will need some additional skills to get a job. Having a good resume and knowing how to successfully interview for a job will help you to obtain your dream job.

Your Resume

A resume is a snapshot of your education and experience. It is generally one page in length. You will need a resume to apply for scholarships or part-time jobs, or find a position after you graduate. Start with a file of information you can use to create your resume. Keep your resume on file in your computer or on your flash drive so that you can revise it as needed. A resume includes the following:

- Contact information: your name, address, telephone number, and email address
- A brief statement of your career objective

- A summary of your education:
  - Names and locations of schools
  - Dates of attendance
  - Diplomas or degrees received
- A summary of your work and/or volunteer experience
- If you have little directly related work experience, a list of courses you have taken that would help the employer understand your skills for employment
- Special skills, honors, awards, or achievements
- References (people who can recommend you for a job or scholarship)

Your resume is important in establishing a good first impression. There is no one best way to write a resume. Whatever form you choose, write clearly and be brief, neat, and honest. If your resume is too lengthy or difficult to read, it may wind up in the trash can. Adjust your resume to match the job for which you are applying. This is easy to do if you have your resume stored on your computer. Update your resume regularly.

Ask for a letter of reference from your current supervisor at work or someone in a position to recommend you, such as a college professor or community member. Ask the person to address the letter "To Whom It May Concern" so that you can use the letter many times. The person recommending you should comment on your work habits, skills, and personal qualities. If you wait until you graduate to obtain letters of reference, potential recommenders may no longer be there or may not remember who you are. Always ask if you can use a person's name as a reference. When you are applying for a job and references are requested, phone the people who have agreed to recommend you and let them know to expect a call.

Print your resume so that it looks professional. Use a good-quality white, tan, or gray paper.

You will probably need to post your resume online to apply for some scholarships and job opportunities. Having your resume on the computer will make this task easier.

The Cover Letter

When you respond to job announcements, you will send a cover letter with your resume attached. Address your letter to a specific person at the company or organization and spell the name correctly. You can call the personnel office to obtain this information. The purpose of the cover letter is to state your interest in the job, highlight your qualifications, and get the employer to read your resume and call you for an interview. The cover letter should be brief and to the point. Include the following items:

- State the job you are interested in and how you heard about the opening.
- Briefly state how your education and experience would be assets to the company.
- Ask for an interview and tell the employer how you can be contacted.
- Attach your resume.
- Your cover letter is the first contact you have with the employer. Make it neat and free from errors.
- Use spell check and grammar check, read it over again, and have someone else check it for you.

The Job Interview

Knowing how to be successful in an interview will help you to get the job that you want. Here are some ideas for being prepared and making a good impression.

- **Learn about the job.** Before the interview, it is important to research both the company and the job. This research will help you in two ways: you will know if the job is really the one you want, and you will have information that will help you to succeed at the interview. If you have taken the time to learn about the company before the interview, you will make a good impression and show that you are really interested in the job. Here are some ways that you can find this information:
  - Your college or public library may have a profile describing the company and the products it produces. This profile may include the size of the company and the company mission or philosophy.
  - Do you know someone who works for the company? Do any members of your family, friends, or teachers know someone who works for the company? If so, you can find out valuable information about the company.
  - The personnel office often has informational brochures that describe the employer.
  - Visit the company website on the Internet.

- **Understand the criteria used in an interview.** The interviewer represents the company and is looking for the best person to fill the job. It is your job to show the interviewer that you will do a good job. Of course you are interested in salary and benefits, but in order to get hired you must first convince the interviewer that you have something to offer the company. Focus on what you can offer the company based on your education and experience and what you have learned about the company. You may be able to obtain information on salary and benefits from the personnel office before the interview.

  Interviewers look for candidates who show the enthusiasm and commitment necessary to do a good job. They are interested in hiring someone who can work as part of a team. Think about your education and experience and be prepared to describe your skills and give examples of how you have been successful on the job. Give a realistic and honest description of your work.

- **Make a good impression.** Here are some suggestions for making a good impression:
  - Dress appropriately for the interview. Look at how the employees of the company dress and then dress a little better. Of course, your attire will vary with the type of job you are seeking. You will dress differently if you are interviewing for a position as manager of a surf shop or an entry-level job in an engineering firm. Wear a conservative dark-colored or neutral suit for most professional positions. Do not wear too much jewelry, and hide excess body piercings (unless you are applying at a piercing shop). Cover any tattoos if they are not appropriate for the workplace.
  - Relax during the interview. You can relax by preparing in advance. Research the company, practice interview questions, and visualize yourself in the interview room feeling confident about the interview.
  - When you enter the interview room, smile, introduce yourself, and shake hands with the interviewer. If your hands are cold and clammy, go to the restroom before the interview and run warm water over your hands or rub them together.
  - Maintain eye contact with the interviewer and sit up straight. Poor posture or leaning back in your chair could be seen as a lack of confidence or interest in the job.

- **Anticipate the interview questions.** Listen carefully to the interview questions. Ask for clarification of any question you do not understand. Answer the questions concisely and honestly. It helps to anticipate the questions that are likely to be asked and think about your answers in advance. Generally, be prepared to talk about yourself, your

Tips for a Successful Job Interview

- Learn about job
- Understand criteria of interview
- Make a good impression
- Anticipate interview questions
- Send thank-you note

Making a Good Impression

- Dress appropriately
- Relax
- Prepare in advance
- Smile
- Shake hands
- Introduce yourself
- Maintain eye contact
- Sit up straight

goals, and your reasons for applying for the job. Following are some questions that are typically asked in interviews and some suggestions for answering them:

1. **What can you tell us about yourself?** Think about the job requirements, and remember that the interviewer is looking for someone who will do a good job for the company. Talk about your education and experience as they relate to the job. You can put in interesting facts about your life and your hobbies, but keep your answers brief. This question is generally an icebreaker that helps the interviewer get a general picture of you and help you relax.

2. **Why do you want this job? Why should I hire you?** Think about the research you did on this company and several ways that you could benefit the company. A good answer might be, "I have always been good at technical skills and engineering. I am interested in putting these technical skills into practice in your company." A not-so-good answer would be, "I'm interested in making a lot of money and need health insurance."

3. **Why are you leaving your present job?** Instead of saying that the boss was horrible and the working conditions were intolerable (even if this was the case), think of some positive reasons for leaving, such as:

   • I am looking for a job that provides challenge and an opportunity for growth.

   • I received my degree and am looking for a job where I can use my education.

   • I had a part-time job to help me through school. I have graduated and am looking for a career.

   • I moved (or the company downsized or went out of business).

   Be careful about discussing problems on your previous job. The interviewers might assume that you were the cause of the problems or that you could not get along with other people.

4. **What are your strengths and weaknesses?** Think about your strengths in relation to the job requirements, and be prepared to talk about them during the interview. When asked about your weaknesses, smile and try to turn them into strengths. For example, if you are an introvert, you might say that you are quiet and like to concentrate on your work, but you make an effort to communicate with others on the job. If you are an extrovert, say that you enjoy talking and working with others, but you are good at time management and get the job done on time. If you are a perfectionist, say that you like to do an excellent job, but you know the importance of meeting deadlines, so you do the best you can in the time available.

Tips for Answering Questions

• Listen carefully
• Ask for clarification
• Answer concisely and honestly

5. **Tell us about a difficulty or problem that you solved on the job.** Think about some problem that you successfully solved on the job and describe how you did it. Focus on what you accomplished. If the problem was one that dealt with other people, do not focus on blaming or complaining. Focus on your desire to work things out and work well with everyone.

6. **Tell us about one of your achievements on the job.** Give examples of projects you have done on the job that have turned out well and projects that gave you a sense of pride and accomplishment.

7. **What do you like best about your work? What do you like least?** Think about these questions in advance and use the question about what you like best to highlight your skills for the job. For the question about what you like the least, be honest but express your willingness to do the job that is required.

8. **Are there any questions that you would like to ask?** Based on your research on the company, think of some specific questions that show your interest in the company. A good question might be, "Tell me about your company's plans for the future." A not-so-good question would be, "How much vacation do I get?"

9. **Write a thank-you note.** After the interview, write a thank-you note and express your interest in the job. It makes a good impression and causes the interviewer to think about you again.

Journal Entry #4

A friend is looking for a job. What advice would you give him or her about the resume and job interview?

KEYS TO SUCCESS · Life Is a Dangerous Opportunity

Even though we may do our best in planning our career and education, life does not always turn out as planned. Unexpected events happen, putting our life in crisis. The crisis might be loss of employment, divorce, illness, or death of a loved one. How we deal with the crisis events in our lives can have a great impact on our current well-being and the future.

The Chinese word for crisis has two characters: one character represents danger and the other represents opportunity. Every crisis has the danger of loss of something important and the resulting emotions of frustration, sorrow, and grief. But every crisis also has an opportunity. Sometimes it is difficult to see the opportunity because we are overwhelmed by the danger. A crisis, however, can provide an impetus for change and growth. A crisis forces us to look inside ourselves to find capabilities that have always been there, although we did not know it. If life goes too smoothly, there is no motivation to change. If we get too comfortable, we stop growing. There is no testing of our capabilities. We stay in the same patterns.

To find the opportunity in a crisis, focus on what is possible in the situation. Every adversity has the seed of a greater benefit or possibility. Expect things to work out well. Expect success. To deal with negative emotions, consider that feelings are not simply a result of what happens to us, but of our interpretation of events. If we focus on the danger, we cannot see the possibilities.

As a practical application, consider the example of someone who has just lost a job. John had worked as a construction worker for nearly 10 years when he injured his back. His doctor told him that he would no longer be able to do physical labor. John was 30 years old and had two children and large house and truck payments. He was having difficulty finding a job that paid as well as his construction job, and was suffering from many negative emotions resulting from his loss of employment.

John decided that he would have to use his brain rather than his back. As soon as he was up and moving, he started taking some general education courses at the local college. He assessed his skills and identified his strengths. He was a good father and communicated well with his children. He had wanted to go to college, but got married early and started to work in construction instead. John decided that he would really enjoy being a marriage and family counselor. It would mean getting a bachelor's and a master's degree, which would take five or more years.

John began to search for a way to accomplish this new goal. He first tackled the financial problems. He investigated vocational rehabilitation, veteran's benefits, financial aid, and scholarships. He sold his house and his truck. His wife took a part-time job. He worked out a careful budget. He began to work toward his new goal with a high degree of motivation and self-satisfaction. He had found a new opportunity.

At times in life, you may face a crisis or setback which causes an unexpected change in plans. If you think positively about the situation, you can think of some new opportunities for the future. This situation is called a dangerous opportunity. Describe a dangerous opportunity you have faced in your life. What were the dangers and what opportunities did you find?

> "Life is not about waiting for the storms to pass . . . it's about learning how to dance in the rain."
>
> Vivian Greene

JOURNAL ENTRIES

Planning Your Career and Education

Go to http://www.collegesuccess1.com/JournalEntries.htm for Word files of the Journal Entries

Success over the Internet

Visit the *College Success Website* at http://www.collegesuccess1.com/

The *College Success Website* is continually updated with new topics and links to the material presented in this chapter. Topics include:

- Future trends
- Planning your major
- Job descriptions
- Career outlooks
- Career information
- Salary
- Interests
- Self-assessment
- Exploring careers
- Hot jobs for the future
- Profiles of successful people
- Resume writing
- Interviewing
- The personal side of work
- Using the Internet for a job search
- Job openings
- Decision making
- How to write a resume and cover letter
- How to post your resume online

Contact your instructor if you have any problems in accessing the *College Success Website*.

Notes

1. Michael T. Robinson, "Top Jobs for the Future," from www.careerplanner.com, 2004.

2. Gail Sheehy, *New Passages* (New York: Random House, 1995), 34.

3. U.S. National Center for Health Statistics, National Vital Statistics Reports (NVSR), *Deaths: Final Data for 2006*, Vol. 57, No. 14, April 17, 2009.

4. Jeff Giles, "Generalization X," *Newsweek*, June 6, 1994.

5. Jane Bryant Quinn, "The Luck of the Xers, Comeback Kids: Young People Will Live Better Than They Think," *Newsweek*, 6 June 1994, 66–67.

6. Ellen Neuborne, http://www.businessweek.com, 1999.

7. Claudia Smith Brison, http://www.thestate.com, 14 July 2002.

8. Neil Howe and William Strauss, *Millennials Rising: The Next Great Generation* (New York: Vintage Books, 2000).

9. Neuborne, www.businessweek.com, 1999.

10. John Naisbitt, Patricia Aburdeen, and Walter Kiechel III, "How We Will Work in the Year 2000," *Fortune*, 17 May 1993, 41–52.

11. U.S. Bureau of Labor Statistics, *Occupational Outlook Handbook*, 2010–11 Edition, "Overview of the 2008–18 Projections," accessed from http://data.bls.gov

12. Ibid.

13. Ibid.

14. Ibid.

15. Joyce Lain Kennedy, *Joyce Lain Kennedy's Career Book* (Chicago, IL: VGM Career Horizons, 1993), 32.

16. U.S. Bureau of Labor Statistics, "Overview of the 2008–18 Projections."

17. *The Wall Street Journal*, "E-Commerce Growth Slows, But Still Out-Paces Retail," accessed March 2010, http://blogs.wsj.com

18. Bill Gates, "Microprocessors Upgraded the Way We Live," *USA Today*, 22 June 1999.

19. From "The Microsoft Future According to Bill Gates," accessed from http://www.ameinfo.com/33384.html, 2004.

20. Bill Gates, *Business @ the Speed of Thought: Using a Digital Nervous System* (Warner, 1999). Excerpts available at www.speed-of-thought.com.

21. U.S. Bureau of Labor Statistics, "Overview of the 2008–18 Projections."

22. "Tomorrow's Best Careers," from http://www.future-trends.com, 2004.

23. Dan Tynan, "The Next 25 Years in Tech," www.pcworld.com, January 30, 2008.

24. Anne Foerst, "A New Breed of 'Replicants' Is Redefining What It Means to Be Human," *Forbes ASAP*, 1999.

25. Michael T. Robinson, "Offshoring of America's Top Jobs," from http://www.careerplanner.com, 2004.

26. "Tomorrow's Best Careers," from http://www.future-trends.com, 2004.

27. U.S. Bureau of Labor Statistics, "Overview of the 2008–18 Projections."

28. Roxanne Khamsi, "Paralyzed Man Sends E-Mail by Thought," *News @ Nature.Com*, October 13, 2004.

29. Judith Kautz, "Entrepreneurship Beyond 2000," from www.smallbusinessnotes.com, 2004.

30. Faith Popcorn and Lys Marigold, *Clicking: 16 Trends to Future Fit Your Life, Your Work, and Your Business* (New York: HarperCollins, 1996).

31. James E. Challenger, "Career Pros: Terrorism's Legacy," from www.jobjournal.com, 2003.

32. Michael T. Robinson, "Top Jobs for the Future," CareerPlanner.com, 2008.

33. T. J. Grites, "Being 'Undecided' Could Be the Best Decision They Could Make," *School Counselor* 29 (1981): 41–46.

34. Secretary's Commission on Achieving Necessary Skills (SCANS), *Learning a Living: A Blueprint for High Performance* (Washington, DC: U.S. Department of Labor, 1991).

35. U.S. Bureau of Labor Statistics, "Overview of the 2008–18 Projections."

36. Quoted in Rob Gilbert, ed., *Bits and Pieces,* 7 October 1999.

Sample Cover Letter

Sara Student
222 College Avenue
San Diego, CA 92019
(619) 123-4567

June 20, 2010

Mr. John Smith
Director of Human Resources
Future Technology Company
111 Technology Way
La Jolla, CA 92111

Dear Mr. Smith:

At our college job fair last week, I enjoyed speaking with you about some new engineering jobs available at Future Technology Company. As you suggested, I am sending my resume. I am interested in your opening for an electrical engineer. Is there anything else I need to do to apply for this position?

While at UCSD, I gained experience in laboratory projects, writing scientific reports, and preparing technical presentations. Some engineering projects that I completed relate to work done at your company:

- Constructed a programmable robot with motor and sensors
- Worked with a group of students on the design of a satellite communications system
- Completed lab projects on innovative fiber-optic fabrication techniques
- Proposed a design for a prosthetic device to help the visually impaired

For my senior design project, I used my knowledge of digital signal processing and systems integration to design and construct a voice modulator. This project involved applying theory to hardware and understanding information processing as well as the relation of a computer to its controlled devices.

I am excited about the possibility of continuing work in this field and would enjoy the opportunity to discuss my qualifications in more detail. I am available for an interview at your convenience. I look forward to hearing from you.

Sincerely,

Sara Student

Encl.: Resume

Sample Resume for a Recent College Graduate

Sara Student
222 College Avenue; San Diego, CA 92019
(619) 123-4567
saraengineer@aol.com

OBJECTIVE	Electrical Engineer
HIGHLIGHTS	Recent degree in Electrical Engineering Specialized coursework in electromagnetism, photonics and lasers, biomedical imaging devices, and experimental techniques
EDUCATION	B.S., Electrical Engineering, University of California, San Diego, CA, 2010 A.S. with Honors, Cuyamaca College, El Cajon, CA, 2008

KEY RELATED COURSES
- **Circuits and systems:** solving network equations, Laplace transforms, practical robotics development
- **Electromagnetism:** Maxwell's equations, wave guides and transmission, electromagnetic properties of circuits and materials
- **Experimental techniques:** built and programmed a voice processor; studied transducers, computer architecture, and interfacing; applied integrated construction techniques
- **Photonics and lasers:** laser stability and design, holography, optical information processing, pattern recognition, electro-optic modulation, fiber optics
- **Biomedical imaging devices:** microscopy, x-rays, and neural imaging; designed an optical prosthesis
- **Quantum physics:** uncertainty principle, wave equation and spin, particle models, scattering theory and radiation

SKILLS	**Computer Skills:** PSpice, Matlab, Java, DSP, Assembly Language, Unix, Windows, Microsoft Word, Excel, and PowerPoint **Technical Skills:** Microprocessors, circuits, optical components, oscilloscope, function generator, photovoltaics, signal processing, typing, SQUID testing **Personal Skills:** Leadership, good people skills, organized, responsible, creative, motivated, hardworking, good writing skills
EMPLOYMENT	Intern, Quantum Design, La Jolla, CA, Summer 2009 Computer Lab Assistant, UCSD, La Jolla, CA, 2008–2010 Teacher's Aide, Cuyamaca College, El Cajon, CA, 2005–2007 Volunteer, Habitat for Humanity, Tijuana, Mexico, 2003–2005
INTERESTS	Optics, computing, programming, physics, electronic music, sampling, marine biology, and scuba diving
ACHIEVEMENTS	Advanced Placement Scholar Dean's List, Phi Theta Kappa Honor Society Provost's Honors List

Resume Worksheet for Your Ideal Career

Name _____   Date _____

Use this worksheet to prepare a resume similar to the sample on the previous page. Assume that you have graduated from college and are applying for your ideal career.

1. What is the specific job title of your ideal job?

2. What are two or three qualifications you possess that would especially qualify you for this job? These qualifications can be listed under Highlights on your resume.

3. List your degree or degrees, major, and dates of completion.

4. List five courses you will take to prepare for your ideal career. For each course, list some key components that would catch the interest of your potential employer. Use a college catalog to complete this section.

5. List the skills you would need in each of these areas.

Computer skills:

Technical or other job-related skills:

Personal skills related to your job objective:

6. List employment that would prepare you for your ideal job. Consider internships or part-time employment.

7. What are your interests?

8. What special achievements or awards do you have?

Name _____ Date _____

Answer the following questions to prepare for the interview for your ideal job. If you do not know what your ideal job is, pretend that you are interviewing for any professional job. You may want to practice these questions with a classmate.

1. What can you tell us about yourself?

2. Why are you leaving your present job?

3. What are your strengths and weaknesses?

4. Tell us about a difficulty or problem that you solved on the job.

5. Tell us about one of your achievements on the job.

6. What do you like best about your work? What do you like least?

7. Are there any questions that you would like to ask?

Rate Your Skills for Success in the Workplace

Name _____ Date _____

Read each statement relating to skills needed for success in the workplace. Use the following scale to rate your competencies:

5 = Excellent   4 = Very good   3 = Average   2 = Needs improvement   1 = Need to develop

_____ 1. I have good reading skills. I can locate information I need to read and understand and interpret it. I can pick out the main idea and judge the accuracy of the information.

_____ 2. I have good writing skills. I can communicate thoughts, ideas, and information in writing. I know how to edit and revise my writing and use correct spelling, punctuation, and grammar.

_____ 3. I am good at arithmetic. I can perform basic computations using whole numbers and percentages. I can make reasonable estimates without a calculator and can read tables, graphs, and charts.

_____ 4. I am good at mathematics. I can use a variety of mathematical techniques including statistics to predict the occurrence of events.

_____ 5. I am good at speaking. I can organize my ideas and participate in discussions and group presentations. I speak clearly and am a good listener. I ask questions to obtain feedback when needed.

_____ 6. I am a creative thinker. I can come up with new ideas and unusual connections. I can imagine new possibilities and combine ideas in new ways.

_____ 7. I make good decisions. I can specify goals and constraints, generate alternatives, consider risks, and evaluate alternatives.

_____ 8. I am good at solving problems. I can see when a problem exists, identify the reasons for the problem, and devise a plan of action for solving the problem.

_____ 9. I am good at mental visualization. I can see things in my mind's eye. Examples include building a project from a blueprint or imagining the taste of a recipe from reading it.

_____ 10. I know how to learn. I am aware of my learning style and can use learning strategies to obtain new knowledge.

_____ 11. I am good at reasoning. I can use logic to draw conclusions and apply rules and principles to new situations.

_____ 12. I am a responsible person. I work toward accomplishing goals, set high standards, and pay attention to details. I usually accomplish tasks on time.

_____ 13. I have high self-esteem. I believe in my self-worth and maintain a positive view of myself.

_____ 14. I am sociable, understanding, friendly, adaptable, polite, and relate well to others.

_____ 15. I am good at self-management. I know my background, skills, and abilities and set realistic goals for myself. I monitor my progress toward completing my goals and complete them.

_____ 16. I practice integrity and honesty. I recognize when I am faced with a decision that involves ethics and choose ethical behavior.

_____ 17. I am good at managing my time. I set goals, prioritize, and follow schedules to complete tasks on time.

_____ 18. I manage money well. I know how to use and prepare a budget and keep records, making adjustments when necessary.

_____ 19. I can manage material and resources. I can store and distribute materials, supplies, parts, equipment, space, or products.

_____ 20. I can participate as a member of a team. I can work cooperatively with others and contribute to group efforts.

_____ 21. I can teach others. I can help others to learn needed knowledge and skills.

_____ 22. I can exercise leadership. I know how to communicate, encourage, persuade, and motivate individuals.

_____ 23. I am a good negotiator. I can work toward an agreement and resolve divergent interests.

_____ 24. I can work with men and women from a variety of ethnic, social, or educational backgrounds.

_____ 25. I can acquire and evaluate information. I can identify a need for information and find the information I need.

_____ 26. I can organize and maintain information. I can find written or computerized information.

_____ 27. I can use computers to process information.

_____ 28. I have an understanding of social, organizational, and technological systems and can operate effectively in these systems.

_____ 29. I can improve the design of a system to improve the quality of products and services.

_____ 30. I can use machines and computers to accomplish the desired task.

_____ Total

Score your skills for success in the workplace.

150–121	Excellent
120–91	Very good
90–61	Average
Below 60	Need improvement

From the previous list of workplace skills, make a list of five of your strong points. What do you do well?

From the list of workplace skills, make a list of areas you need to improve.

The Planful Decision Strategy

Name _____ Date _____

Read the following scenario describing a college student in a problem situation. Then, answer the questions that follow to practice the planful decision strategy. You may want to do this as a group activity with other students in the class.

> Rhonda is an 18-year-old student who is trying to decide on her major. She was a good student in high school, earning a 3.4 grade point average. Her best subjects were English and American history. She struggled with math and science but still earned good grades in these subjects. While in high school, she enjoyed being on the debate team and organizing the African American Club. This club was active in writing letters to the editor and became involved in supporting a local candidate for city council.
>
> Rhonda is considering majoring in political science and has dreams of eventually going to law school. Rhonda likes being politically involved and advocating for different social causes. The highlight of her life in high school was when she organized students to speak to the city council about installing a traffic light in front of the school after a student was killed trying to cross the street. The light was installed during her senior year.
>
> Rhonda's family has always been supportive, and she values her family life and the close relationships in the family. She comes from a middle-income family that is struggling to pay for her college education. Getting a bachelor's degree in political science and going to law school would take seven years and be very expensive. There is no law school in town, so Rhonda would have to move away from home to attend school.
>
> Rhonda's parents have suggested that she consider becoming a nurse and attending the local nursing college. Rhonda could finish a bachelor's degree in nursing in four years and could begin working part-time as a nurse's aide in a short time. A cousin in the family became a nurse and found a job easily and is now earning a good income. The cousin arranged for Rhonda to volunteer this summer at the hospital where she works. Rhonda enjoys helping people at the hospital. Rhonda is trying to decide on her major. What should she do?

1. State the problem.

2. Describe Rhonda's values, hopes, and dreams.

3. What special interests, talents, or aptitudes does she have?

4. What further information would be helpful to Rhonda in making her decision?

5. What are the alternatives and the pros and cons of each?

Alternative 1

Pros:	Cons:

Alternative 2

Pros:	Cons:

Alternative 3 (be creative!)

Pros:	Cons:

6. Only Rhonda can choose what is best for her. If you were Rhonda, what would you do and why? Use a separate piece of paper, if necessary, to write your answer.